Paul the Reluctant Witness

Paul the Reluctant Witness
Power and Weakness in Luke's Portrayal

Blake Shipp

Cascade Books
A division of *Wipf & Stock Publishers*
199 West 8th Avenue, Suite 3 • Eugene OR 97401

PAUL THE RELUCTANT WITNESS
Power and Weakness in Luke's Portrayal

Copyright © 2005 Blake Shipp. All rights reserved. Except for brief quotations in critical publications or reviews, no part of this book may be reproduced in any manner without prior written permission from the publisher. Write: Permissions, Wipf & Stock Publishers, 199 W. 8th Ave., Suite 3, Eugene, OR 97401.

Cascade Books
A Division of Wipf & Stock Publishers
199 W. 8th Ave., Suite 3
Eugene, OR 97401

ISBN: 1-59752-400-X

Cataloging-in-publication information

Shipp, Blake
    Paul the reluctant witness: power and weakness in Luke's portrayal / Blake Shipp

       p. cm.

       Includes bibliographical references.
       ISBN: 1-59752-400-X

1. Bible. N.T. Acts—Criticism, interpretation, etc. 2. Bible. N.T. Acts—Language, style. 3. Paul, the Apostle, Saint. I. Title.

BS2506 .S54 2005

Manufactured in the U.S.A.

Contents

List of Figures — vii

List of Tables — ix

Abbreviations — xi

Acknowledgments — xiii

1. Luke and the Multiple Damascus Accounts — 1
2. Saul, the Overcome and Empowered Enemy — 27
3. Paul, the Overcome Witness — 62
4. Paul the Witness — 93
5. Conclusion — 114

Appendix — 121

Bibliography — 159

Figures

1. The Lukan Paradigm for Saul's Character Transformation   61

2. The Interrupted Transformation of Paul's Character   92

3. The Projected Transformation of Paul's Character   113

4. The Lukan Literary Use of the Damascus Narrative   118

Tables

1. The Overcome Saul (Acts 9:1-9)	50
2. God and Ananias (Acts 9:10-16)	53
3. The Restored Saul (Acts 9:17-19a)	56
4. Saul the Empowered Witness (Acts 9:19b-26a)	59
5. Paul in Chains (Acts 21:33-40; 22:2)	75
6. Paul Remains in Chains (Acts 22:22-24a)	76
7. Saul the Persecutor (Acts 22:4-11)	86
8. Saul and Ananias (Acts 22:12-16)	88
9. Saul the Resistant Witness (Acts 22: 17-21)	90
10. Paul before Agrippa (Acts 25:23—26:1)	100
11. Paul the Ineffective Witness (Acts 26:24-32)	102
12. Saul, the Overcome Persecutor (Acts 26:9-18)	108
13. Saul, the Obedient Witness (Acts 26:19-21)	109

Abbreviations

AB	Anchor Bible
ABR	*Australian Biblical Review*
AKGWG	Abhandlungen der Königlichen Gesellschaft der Wissenschaften zu Göttingen Philologisch Historische Klasse
BETL	Bibliotheca Ephemeridum theologicarum Lovaniensium
Bib	*Biblica*
BibSac	*Bibliotheca Sacra*
BR	*Biblical Research*
BTB	*Biblical Theology Bulletin*
CBQ	*Catholic Biblical Quarterly*
CV	*Communio Viatorum*
EHPR	Études d'Histoire et de Philosophie Religieuses
EKKNT	Evangelisch-Katholischer Kommentar zum Neuen Testament
ETL	*Ephemerides theologicae Lovanienses*
EvTh	*Evangelische Theologie*
FRLANT	Forschungen zur Religion und Literatur des Alten und Neuen Testaments
GBS	Guides to Biblical Scholarship
HTR	Harvard Theological Review
ICC	*International Critical Commentary*
Int	*Interpretation*

JBL	*Journal of Biblical Literature*
JSNT	*Journal for the Study of the New Testament*
JSNTSS	Journal for the Study of the New Testament Supplement Series
JSOTSS	Journal for the Study of the Old Testament Supplement Series
KEKNT	Kritisch-exegetischer Kommentar über das Neue Testament
LEC	Library of Early Christianity
LCL	Loeb Classical Library
LSt	*Louvain Studies*
NAC	New American Commentary
NarrComm	Narrative Commentary
NICNT	New International Commentary on the New Testament
NovT	*Novum Testamentum*
NovTSup	Novum Testamentum Supplements
NTS	*New Testament Studies*
NTTS	New Testament Tools and Studies
RevExp	*Review and Expositor*
SBLDS	Society of Biblical Literature Dissertation Series
SBLMS	Society of Biblical Literature Monograph Series
SBLSBS	Society of Biblical Literature Sources for Biblical Study
SBLSP	Society of Biblical Literature Seminar Papers
SecCent	*The Second Century: A Journal of Early Christian Studies*
SNTSMS	Society for New Testament Studies Monograph Series
StTh	*Studia Theologica*
SWJT	*Southwestern Journal of Theology*
ThQ	*Theologische Quartalschrift*
WUNT	Wissenschaftliche Untersuchungen zum Neuen Testament
ZNW	*Zeitschrift für die neutestamentliche Wissenschaft*

Acknowledgments

The completion of any project of magnitude is never an individual achievement. The following work has become a reality only through the love, support, dedication, and vision of those who surrounded me. I can never say enough thanks to those who nurtured me along my path of questioning and discovery. I must first thank my parents, educators who passed on their love of learning to me. Thanks must be given to Philip Ervin for teaching me to ask questions of the biblical text and showing an interest in my further study. I must thank Bethel Baptist Church and New Henleyfield Southern Baptist Church for their love, support, and understanding for their pastor as he traveled along this road. Thanks to my fellow students and companions in scholarship: Brad Arnett, Norris Grubbs, and Viktor Roudkovski. Their open ears as I spoke about Acts and willingness to help proof the following work are greatly appreciated. Thank you also to the library staff of the New Orleans Baptist Theological Seminary. Your perseverance in tracking down articles and finding rare books is greatly appreciated. Thanks must be given to Gerald L. Stevens. Thank you for your open door, your patience with my many questions, your willingness to journey with me as I studied rhetoric, and your example of Christ-like love and scholarship. Finally, I must thank my wife. She has faithfully endured throughout this journey. Thank you for your never-failing support and encouragement. Thank you for the sacrifice of allowing me the time to read and research without ever complaining. Without your love and support I never would have finished." Ὡς κρίνον ἐν μέσω ἀκανθῶν οὕτως ἡ πλησίον μου ἀνὰ μέσον τῶν θυγατέρων. Song of Songs 2.2 (LXX)

1

Luke and the Multiple Damascus Accounts

Introduction

One of the most puzzling issues pertaining to the interpretation of Acts is the presence of multiple reports of Paul's Damascus Road experience in the narrative.[1] As Paul Schubert noted, the presence of the repeated narrative leads one to questions concerning the literary structure of Acts as a whole. "What is Luke's intention in this threefold, elaborate telling of

---

[1] A vast sea of questions arise in the mind of the modern interpreter concerning the repeated Damascus Road narratives of Acts. Why did Luke choose to include three accounts of Paul's Damascus Road experience in the text of Acts? Why do these three accounts bear a striking similarity to each other and yet stand in stark contrast in key details and narrative themes? Why do the narratives occur within their specific locations in Acts? Why did the author include three and not four, five, six, or more tellings of this story? Why was one telling of the story not sufficient? Were these tellings the only time Paul related his Damascus experience? Was Luke trying to underscore a theological point? Was he attempting to remind the reader of a key event in the history of the early church? Did Luke simply suffer from a mild form of literary amnesia, forgetting what he had previously narrated for his readers?

the same story? This is, specifically, one of the most perplexing and revealing questions concerning the literary structure of Acts as a whole. Why should this story in this comparatively short book—although Luke-Acts comprises 27% of the whole NT—be told three times?"[2] In a work such as Acts—a work that moves forward with narrative beauty and poise, surveying in the briefest manner great characters and events of the early New Testament church—a repetition such as that of the Damascus Road account readily stands out. Certainly, Luke must have had some literary purpose for including these multiple accounts of Paul's Damascus Road experience in Acts.[3]

The purpose for the following book is to analyze the multiple accounts of the Damascus Road narrative in order to determine their literary-rhetorical function in Acts. In order to do this, this study will incorporate a proposed literary-rhetorical methodology. Before such a proposal, one must first consider a brief review of literature that surveys the use of rhetorical methodology as applied to the text of Acts and various attempts to answer questions surrounding the literary purpose of the repeated Damascus Road narratives. The purpose of such a review is to demonstrate that a new rhetorical methodology is needed as is a fresh proposal concerning the Lukan literary agenda for the multiple Damascus Road accounts in Acts.

Review of Literature

Application of Rhetoric to the Text of Acts

The application of the principles and forms of rhetoric to the text of Acts as an interpretive tool is a recent phenomenon. Stephen Lösch first addressed the possibility of using rhetoric as a means of analyzing the text of Acts when he tentatively compared the speech of Tertullus in Acts 24:1-4 to fourth century classical speech techniques found in the papyri and Menander.[4] Since Lösch's introductory study, only a few scholars have

---

[2] Paul Schubert, "The Final Cycle of Speeches in the Book of Acts," *JBL* 87 (1968) 11.
[3] "Luke" is used for conventional reasons. However, the thesis does not depend upon the historical issue of authorship.
[4] Stephen Lösch, "Die Dankesrede des Tertullus, Apg 24.1-4," *ThQ* 112 (1931) 295–319.

attempted to apply rhetoric in any form of interpretive analysis to the text of Acts. The works of those interpreters who have utilized rhetoric fall into three broad categories.

The first attempts to use the principles of rhetoric to interpret Acts were comparative studies. In these studies, scholars compared various textual units in Acts to similarly structured or functioning texts in classical works or to principles and guidelines outlined in rhetorical handbooks for the formulation of these texts. Most often, researchers analyzed these classical texts for the purpose of discovering rhetorical patterns that might explain similar patterns found in the text of Acts.[5] Several have compared classical rhetorical texts with portions of Acts for the purpose of identifying the presence of rhetoric in Acts.[6] Finally, a few have scoured classical texts in attempts to provide handles for identifying the genre of Acts.[7]

---

[5] See Lösch, "Die Dankesrede des Tertullus," 295–319; Fred Veltman, "The Defense Speeches of Paul in Acts," in *Perspectives on Luke-Acts*, ed. Charles H. Talbert, Perspectives in Religious Studies 5 (Edinburgh: T. & T. Clark, 1978), 243–56; Thomas Craig Alexander, "Paul's Final Exhortation to the Elders from Ephesus: The Rhetoric of Acts 20:17-38" (PhD diss., Emory University, 1990); Conrad Gempf, "Public Speaking and Published Accounts," in *The Book of Acts in Its First Century Setting*, vol. 1: *The Books of Acts in Its Ancient Literary Setting*, ed. Bruce W. Winter and Andrew D. Clarke (Grand Rapids: Eerdmans, 1993), 259–303; Bruce Winter, "Official Proceedings and the Forensic Speeches in Acts 24–26," in *The Book of Acts in Its First Century Setting*, vol. 1: *The Book of Acts in Its Ancient Literary Setting*, ed. Bruce W. Winter and Andrew D. Clarke (Grand Rapids: Eerdmans, 1993), 306–36; Charles H. Talbert, *Literary Patterns, Theological Themes and the Genre of Luke-Acts*, SBLMS 20 (Missoula, Mont.: Scholars, 1974), 125–40; Vernon K. Robbins, "Narrative in Ancient Rhetoric and Rhetoric in Ancient Narrative," in *SBLSP* (Atlanta: Scholars, 1996), 368–84; and Lawrence Wills, "The Form of the Sermon in Hellenistic Judaism and Early Christianity," *HTR* 77 (1984) 277–99.

[6] See Philip E. Satterthwaite, "Acts Against the Background of Classical Rhetoric," in *The Book of Acts in Its First Century Setting*, vol. 1: *The Book of Acts in Its Ancient Literary Setting*, ed. Bruce W. Winter and Andrew D. Clarke (Grand Rapids: Eerdmans, 1993), 337–79; and William S. Kurz, "Hellenistic Rhetoric in the Christological Proof of Luke-Acts," *CBQ* 42 (1980) 171–95.

[7] See Talbert, *Literary Patterns*, 125–40; Daryl D. Schmidt, "Rhetorical Influences and Genre: Luke's Preface and the Rhetoric of Hellenistic Historiography," in *Jesus and the Heritage of Israel*, vol. 1: *Luke the Interpreter of Israel*, ed. David P. Moessner and David L. Tiede (Harrisburg, Pa.: Trinity, 1999), 27–60; and Ben Witherington III, "Finding Its Niche: The Historical and Rhetorical Species of Acts," in *SBLSP* (Atlanta: Scholars, 1996), 67–97.

The use of classical texts to identify genre and patterns in Acts is insightful. By analyzing the ways in which classical authors constructed texts, one may gain a better understanding of the literary surroundings that influenced Luke as he wrote Acts. Further, the use of comparison to identify the genre of Acts provides some clarity to the much-debated issue of genre. Finally, by comparing Acts with classical texts, researchers have been able to establish that Luke knew and used some elements of Hellenistic rhetoric. While the comparison of classical texts with the text of Acts provides a great deal of information and insight about the form, background, and genre of Acts, scholars have not illuminated the thematic and literary development of the individual Book of Acts using this method.

A second approach to the application of rhetoric to the text of Acts is the formal rhetorical analysis of portions of the text. This approach involves analyzing various portions of the text of Acts in light of commonly accepted principles and rules for constructing speeches and narratives, most often found within rhetorical handbooks. This approach, only a little over twenty years old, has grown out of the influential works of George Kennedy and Hans Dieter Betz.[8] Very few researchers have attempted to apply this method on a large scale, instead opting to analyze individual pericopes and speeches.[9] The handful of scholars who have attempted to utilize

---

[8]Hans Dieter Betz, *Galatians,* Hermeneia (Philadelphia: Fortress, 1979); and George A. Kennedy, *New Testament Interpretation through Rhetorical Criticism* (Chapel Hill: Univ. of North Carolina Press, 1984).

[9]See Alexander, "Paul's Final Exhortation"; Dean Zweck, "The *Exordium* of the Areopagus Speech, Acts 17.22, 23," *NTS* 35 (1989) 94–103; Burton L. Mack, *Rhetoric and the New Testament,* GBS (Minneapolis: Fortress), 88–92; Duane F. Watson, "Paul's Speech to the Ephesian Elders (Acts 20.17-38): Epideictic Rhetoric of Farewell," in *Persuasive Artistry: Studies in New Testament Rhetoric in Honor of George A. Kennedy,* ed. Duane F. Watson, JSNTSS 50 (Sheffield: Sheffield Academic, 1991), 184–208; Karl Olav Sandnes, "Paul and Socrates: The Aim of Paul's Areopagus Speech," *JSNT* 50 (1993) 13–26; Todd C. Penner, "Narrative as Persuasion: Epideictic Rhetoric and Scribal Amplification in the Stephen Episode in Acts," in *SBLSP* (Atlanta: Scholars, 1996), 352–67; Jacques Dupont, "La structure oratoire du discours d'Étienne," *Bib* 66 (1985) 153–67; C. Clifton Black, "The Rhetorical Form of the Hellenistic Jewish and Early Christian Sermon: A Response to Lawrence Wills," *HTR* 81 (1998) 1–18; Frank Crouch, "The Persuasive Moment: Rhetorical Resolutions in Paul's Defense Before Agrippa," in *SBLSP* (Atlanta: Scholars, 1996), 333–42; and Petrus Maryano, "Luke's Use of Biblical History and Promise in Acts 13:16-41" (PhD diss., Dallas Theological Seminary, 2001).

rhetorical analysis on a larger scale have analyzed extended sections, series of speeches, and the text of Acts as a whole.[10]

The application of formal rhetorical analysis is the most promising area of rhetorical study for the text of Acts. With comparative studies, scholars only identified the presence and use of rhetoric in Acts, while with formal analysis, the purpose, argumentative logic, and thematic unity of the text is discovered, as well as some insight into audience analysis. Yet, the promise of these studies is offset by their deficiencies. First, many who apply formal rhetorical analysis display a lack of discernment in their application of the rhetorical handbooks. Many weigh equally the comments of Aristotle, Quintilian, Cicero, and numerous others, including insights from the philosophically based *New Rhetoric* movement.[11] Second, rarely will an interpreter, using a formal rhetorical analysis, seek to develop themes outside the immediately studied pericope. No attention is given to the place of the pericope within the wider text as a whole. Third, a common practice is to force the rules of rhetoric upon texts that follow no such standards.[12] Fourth, many corrupt their method by incorporating and reading ancient rhetoric through the eyes of modern discourse and literary theories.[13] Finally, no unified theory or method for the application of formal rhetorical analysis exists. Each interpreter approaches the text with a different understanding of rhetoric, an assorted number of rhetorical handbooks, and a peculiar manner of applying the principles contained therein.

---

[10] See Donald Galen Meyer, "The Use of Rhetorical Technique by Luke in the Book of Acts (Volumes I and II)" (PhD diss., University of Minnesota, 1987); William R. Long, "The Trial of Paul in the Book of Acts: Historical, Literary, and Theological Considerations" (PhD diss., Brown University, 1982); and Paul Meierding, "Jews and Gentiles: A Narrative and Rhetorical Analysis of the Implied Audience in Acts (Luke-Acts)" (PhD diss., Luther Northwestern Theological Seminary, 1992).

[11] See Alexander, "Paul's Final Exhortation"; Meyer, "Rhetorical Technique"; Zweck, "The *Exordium*"; Long, "The Trial of Paul"; and Maryono, "Biblical History." The issue of the conflation of rhetorical handbooks is discussed in the appendix on methodology.

[12] See Meyer, " Rhetorical Technique."

[13] Ibid. See also Marion L. Soards, *The Speeches in Acts: Their Content, Context, and Concerns* (Louisville: Westminster John Knox, 1994). Consider, especially, Maryono, "Biblical History." Maryono's methodological approach is an interesting blend of classical rhetorical theory, New Rhetoric, and modern secular literary analysis.

The third and most recent application of rhetoric to the text of Acts is the socio-rhetorical method. This method, first articulated by Vernon Robbins, is actually the melding of numerous methodologies: social-scientific criticism, rhetorical criticism, postmodern criticism, and historical-theological approaches.[14] With this method, one attempts to analyze a text from numerous interpretive angles using multiple critical disciplines in a mutually dependent and informing manner.[15] The idea, in theory, is applaudable. In practice, the result is often anemic. A prime example is Ben Witherington's application of the socio-rhetorical method to the text of Acts.[16]

Witherington's attempt to utilize the socio-rhetorical method for interpreting Acts produced mixed results at best. Witherington—like most socio-rhetorical exegetes—applied various interpretive methods, including rhetorical criticism, in an overlapping, simultaneous manner. The reasoning behind simultaneously applying these divergent methods is the desire to integrate the various methods, resulting in a singular, homogeneous interpretive result. In the application of the method, as discussed by Robbins, one is to work systematically through four textual arenas or interpretive angles of a text: (1) Inner texture; (2) Intertexture; (3) Social and Cultural Texture; and (4) Ideological Texture.[17] Witherington, on the other hand, did not separate his interpretation of the text into different textual arenas. Instead, he combined all of his analysis into one running commentary. Perhaps the attempt was to add the flavor of homogeneity

---

[14] Vernon K. Robbins, *Exploring the Texture of Texts: A Guide to Socio-Rhetorical Interpretation* (Valley Forge, Pa.: Trinity, 1996), 2. See also idem, *The Tapestry of Early Christian Discourse: Rhetoric, Society and Ideology* (London: Routledge, 1996), 1–43. This method is not truly a rhetorical approach to the text, nor does this method have much in common with a rhetorical approach. Socio-rhetorical criticism is mentioned here because of the equating of this method with rhetorical approaches in recent years. In the appendix on methodology, socio-rhetorical criticism is set aside and apart from rhetorical criticism as an entirely separate method.

[15] For illustrations of the above method as applied to the text of Acts see Istvan Czachesz, "Socio-Rhetorical Exegesis of Acts 9.1-30," *CV* 37 (1995) 5–32; Randall C. Webber, "'Why Were the Heathen So Arrogant?' The Socio-Rhetorical Strategy of Acts 3–4," *BTB* 22 (1992) 19–25; and Ben Witherington III, *The Acts of the Apostles: A Socio-Rhetorical Commentary* (Grand Rapids: Eerdmans, 1998).

[16] Witherington, *Acts*.

[17] Robbins, *Tapestry*, 27–43. A similar approach is noted in Czachesz, "Acts 9.1-30."

to the interpretive result, but the ensuing interpretive result is actually heterogeneous. No one interpretive method is fully applied to the text of Acts, nor does the reader know when certain methods are being applied and which critical disciplines are generating the current analyses. Where interpretive methods are openly applied, they are applied to the exclusion of the other methods, leaving portions of the text lacking in key insights and, in the case of rhetorical criticism, lacking in fundamental rhetorical insights. In the end, the reader is not presented with a full understanding of the text from any one critical perspective but is met with a dizzying array of competing analyses, which leads to hermeneutical confusion.[18]

While the applications of rhetoric to the text of Acts as an interpretive tool are few in number, the potential interpretive value of this method is significant. In order to capitalize on the potential value of this method, several steps must be taken. First, a method that makes consistent and judicious use of the rhetorical handbooks, making note of their influence and date of authorship, must be proposed. Second, a method that places the individual textual unit within the larger rhetorical movement of the text, observing the careful construction of logic and thematic development, is needed. Finally, for the purpose of the proposed thesis, this method will be applied to the multiple Damascus Road accounts in the text of Acts.[19]

Interpretations of the Damascus Road Narratives

Few scholars investigated the reasoning behind the triple Damascus narrative found in Acts until the end of the nineteenth century. Even after scholars began to question the purpose and function of the multiple Damascus narratives, few gave significant attention to the issue. Most early exegetes dismissed the issue with a few paragraphs or pages. Later

---

[18]The above critiques are not designed to dissuade researchers from the application of the socio-rhetorical method. As stated, the method is sound in theory, as no single critical approach will provide insight into all aspects of a text. Instead, exegetes would find greater consistency by fully applying various critical approaches independently and then integrating the results in a round table or seminar format. Further discussion of the socio-rhetorical method is found in the appendix on methodology below.

[19]At this date, no published rhetorical analysis has been found interpreting the multiple Damascus accounts in Acts.

researchers have dedicated short journal articles and excurses to the question, but none to date has sought to investigate the literary function of the repetition of the Damascus narrative in an extended manner.

Early analyses centered upon questions of sources used by Luke in his composition of Acts. Dissatisfied with the results of such source analysis, scholars turned to other interpretive methods. Most have examined the Damascus narratives through what has come to be known as literary and narrative criticisms, but a handful have sought to apply an eclectic collection of historical, form, and socio-rhetorical criticisms.

Source Analysis

When confronted with the dilemma of explaining the reasoning behind the Lukan inclusion of three narratives of Paul's Damascus experience, early scholars argued that the repetition was due to Luke's possession of more than one account of the event. Most posited that Luke had at least two, possibly three, sources, which he failed to harmonize, either through carelessness or lack of literary artistry.[20] Emanuel Hirsch provided the definitive source analysis from which few source critics after him fully departed. Hirsch argued that Luke possessed two sources of the Pauline Damascus experience: a legendary source from Damascus and a source connected to Paul himself. Hirsch hypothesized that Luke used the

---

[20]See Friedrich Spitta, *Die Apostelgeschichte: Ihre Quellen und deren Geschichtlicher Wert* (Halle: Waisenhauses, 1891), 144–45, 270–77; Johannes Jüngst, *Die Quellen der Apostelgeschichte* (Gotha: Perthes, 1895), 83–86, 223–26; Julius Wellhausen, *Kritische Analyse der Apostelgeschichte*, AKGWG 15/2 (Berlin: Weidmann, 1914), 16–18; Hans Hinrich Wendt, *Die Apostelgeschichte*, KEKNT 5 (Göttingen: Vandenhoeck & Ruprecht, 1899), 186–89, 352–53; F. J. Foakes-Jackson and Kirsopp Lake, "The Internal Evidence of Acts," in *The Beginnings of Christianity, Part 1: The Acts of the Apostles,* vol. 2, ed. F. J. Foakes-Jackson and Kirsopp Lake, *Prolegomena II, and Criticism* (London: Macmillan, 1922), 121–206; Kirsopp Lake, "The Conversion of Paul and the Events Immediately Following It," in *The Beginnings of Christianity: Part 1 The Acts of the Apostles*, vol. 5, ed. F. J. Foakes-Jackson and Kirsopp Lake, *Additional Notes to the Commentary* (London: Macmillan, 1933), 188–95; Emanuel Hirsch, "Die drei Berichte der Apostelgeschichte über die Bekehrung des Paulus," *ZNW* 28 (1929) 305–12; and Étienne Trocmé, *Le "Livre Des Actes" et L'Histoire*, EHPR 45 (Paris: Presses Universitaires de France, 1957), 179.

legendary source as the basis of the Acts 9 account and the Pauline source as the basis for the Acts 26 account. Hirsch proposed that Luke had these two sources before him and did not wish to discard either; therefore, he blended the legendary and Pauline sources to form the account of Acts 22.²¹

Hirsch and other source critics were able to explain, from a source critical perspective, the presence of the three Damascus narratives in Acts, but they were unable or did not attempt to explain the accounts' placement within the narrative. Nor were the source critics able to provide an adequate argument for Luke's integration of functional intent for the narrative in the text of Acts. The most telling critique of the source critical position came early when Ernst von Dobschütz asked the obvious question, "Warum wählte er nicht aus den drei vorliegenden Berichten den einen ihm am besten dünkenden aus oder verschmolz sie alle zu einem?"²² Recently, critics have abandoned the effort to identify the sources behind the text of Acts. Most agree that the author of Acts did use sources, but he blended them with such great skill as to nullify any attempt to isolate them.

Form, Literary, and Narrative Analyses

Von Dobschütz's criticism signaled the beginning of the end for the application of source criticism to the question of the repeated Damascus narrative and the beginning of the application of literary and narrative approaches. Von Dobschütz began his analysis of the Damascus narratives by asking a different question. Instead of asking about the origins or sources of the three accounts—as the source critics had been asking—von Dobschütz asked why the three accounts of Paul's Damascus experience were present in Acts.²³ Von Dobschütz concluded:

---

²¹Hirsch, "Die drei Berichte," 305–12.
²²Ernst von Dobschütz, "Die Berichte über die Bekehrung des Paulus," *ZNW* 29 (1930) 144. "Why did he not select one of the three present reports that seemed best to him or merge all into one?" Translations of German are made by the author unless otherwise stated.
²³Ibid.

> Es ist einleuchtend, daß damit diese Geschichte als ganz besonders wichtig hervorgehoben wird, und das mag ein Motiv des Schriftstellers sein, sie den Lesern nachdrücklich einzuprägen. Aber daß er dies dreimal tut, und zwar einmal in der Form der Erzählung, das zweite und dritte Mal in der Form eines von Paulus selbst erstatteten Berichtes, das scheint doch noch einen anderen Grund zu haben. Ich vermute ihn in einer literarischen Stilregel der antiken Geschichtsschreibung.[24]

His suggestion that Luke may have included three accounts of Paul's Damascus experience to emphasize the event, using techniques that possibly were modeled on ancient historiography, was the first such suggestion opening new avenues for research.

Not all interpreters have followed von Dobschütz's suggestion. After the demise of the source-critical approach, a handful of scholars endeavored to apply the principles of form criticism in an attempt to answer the vexing question of repetition in Acts and the multiple Damascus narratives.[25] These scholars have generated two conclusions from their attempts. First, Cadbury concluded that repetition was a feature of Lukan style.[26] Löning and Steck both concluded that Luke utilized a single *Saulustradition* and varied this tradition to fit the context of the narrative, adding additional accents as necessary.[27] Pesch concluded that several *Saulustraditions* lay behind the single conversion story. Luke had combined these traditions into a single narrative to fit the context.[28] While the results of these studies

---

[24]Ibid., 147. "It is plausible, that this history as a whole is accentuated as particularly important, and such may be a motive of the author, to emphasize it emphatically to the readers. But that he does this three times, the second and third times in the form of Paul's speeches, this seems to have another reason altogether. I suspect this is a literary style rule of antique historiography."

[25]See Henry J. Cadbury, "Four Features of Lucan Style," in *Studies in Luke-Acts*, ed. Leander E. Keck and J. Louis Martyn (Nashville: Abingdon, 1966), 88–97; Karl Löning, *Die Saulustradition in der Apostelgeschichte* (Münster: Aschendorff, 1973), 14–19; Odil Hannes Steck, "Formgeschichtliche Bemerkungen zur Darstellung des Damaskusgeschehens in der Apostelgeschichte," *ZNW* 67 (1976) 20–28; Rudolf Pesch, *Die Apostelgeschichte*, vol. 1: *Apg 1–12*, EKKNT 5/1 (Zurich: Benziger, 1986), 301–2; and idem, *Die Apostelgeschichte*, vol. 2: *Apg 13–28*, EKKNT 5/2 (Zurich: Benziger, 1986), 230, 275.

[26]Cadbury, "Features of Lucan Style," 88–97.

[27]Löning, 14–19; and Steck, "Formgeschichtliche," 20–28.

[28]Pesch, *Apostelgeschichte (Apg 1–12)*, 302; and *idem, Apostelgeschichte (Apg 13–28)*, 230, 275.

remain insightful, they contribute little to an understanding of the literary nature and placement of the Lukan repetitions of the Damascus event.

However, most interpreters, utilizing various literary and narrative methodologies, have followed von Dobschütz's reasoning. Exegetes have proposed that Luke employed the triple Damascus narrative primarily for emphasis. Two German scholars are representative of this stream of interpretation. Ernst Haenchen asked, "Why did Luke recount Paul's conversion three times? Luke employs such repetitions only when he considers something to be extraordinarily important and wishes to impress it unforgettably on the reader."[29] Or similarly, Otto Bauernfeind wrote:

> Wie aus dem großen Verfolger der große Bekenner wurde, hat Lk nicht weniger als dreimal erzählt. Gewiß nicht deschlab, weil ihm beim Niederschreiben der Paulusreden Kp 22 u 26 der Gedanke aufgegangen wäre, hier seinen nunmehr Variationen des Kp 9 Berichteten am Platze, auch nicht, weil seine Quellen ihn unausweichlich dazu gedrängt hätten; die Dreimaligkeit gehört vielmehr von vornherein in seinen Gesamtplan: Die Geschichte von der Paulusbekehrung enthält eine Wahrheit, die unbedingt—durch doppelte Wiederholung—eingeschärft werden soll.[30]

Both Haenchen and Bauernfeind explained the repetition as a Lukan device to impress a central truth upon the reader. This explanation is a development of von Dobschütz's proposal.

Almost every interpreter after von Dobschütz has contended that the issue Luke wished to underscore was the importance of the Gentile mission. Scholars have noted the specific nuances of this emphasis with overlapping suggestions. Interpreters have asserted that the repetition of the Damascus

---

[29]Ernst Haenchen, *The Acts of the Apostles: A Commentary*, trans. Bernard Noble et al. (Philadelphia: Westminster, 1971), 327.
[30]Otto Bauernfeind, *Kommentar und Studien zur Apostelgeschichte*, WUNT 22 (Tübingen: Mohr/Siebeck, 1980), 129. "As he (Paul) went from the largest persecutor to the biggest confessor, Luke told *the story* no less than three times. Certainly not on this account, because the thought would have come to him as he wrote down the Pauline speeches in Chapter 22 and 26, here his only variation from Chapter 9 is the reporting of the place, also not, because his sources would have pressed him unavoidably to it; the triple *story* belongs to his total plan from the start: The history of Paul's conversion contains a truth, an absolute—through double repetition—that should be impressed."

narrative emphasized a call to Gentile mission, a defense of Paul's Gentile mission, an apology of Paul because of his Gentile mission, an emphasis on God's initiative in calling Paul to a Gentile mission, or even possibly an emphasis on Paul's call to a Gentile mission.[31]

While numerous scholars have addressed the issue of the triple Damascus narrative over the last seventy years, the primary solution to the dilemma of the literary function of the multiple accounts has not progressed beyond the suggestion of von Dobschütz. Interpreters have

---

[31] Ibid., 327–28. See also Gerhard Lohfink, *The Conversion of St. Paul: Narrative and History in Acts*, trans. Bruce J. Malina, Herald Scripture Library (Chicago: Franciscan Herald, 1976), 87–88; Roy A. Harrisville, "Acts 22:6-21," *Int* 42 (1988) 181–85; Joseph A. Fitzmyer, *The Acts of the Apostles*, AB 31 (New York: Doubleday, 1998), 420; John B. Polhill, *Acts*, NAC 26 (Nashville: Broadman, 1992), 231; James D. G. Dunn, *The Acts of the Apostles*, NarrComm (Valley Forge, Pa.: Trinity, 1996), 117–18; Raymond F. Collins, "Paul's Damascus Experience: Reflections on the Lukan Account," *LSt* 11 (1986) 112–18; Robert C. Tannehill, *The Narrative Unity of Luke-Acts: A Literary Interpretation*, vol. 2: *The Acts of the Apostles* (Minneapolis: Fortress, 1994), 116, 275; David M. Stanley, "Paul's Conversion in Acts: Why the Three Accounts?" *CBQ* 15 (1953) 315–38; Dennis Hamm, "Paul's Blindness and Its Healing: Clues to Symbolic Intent (Acts 9, 22 and 26)," *Bib* 71 (1990) 63–72; Willy Rordorf, "Paul's Conversion in the Canonical Acts and in the Acts of Paul," *Semeia* 80 (1997) 137–44; Edward Schillebeeckx, *Jesus: An Experiment in Christology*, trans. Hubert Hoskins (New York: Crossroad, 1979, reprinted 1995), 360–79 (page citations are to the reprint edition); John T. Carroll, "Literary and Social Dimensions of Luke's Apology for Paul," in *SBLSP* (Atlanta: Scholars, 1988), 115–18; Steven Richard Bechtler, "The Meaning of Paul's Call and Commissioning in Luke's Story: An Exegetical Study of Acts 9, 22, and 26," *Studia Biblica et Theologica* 15 (1987) 53–77; Norman A. Beck, "The Lukan Writer's Stories About the Call of Paul," in *SBLSP* (Chico: Scholars, 1983), 213–18; Richard I. Pervo, *Luke's Story of Paul* (Minneapolis: Fortress, 1990), 86; Robert L. Brawley, *Luke-Acts and the Jews: Conflict, Apology, and Conciliation*, SBLMS 33 (Atlanta: Scholars, 1987), 51–67; Sten Lundgren, "Ananias and the Calling of Paul in Acts," *StTh* 25 (1971) 117–22; Marie-Eloise Rosenblatt, "Recurrent Narration as a Lukan Literary Convention in Acts: Paul's Jerusalem Speech in Acts 22:1-21," in *New Views on Luke and Acts*, ed. Earl Richard (Collegeville, Minn.: Liturgical, 1990), 94–105; Robert Allen Black, "The Conversion Stories in the Acts of the Apostles: A Study of Their Forms and Functions" (PhD diss., Emory University, 1985), 147, 174; Benjamin J. Hubbard, "The Role of Commissioning Accounts in Acts," in *Perspectives on Luke-Acts*, Perspectives in Religious Studies, ed. Charles H. Talbert, no. 5 (Edinburgh: T. & T. Clark, 1978), 187–98; Bauernfeind, *Apostelgeschichte*, 130; Jacob Jervell, *Die Apostelgeschichte*, KEKNT 17 (Göttingen: Vandenhoeck & Ruprecht, 1998), 278–79, 531–33, 590; and Alan F. Segal, *Paul the Convert: The Apostolate and Apostasy of Saul the Pharisee* (New Haven: Yale Univ. Press, 1990), 8.

debated only the fine nuances of what Luke was emphasizing. With his inclusion of the three narratives, was Luke underscoring Paul's call to the Gentile mission or God's initiative in calling Paul to such a mission? Was Luke highlighting the authenticity of the Gentile mission or urging his generation to continue the Gentile mission? Regardless of the nuance proposed, the answer to Luke's employment of the narratives is singular, that of repetition for emphasis. Such a proposal is a valid literary and narrative observation. Certainly, as Haenchen contended, Luke's repetition of Paul's Damascus experience would impress such an event on the reader.[32] Furthermore, Paul's experience as he traveled to Damascus for the Gentile mission in the text of Acts is literarily important. The event is necessary to transform Saul, the one who persecutes the members of "The Way," into Paul, the one who purposefully journeys in order to evangelize among the Gentiles.

That the Gentile mission is an important theme in the last half of Acts is undeniable, but one cannot claim that this mission is the only theme. Neither, according to the text, is this mission the only mission in which Paul engages. The majority of scholars agree that the primary theme of Acts is the forward expansion of the gospel to the ends of the earth (Acts 1:8). This expansion includes both Jews and Gentiles, a fact not lost literarily upon the character Paul in his journeys. The Paul that Luke described in the text of Acts evangelized both Jews and Gentiles, not Gentiles exclusively. Interestingly, when possible, the Paul of Acts evangelized Jews first.[33] The Saul that was called/commissioned on the Damascus Road was engaged in a mission not just to Gentiles—nor even primarily to Gentiles—but in a mission to all people, a mission fitting with the overall theme of the text of Acts. Therefore, any emphasis given by the repetition of the Damascus narrative to Paul's mission is to the overall forward progress of the gospel, of which the Gentile mission is only a part. The authors of the above studies have failed to integrate the

---

[32]Haenchen, *Acts*, 327.
[33]Acts 13:5, 14-48; 14:1; 16:13; 17:1-4, 11-12, 17; 18:4; and 28:17-28. Jacob Jervell emphasized the Jewish nature of Paul's mission as a corrective to those who emphasize Paul's Gentile mission. He stated, "Die Mission des Paulus greift weiter als die der Zwölf, denn Paulus missioniert, als der einzige Völkerapostel und Welzeuge, sowohl für Israel, Juden, als auch für Heiden. Seine Mission ist nicht vornehmlich eine Heidenmission, sondern gilt in erster Linie dem Volk, den Juden," Jervell, *Apostelgeschichte*, 594.

emphasis upon Gentile mission into the overall thematic unity of Acts. The narrative movement in the text of Acts and the character of Paul is the forward progress of the gospel to all people, to the ends of the earth, not just to the Gentiles. A proposal is needed that integrates the emphasis upon Paul's mission with the overall theme of Acts, the forward progress of the gospel.

One must level two further critiques against the above studies. While exegetes in the above-mentioned studies have striven to account for the presence of the repeated Damascus narrative, they have not sought to identify the reasoning behind the placement of such narratives. Such a lacuna is somewhat amazing when most of them employ literary and narrative methods. By their very nature, these methods should allow insight into authorial purpose and narrative agenda.

Robert Tannehill came the closest to any attempt of suggesting narrative/literary purpose behind the placement of the Damascus narratives when he noted, "The triple narration of this event is an indication of its key importance for understanding Paul's mission. The placement of the three accounts supports this observation. The first appears at the beginning of Paul's mission as its foundation, the second and third in the two major defense speeches at the beginning and end of the defense sequence in Acts 22–26, all prominent positions."[34] While Tannehill has correctly noted that Luke placed the Damascus narrative in prominent positions, he has not explained why the author placed this episode in these positions, beyond the explanation of emphasis. Again, von Dobschütz's conclusions are the limit of the present research. Certainly, the beginning of Paul's mission and the trial sequences in Acts are important positions in Luke's narration of the character of Paul in Acts. Yet, in other important and prominent points in the narrative Luke did not include an account of Paul's Damascus road experience. Paul stood on trial before Gallio the proconsul of Achaia, yet Luke included no Damascus narrative.[35] Luke recorded that Paul's greatest evangelistic success was in the city of Ephesus, and yet he included no Damascus narrative.[36] One could continue with references to Lystra, the Jerusalem council, Thessalonica, and Athens. Why did Luke choose

---

[34]Tannehill, *Narrative Unity*, 275.
[35]Acts 18:12-17.
[36]Acts 19:1—20:1.

to repeat Paul's Damascus experience where he did in the text of Acts? The question remains unanswered. A proposal is needed that accounts for Luke's narrative agenda and placement of these repeated accounts.

One final charge remains to be leveled against the argument for emphasis alone. Interpreters have aspired, in the above studies, to link the repetition of the Damascus narrative solely to the theme of the Gentile mission. Such a theme, as noted above, is integrally connected to the over-arching theme of Acts, the forward progress of the gospel. Yet, as Gerald Stevens has argued in his presentation at the 1999 Southwest Regional meeting of the Society of Biblical Literature, at least two other major themes exist in the text of Acts that interact literarily with the theme of the progressing gospel. Stevens argues that in the Stephen speech of Acts 7, Luke introduced the themes of *God Active* and *God Resisted*. Stevens went beyond the identification of these themes in the speech of Stephen by demonstrating how these themes constituted a major part of Luke's narrative agenda, including the story of Saul/Paul.[37] A proposal is needed that accounts for these narrative themes identified by Stevens.

Against the direction of the majority of research, a few scholars in recent days have attempted to advance beyond the conclusions of von Dobschütz. Charles Hedrick was the first to make such an attempt in his seminal article, "Paul's Conversion/Call: A Comparative Analysis of the Three Reports in Acts."[38] Hedrick did not dismiss the idea of sources, nor did he deny the use of repetition for emphasis. Instead, he compared the structure of the three reports from the perspective of Luke's literary method. He concluded that the Damascus narratives worked in an integrated/cumulative manner. According to Hedrick, the Damascus story of Acts 9 was a traditional story upon which Luke built the later accounts in Acts 22 and 26. Luke advanced the story, building upon Acts 9 in a correcting and clarifying manner and using differences and contradictions to tell the story of Paul's experience as he journeyed to Damascus. Since the later narratives built upon that of Acts 9, Hedrick argued that all three accounts

---

[37]Gerald L. Stevens, "Luke's Perspective on Paul's Jerusalem Visit in Acts 19–23" (paper presented at the AAR/SBL Southwest Regional Meeting, Dallas, Texas, March 6, 1999), photocopied, 1–16. Further discussion of Stevens's argument is included below.

[38]Charles W. Hedrick, "Paul's Conversion/Call: A Comparative Analysis of the Three Reports in Acts," *JBL* 100 (1981) 415–32.

are needed to understand Paul's story as Luke understood the story. No one story is complete in and of itself. Instead, one must read each narrative in light of the previous accounts.[39]

Hedrick's contribution was enormous. He had proposed for the first time that the repeated narratives could work together in a manner other than the building of emphasis. The reasoning thus follows that if one could interpret how the stories function together, then one could understand Luke's narrative agenda. Furthermore, one should be able to discern the reason for Luke's placement of the narratives as well as the manner in which he employed these repeated narratives to further the themes of his book.

By and large, most scholars have overlooked Hedrick's most significant contribution, namely that Luke meant to integrate the Damascus narratives in order to create a cumulative effect. A handful of scholars, however, have wrestled with Hedrick's conclusions and endeavored to apply them to the text of Acts. Most recently, Witherington made plain his dependence upon the work of Hedrick by repeating Hedrick's conclusions in his commentary on Acts. Witherington wrote, "That is, Luke does not include all the details he wishes to convey in any one telling of the story, but adds fresh details in the accounts subsequent to Acts 9, not merely for the sake of stylistic variation but so that there is a cumulative effect on the hearer. The full picture is not gained until one has heard Acts 26."[40] Several additional scholars have provided significant contributions to understanding the triple Damascus narrative in Acts based upon an interaction between the three narratives.

Beverly Gaventa noted, in her presentation at the 1985 national Society of Biblical Literature meeting, that Luke used the Damascus narratives to establish an identity for Paul in Acts.[41] Specifically, she proposed that Luke established an identity for Paul in Acts 9, which he then referred to in Acts 22 and 26. The identity of Paul that Luke created in Acts 9 was that of the reversed enemy of God. Paul's story was that of Saul, overcome

---

[39]Ibid.
[40]Witherington, *Acts*, 666, and n.91. See also C. J. A. Hickling, "The Portrait of Paul in Acts 26," in *Les Actes des Apôstres: Traditions, rédaction, théologie,* ed. J. Kremer, BETL 48 (Leuven: Leuven Univ. Press, 1979), 499–503.
[41]Beverly Roberts Gaventa, "The Overthrown Enemy: Luke's Portrait of Paul," in *SBLSP* (Atlanta: Scholars, 1985), 439–49.

as the enemy of God and then restored to become Paul the proclaimer. Ironically, according to Gaventa, the identity of Paul remains that of enemy in the subsequent Damascus narratives. Gaventa contended, "Even when Paul emerges as ardent proclaimer, the question concerning his identity does not disappear. He remains the enemy, although now the enemy who has been overthrown. Because the second and third accounts of Paul's conversion emphasize his vocation to preach among the Gentiles, we might expect this portrait of the 'overthrown enemy' to fade, but it does not."[42] Gaventa's chief contribution is her suggestion that Luke utilized the repeated Damascus narrative to characterize Paul. Further, this building of character began with a paradigmatic characterization in Acts 9. Paul began his career as Saul the enemy, an identity that remained with him throughout the text of Acts.

Ronald Witherup, in two articles published in the *Journal for the Study of the New Testament*, advanced the suggestion that Luke employed multiple Damascus narratives as a type of functional redundancy to characterize Paul.[43] Witherup defined functional redundancy as a "narrative technique of repetition and variation which serves as a 'counterbalance designed to ensure a full and unambiguous reception of the message' that any particular piece of literature might contain."[44] He suggested that the message that Luke emphasized with such redundancy was that of Paul growing in his status as a witness to the gospel to the ends of the earth. According to Witherup, with each telling of Paul's Damascus experience, his stature as a witness grows through the presence of variations between the accounts.[45] The contribution of Witherup's analysis is his linking of Luke's development of Paul's character to the larger narrative scheme of Acts. Witherup argued that the manipulation of the Pauline character was a Lukan device in service of the overall narrative plot of the spread of the gospel to the ends of the earth.[46] However, one might question whether this Lukan manipulation truly represents a growth in Paul's character as witness.

---

[42]Ibid., 448.
[43]Ronald D. Witherup, "Functional Redundancy in the Acts of the Apostles: A Case Study," *JSNT* 48 (1992) 67–86; and *idem*, "Cornelius Over and Over and Over Again: 'Functional Redundancy' in the Acts of the Apostles," *JSNT* 49 (1993) 45–66.
[44]Witherup, "Cornelius Over and Over," 47.
[45]Witherup, "Functional Redundancy," 82–83.
[46]Witherup, "Cornelius Over and Over," 64.

In the narrative context of the first account, Saul the persecutor is transformed into Paul the witness. In this context, growth of the Pauline witness is observed.[47] This witness is powerful and effective, resulting in an attempt on Paul's life. If Witherup is correct in his assessment that the Pauline witness continues to grow, then the second Damascus account should occur within a context of an even greater and more effective Pauline witness. Yet, when the larger literary context of the second Damascus narrative is considered, one finds no such witness. Instead, the Pauline witness has decreased, not increased. Beginning with his arrest outside the Temple until after the second Damascus account, Paul is totally ineffective in verbally presenting his defense, and at no time does Luke record that Paul shared the gospel. Luke recorded neither forward progress for the gospel nor any opportunities for Paul to preach (Acts 21:27—24:33). If Paul's character as a witness has grown then literarily one should observe an increase in Paul's effectiveness as a witness and in opportunities to bear witness. Neither is observed. One does observe—as Witherup has proposed—a manipulation of the Pauline character of witness, only this manipulation is a regression of Paul's character of witness instead of growth.

Finally, Daniel Marguerat suggested that the Lukan repetition of the Damascus narrative served a theological purpose.[48] He carefully delineated that the three narratives do not totally function on the same plane. While a level of connectivity exists across the three reports, each functions differently.[49] Marguerat drew several conclusions, one of which was that the repetition of the "Damascus road event allows the author of Acts to unfold the theological theme that he cherishes beyond everything else; the theme of the power of the Risen One as a transforming force within history."[50] According to Marguerat, each of the Damascus narratives functions in a different way to reveal the transforming power of Jesus.

Which of the above suggestions concerning Luke's employment of the Damascus narrative is correct? Did Luke repeat Paul's Damascus experience to portray Paul as a witness, an enemy, or to demonstrate the

---

[47] Acts 9:1-25.
[48] Daniel Marguerat, "Saul's Conversion (Acts 9, 22, 26) and the Multiplication of Narrative in Acts," in *Luke's Literary Achievement: Collected Essays*, JSNTSS 116 (Sheffield: Sheffield Academic, 1995), 127–55.
[49] Ibid., 137.
[50] Ibid., 155.

transforming power of Jesus? Perhaps all three are correct; that is, each exegete has identified one of several interlaced facets present in the repetition of the Damascus narrative. How can one fuse these seemingly non-related suggestions concerning the Lukan repetitions? One finds guidance in the work of Stevens.

As noted above, Gerald Stevens argued that Luke presented two interrelated themes in the Stephen speech of Acts 7, *God Active* and *God Resisted*. He proposed that with the Stephen speech, Luke suggested that God was always active, working outside the land of promise among new peoples and in new ways to facilitate the growth of his kingdom. God was always active, but whenever and wherever God was active, resistance was present. People—ironically even God's own people—resisted God's activity. Stevens contended that these themes were fundamental to the plot development of Acts. As Luke developed his overarching theme of Acts—the outward progression of the gospel—he utilized characters and events in order to elaborate the significance of the two themes of *God Active* and *God Resisted* throughout the entire text of Acts. This elaboration becomes especially important in the presentation of the character and ministry of Paul in Acts.

Central to his presentation, Stevens identified the presence and function of these two themes in Luke's articulation of Paul's narrative ethos at the beginning of his second missionary journey. Stevens determined that with the beginning of the second missionary journey, Acts 15:37—16:10, the narrative theme present in the ethos of Paul's character was that of *God Resisted*. Stevens stated, "That Paul actually is fighting the Spirit is evident in the way Luke characterizes the launching of this new initiative."[51] He argued that Luke had portrayed Paul as one who resisted God even as God was attempting to act. Paul resisted God's action by striking out on a mission journey guided by his own personal agenda and ambitions. Paul thus found himself hemmed in by the Spirit

---

[51]Stevens, "Luke's Perspective," 14. Stevens argued that, contrary to the success of the first journey and the unity and harmony produced, the second journey began without unity and harmony. He concluded that the fragmentation of the mission team was due in part to the stubbornness and self-reliance of Paul. The mission journey was at Paul's bidding and not that of the Holy Spirit. That Paul was acting outside the bounds of the Holy Spirit is seen in the resistance Paul experiences from the Spirit (13–17).

until he experienced a corrective vision that reoriented his focus and mission objectives.

Stevens concluded his presentation by tracing the themes of *God Active* and *God Resisted* as they applied to Paul's last trip to Jerusalem. He concluded that Paul's last trip to Jerusalem was not God's will but was a journey narrative containing echoes of the resistant spirit of Paul found at the beginning of the second mission journey.[52] Using six key passages, he argued that Paul's journey to Jerusalem—just like the second mission journey—was at Paul's behest and not that of the Holy Spirit.[53] Instead of the journey being God ordained—a commonly assumed exegetical point—Stevens insisted that the author of Acts portrayed a resistance by Paul to the Holy Spirit's guidance toward Rome. Paul's disobedience to the will of the Spirit is therefore a tragic portrayal of the themes of the Stephen Speech of Acts 7.[54]

Stevens noted that the Damascus Road narrative retold in Acts 22 included elements that were integral to the Lukan characterization of Pauline resistance and disobedience to God's will. Stevens posited that Luke's delayed telling of Paul's temple vision created an ironic

---

[52]Stevens, "Luke's Perspective," 17–37.

[53]Ibid., Acts 19:21; 20:22-23; 21:4, 11-12; 22:17-21; 23:11.

[54]Stevens determined that Luke plainly portrayed Paul's resistance to God in his final journey to Jerusalem beginning in Acts 19:21. Having experienced the greatest success of his entire mission career in Ephesus, Paul decided he must travel to Jerusalem and then to Rome. A surface reading of the text indicates that both are part of God's divinely ordained plan. However, Stevens argued that the grammatical structure indicated a dramatic narrative tension between Paul's plans and God's plans. He demonstrated two important observations concerning the grammatical structure of the verse. First, he discussed that ἔθετο was a true middle. Thus, with this verb, Luke identified that the plan to go to Jerusalem was Paul's own plan and not that of God. Stevens then noted that Luke had coupled this true middle with the idiomatic phrase ἐν τῷ πνεύματι, which meant "to make up one's own mind." The use of a true middle verb and the idiomatic phrase with the plan to go to Jerusalem signaled that the plan to travel to Jerusalem was Paul's plan. On the other hand, Stevens contended that a second grammatical feature clearly indicated that the plan to go to Rome was that of the Holy Spirit. He observed that Luke employed the verb of divine necessity, δεῖ, with Rome and not Jerusalem. Stevens concluded that Luke constructed Acts 19:21 to demonstrate that although God had told Paul to go to Rome, Paul had decided on his own account to go to Jerusalem first. Thus, this journey was beginning much like the second journey, at Paul's own bidding and not that of the Holy Spirit.

Stevens demonstrated that the tension between God's plans and Paul's plans only became more apparent as Paul drew nearer to Jerusalem. He noted that in Acts 20:22-23

demonstration of the stubbornness of Paul to the Spirit in the current narrative.⁵⁵ Following Stevens, the barracks vision of Acts 23:11 then served as a "word of grace" that corrected Paul's stubbornness and disobedience.⁵⁶ Interestingly, the second retelling of the Damascus event occurs after this correcting vision of grace but within the same forensic setting as the retelling in Acts 22. The two scenes function almost like bookends of the Pauline trial narrative with the barracks vision occurring in the middle of this larger narrative, Acts 21:33—26:32.

Within the proposals of Stevens are the tools needed to combine the suggestions of Witherup, Gaventa, and Marguerat. According to Gaventa,

---

the verb of divine necessity, δεῖ, was absent with the mention of travel plans. Further, he argued that the warnings from the spirit of the dangers of the journey were anachronistic in light of the divine protection Paul had received on his first two mission journeys and while at Ephesus. The absence of any signal of God's will coupled with the removal of divine protection, according to Stevens, was foreboding signs.

Furthermore, during Paul's stay with the Tyrian disciples, Luke plainly recorded that the disciples warned Paul by the Spirit not to go to Jerusalem. Stevens maintained that the "spirit" mentioned in the text was none other than the Holy Spirit. Thus, any continued journey to Jerusalem was now in open and plain defiance to the expressed will of the Holy Spirit.

Stevens next recognized that in Acts 21:11-12 the presence of the we-section expressed a stark difference of opinion between Paul's character and the narrator. The narrator openly resisted Paul's journey to Jerusalem. In addition to the presence of strains in the relationship between Paul and the narrator, Stevens affirmed that the prophecy of Agabus contained strong echoes of prophetic judgment texts from the LXX. Not only was Paul resisting the Holy Spirit in his traveling to Jerusalem, but God's judgment was about to bind the apostle.

Stevens further noted that in Acts 22:17-21 Luke employed a form of narrative delay to create an ironic effect for the reader. He posited that Luke delayed the telling of the temple vision until the present narrative to highlight Paul's resistant ethos. In the past, God had instructed Paul not to work in Jerusalem. However, Paul is relating this vision from none other than Jerusalem. His presence in the city had always been a problem and was yet again.

Stevens concluded that the narrative ethos of Paul was that of one resisting God who was trying to act. This resistant Paul, if he was to be used for further service of God had to be corrected. Stevens contended that this correction occurred in the vision related in Acts 23:11. In this text Paul receives a vision—much like his vision in Troas—that reorients his character and mission (17–34).

⁵⁵Stevens, "Luke's Perspective," 32.
⁵⁶Ibid., 34.

the first telling of the Damascus event formed a paradigmatic characterization of Saul/Paul, that of an overcome enemy.[57] Saul had resisted the activity of God by persecuting the members of "The Way." In response, God had overcome him. God was active, and one of God's own people, Saul a Jew, resisted and was overcome. This encounter demonstrates the power of Jesus over the enemy Saul and results in his transformation into a witness who will take the gospel towards the ends of the earth.[58] The first Damascus narrative would serve to inform the reader of Saul/Paul's character, a characterization that would be repeated. Saul/Paul is one who is resistant to God. He fights against God as God seeks to move his kingdom forward. God overcomes this resistant one and transforms him into a witness who will help rather than hinder the forward progression of the kingdom of God.

Formally, the process of character transformation in Acts 9 of the character Saul is a full transformation from (1) resisting enemy to (2) overcome enemy to (3) empowered witness. This transformation is in keeping with the overall Lukan narrative strategy of Acts, the progression of the gospel to the ends of the earth (Acts 1:8). For Luke, Paul would play a major role in fulfilling this literary movement. However, Paul cannot function within this role of one who takes the gospel to the ends of the earth as long as his narrative ethos is that of Saul the persecutor. Therefore, Saul the persecutor must be transformed into Paul the witness.

In Acts 22, the resistant spirit of Paul's narrative ethos again rises to the surface. Paul once again, as he did in his character as Saul, resists the forward progression of the gospel. Now, however, instead of resisting through persecution, he resists by refusing to travel to Rome (Acts 19:21). Paul will still function in the text of Acts as the primary means of accomplishing the narrative strategy of Luke. To return Paul's character to this positive role, Luke must show Paul's transformation from one who is resistant into one who is once again obedient to the will of God. In Acts 22 this transformation is begun, but only half of the transformation is completed. Paul is again the enemy and as such has his power as witness vacated. After this vacating of power, Paul's character remains in literary limbo as only overcome enemy. Still awaiting literary development in the Acts plot is Paul's character

---

[57]Gaventa, "Overthrown Enemy," 439–49.
[58]Witherup, "Functional Redundancy," 67–86; and Marguerat, "Saul's Conversion," 127–55.

transformation into Paul the empowered witness. The third stage of the paradigmatic episode showing Saul's character transformation in Acts 9 must be completed in Acts 23–28. If Paul is to continue in his role as a witness, then he must be transformed so that he will help and not hinder the activity of God. Thus, Luke must include narrative development showing Paul's character transformation. This final character transformation is the literary purpose of the third Damascus narrative.

After the transforming "word of grace" in the barracks vision of Acts 23, a third Damascus account appears within the narrative. This third narrative reminds the reader of the transformation previously experienced by Paul's character and models a similar transformation to be anticipated in the following narrative. The overcome Paul will be transformed and empowered as Paul the witness, now headed for Rome, as God originally ordained. Within the text of Acts, Luke utilized the Damascus narratives to recall paradigmatic themes of Paul's narrative ethos: resisting God (disobedience) and subsequent overcoming, as well as obedience toward God and subsequent empowering as a witness.

The proposal for the following work is that the author of Acts utilized multiple accounts of Paul's Damascus Road experience, both individually and collectively, to characterize Paul.[59] This characterization involves the transformation of Paul's character in his role as a witness for the gospel. In the first Damascus Road account, the author of Acts provided the primary and paradigmatic characterization of Paul. This paradigmatic characterization included themes that were central to Paul's narrative ethos in the text of Acts. This paradigmatic characterization included themes that were central to Paul's narrative ethos in the text of Acts. These central themes were (1) resistance and obedience to God's will and (2) restraint and empowerment. In the later Damascus Road narratives, Acts 22 and Acts 26, the author

---

[59]The proposed research will be based upon the assumption that one author penned both the Gospel of Luke and Acts. This work will involve the employment of a literary-rhetorical methodology. Therefore, no investigation will be undertaken concerning the authorship, readership, historical milieu, or source traditions of the text. Second, the literary-rhetorical method to be proposed will be applied solely to the identified multiple accounts of the Damascus narratives, not the entire text of Acts. Third, the proposed thesis will involve no discussion of personal spiritual implications of Paul's Damascus experience; thus, no suggestions will be offered as to Paul's Damascus experience as a call or as a conversion.

manipulated these themes to portray Paul as working inside or outside the will of God. In Acts 22, the author portrayed Paul as one resistant to the will of God. The result of Paul's resistance was the restraining of Paul's witness for the gospel. In Acts 26, the author depicted Paul as one obedient to the will of God, thereby leading to the empowering of Paul's witness for the gospel. These characterizations of Paul fit within the larger authorial intent for the Book of Acts. The gospel progresses to the ends of the earth overcoming all resistance, even resistance that arises internally within the movement. "Thus, when Luke makes his final word in the text of Acts the adverb "unhindered" (Acts 28:31, ἀκωλύτως), he has tied the final ribbon on his narrative strategy."[60]

Having surveyed and found inadequate the past studies of the literary intent behind the repetition of the Damascus Road narrative in Acts, as well as suggesting a new direction of research, one is now prepared to begin a new investigation of the subject. However, before serious investigation may begin, a few comments concerning methodology must be made.

Methodology

The methodology of this book involves the proposal of a new rhetorical method, *Literary-Rhetorical Criticism*. This method is a substantial modification of the principles found in George Kennedy's seminal work, *New Testament Interpretation through Rhetorical Criticism*.[61] The marshaling of rhetorical canons for the purpose of biblical interpretation is not a new phenomenon. However, Kennedy was one of the first modern practitioners of rhetorical criticism. In his pioneering work he made an invaluable contribution to the field. Kennedy was the first modern interpreter to provide a programmatic outline for, and definition of rhetorical criticism. He provided clarity and methodological cohesion to a methodology where ambiguity had previously reigned. Scholars quickly noticed the importance

---

[60]Gerald L. Stevens, personal conversation, January 23, 2003.
[61]Kennedy, *New Testament Interpretation*, 33–38. The above is only an overview of the proposed *Literary-Rhetorical Criticism*—just enough to enable the reader to understand and follow its application, as presented in chapters 2–5. A full statement appears in the Appendix on Methodology. Many readers will find greater profit from this study by reading the Appendix before continuing.

of Kennedy's seminal work and the number of works utilizing his brand of rhetorical methodology swelled. However, in recent days, the number of scholars using Kennedy's methodology has drastically declined, so that the insights and principles set forth by Kennedy have been abandoned. The abandonment of such is due both to certain points of failure in the philosophical and historical presuppositions of Kennedy and to interpreters who have misunderstood and misapplied many of Kennedy's insights.

One of Kennedy's greatest points of failure was the lack of clarity in his own delineation of methodology. Various scholars have struggled to demarcate clear steps within Kennedy's method. Some interpreters have at times divided Kennedy's method into four steps; others have seen five, or even six steps. The methodology seems so clear, but the application has been somewhat chaotic, with varying emphases of the principles presented by Kennedy. Further, Kennedy himself did not draw a clear line between the study of rhetoric and the contribution of rhetoric to the biblical text. As a result, he left open the question of how to read the text in light of rhetorical canons. Finally, faulty philosophical presuppositions plague the methodology. Consequently, there is a universalizing of rhetoric and dependence on modern rhetoric in an avowed classical method.

The faults and lacunas in Kennedy's method, coupled with the lack of clarity in the delineation of the method, have led to the misapplication and failure of Kennedy's rhetorical criticism. The result has been that, after the debunking of Kennedy, the field of rhetorical criticism has returned to the state of methodological chaos that reigned prior to Kennedy. One is left wondering if any life remains at all in rhetorical methodology. Certainly, Kennedy's work suffered from flaws. Yet an outright rejection with no attempts to correct the flaws is unwarranted. If one will retain and modify the methodological framework of Kennedy and correct for the lacunas, then a new form of rhetorical criticism might be proposed that holds the possibility of returning rhetorical criticism to a loose methodological cohesion.

The following work incorporates a methodology that is an attempt to retain Kennedy's basic methodological structure in a modified form, correcting for historical and philosophical anachronisms in the method. The resulting methodology is *Literary-Rhetorical Criticism*. The basic outline of the proposed methodology looks remarkably similar to that of Kennedy. However, the method incorporates significant philosophical and historical departures from that of Kennedy. The framework of the proposed method is as follows. The first step of any literary-rhetorical analysis involves the defining of the rhetorical unit. This definition establishes the bounds of the pericope and the function of the unit in the overall structure of the text. The second step entails the identification of the rhetorical situation of the pericope by distinguishing the possible *stasis,* genre, and overall rhetorical intent of the author. The final step will consist of conducting an analysis of the rhetorical style and literary movement of the unit in order to follow the logic of the text. The purpose of *Literary-Rhetorical Criticism* is to read and interpret the biblical text by comprehending the meaning and message intended by the author, appreciating fully the genre of the text, and following Hellenistic literary and rhetorical principles and rules designed for the construction of such texts. The goal of *Literary-Rhetorical Criticism* is to interpret biblical texts in light of the rhetorical and literary milieu in which they were written.

Data will be gathered from five primary sources and numerous secondary sources. *The Greek New Testament* (4th ed.) will serve as the text for analysis.[62] The rhetorical handbooks of Quintilian, Cicero, Pseudo-Cicero, and Theon will be employed as the basis of the proposed literary-rhetorical method.[63] Numerous secondary sources concerning the practice of rhetorical criticism, the analysis of Paul's Damascus account, and Greco-Roman historiography will also inform the study.

---

[62] *The Greek New Testament*, 4th ed., Kurt Aland et al. (New York: United Bible Societies, 1993).
[63] The following rhetorical handbooks will be employed: Cicero *De Inventione,* trans. H. M. Hubbel, LCL 386 (Cambridge: Harvard Univ. Press, 1949; reprinted, 1993); Cicero, *Rhetorica Ad Herennium,* trans. Harry Caplan, LCL 402 (Cambridge: Harvard Univ. Press, 1954; reprinted, 1989); Quintilian, *Institutio Oratoria,* trans. H. E. Butler, 4 vols. (Cambridge: Harvard Univ. Press, 1920–22; reprinted, 1995–98); and "Theon Θέωνος Σοφιστοῦ Προγυμνάσματα," trans. James R. Butts, in "The Progymnasmata of Theon: A New Text with Translation and Commentary" (PhD diss., Claremont Graduate School, 1986). Unless otherwise stated, translations of the above works will be by the respective translators.

2

Saul, the Overcome and Empowered Enemy

The Rhetorical Unit

The present rhetorical unit of study is Acts 9:1-26a. The unit is bounded by an encircling journey motif of the main character, Saul, from Jerusalem to Damascus and subsequently from Damascus to Jerusalem.[1] The

---

[1]Rudolf Pesch identified the boundaries of the present pericope as vv. 1-22. Pesch, *Apostelgeschichte (Apg 1-12)*, 298. He argued that while the meaning or effects of the story of Saul's Damascus road event extended into the subsequent verses, the story of Saul's experience should be limited to his experience and the immediate effects. Pesch's argument for regarding the Damascus road narrative as complete in v. 22 has some validity. The unit—as identified by Pesch—is surrounded by encircling allusions to binding, leading, Jerusalem, and the high priest (see vv. 1, 2, 21). However, to delimit the end of the passage to v. 22 is to disregard the overall journey narrative of which vv. 1-22 is but a part. The larger narrative includes Saul setting out from Jerusalem for Damascus (v. 2). Saul's purpose is to return once again to Jerusalem (v. 2). Saul is delayed due to unforeseen events that occurred on the road to Damascus. Nonetheless, until Saul returns to Jerusalem, completing his intended journey, the narrative is not complete. Thus, Saul's Damascus road narrative should be considered as 9:1-26a. For arguments similar to those of Pesch, see Jacob Kremer, "Die Dreifache Wiedergabe des Damaskuserlebnisses

rhetorical unit consists of four interlocking narrative panels (vv. 1-9, 10-16, 17-19a, and 19b-26a). The unit is part of the larger framework of Acts, which is the second volume written by Luke to Theophilus concerning the events that have been fulfilled. The contents of this second volume concern the events that occurred after Jesus' ascension (Luke 1:1-4; Acts 1:1-11).

One may outline Luke's second volume to Theophilus in one of three ways. First, one might chart the book as progressing programmatically and geographically following the statement of Jesus in Acts 1:8.[2] A second option is to outline the book thematically.[3] The third and final option is to divide the work according to major characters.[4] Most interpreters follow some form of the first option, acknowledging that Luke's work progresses geographically: Jerusalem, Judea and Samaria, and finally to the ends of the earth. For reasons to be discussed below, this method of arranging the book seems to fit best with the authorial intentions of Luke. The narrative framework Luke applied to his work is that of the progression of the gospel to the ends of the earth in an unhindered fashion.[5] The gospel is first given witness in Jerusalem (Acts 1:12-5:42), then in Judea and Samaria (Acts 6:1—12.25), then unto the ends of the earth (Acts 13:1—28.31).[6]

Pauli in der Apostelgeschichte: Eine Hilfe für das Rechte Verständnis der Lukanischen Osterevangelien," in *The Unity of Luke-Acts,* ed. J. Verheyden, BETL 142 (Leuven: Leuven Univ. Press, 1999), 330; and C. K. Barrett, *A Critical and Exegetical Commentary on the Acts of the Apostles,* 2 vols., ICC (Edinburgh: T. & T. Clark, 1994), 1.439.

[2]The following is a sampling of interpreters who outline the Book of Acts programmatically. See Barrett, *Acts,* 61; F. F. Bruce, *The Book of the Acts,* rev. ed., NICNT (Grand Rapids: Eerdmans, 1988), 36–37; and Hubbard, "Commissioning Accounts," 187–98.

[3]The following is a sampling of interpreters who outline the book of Acts thematically. See Jacob Jervell, *Luke and the People of God: A New Look at Luke-Acts* (Minneapolis: Augsburg, 1972), 158; Charles H. Talbert, *Reading Acts: A Literary and Theological Commentary on the Acts of the Apostles* (New York: Crossroad, 1997), i; and Polhill, *Acts,* 72–76.

[4]For an example of a character-based outline see Brawley, *Luke-Acts,* 43.

[5]Stagg has argued convincingly that the basic premise of the Book of Acts is the triumph of the gospel, overcoming all barriers and progressing to the ends of the earth. See Frank Stagg, *The Book of Acts: The Early Struggle for an Unhindered Gospel* (Nashville: Broadman, 1955).

[6]Acts 6:1 is chosen as the beginning of the second major narrative movement in Acts instead of Acts 8:1. In 8:1 the church in Jerusalem endures a violent persecution and

The present rhetorical unit appears within the second part of the larger narrative, the witness of the gospel in Judea and Samaria (Acts 6:1—12:25).

The Rhetorical Situation

In order to determine the rhetorical situation of the present unit of study, one must understand the genre and rhetorical situation of the Book of Acts as a whole. In general terms, the Book of Acts is a work of narrative prose that is inextricably tied to the Gospel of Luke. The two works are fused by similar prologues addressed to the same audience and bear striking thematic and historical parallels. However, the attempt to define the specific genre of Acts has created something of an ongoing struggle within New Testament scholarship.

Interpreters have not been able to establish or agree upon the genre of Acts. A large part of the dilemma that scholars face in determining the genre of Acts arises from the lack of literary parallels from the surrounding Greco-Roman world with which to compare Acts. Karl Schmidt asserted that Luke and Acts both resist classification among the standard genres of Greco-Roman literature. He contended that the writings of Luke reveal that Luke understood the rudiments of worldly culture and literature, but his efforts fell far short of matching in detail any extant literary document.[7]

The inability to find any firm points of comparison between extant Greco-Roman documents and Acts has not dissuaded interpreters from labeling the genre of Acts. Most often, scholars have pointed to history as the genre of Acts. While this genre label might appear specific on the surface, the label is quite broad and thus has given rise to many varying proposals.

---

scatters to Judea and Samaria. The text appears to provide a natural and logical point of division following the programmatic statement of 1:8. However, the events of Acts 8.1 occur only as narrative developments of the conflict between Stephen and the Hellenistic Jews, a storyline that begins in 6:1. The narrative of 6:1—7:60 lies behind the scattering of the Jerusalem church in 8:1 and cannot be separated from the larger narrative movement observed in Acts 8:1—12:25.

[7]Karl Ludwig Schmidt, *The Place of the Gospels in the General History of Literature*, trans. Byron R. McCane (Columbia: Univ. of South Carolina Press, 2002), 3–13, 27, 78, 84.

Some scholars have been content to classify Acts as a general history. They assert that Luke chose to record the history of the early movement and growth of the church in a manner that generally is in keeping with the historiographical principles of the time.[8] Other interpreters argue that the classification of general history is too broad to be useful. Therefore, attempts have been made to delineate and differentiate between types or sub-genres of Greco-Roman historical prose. The most general of these sub-genres is that of the historical monograph. Darryl Palmer defined the historical monograph as a historical work that consisted of a single book or volume, though the single volume might not fit on a single scroll.[9] Those interpreters who categorize Acts as a historical monograph claim that Luke's intention was to write a one-volume history of the early Christian movement. This literary project was set apart in shape and form from Greco-Roman histories meant to cover vast periods of time, numerous peoples and lands, and fill many volumes.[10] Still other scholars have turned

---

[8] Haenchen, *Acts*, 136–40; Stagg, *Acts,* 17; Étienne Trocmé, "The Beginnings of Christian Historiography and the History of Early Christianity," *ABR* 31 (October 1983) 1–13; David E. Aune, *The New Testament in Its Literary Environment,* LEC (Philadelphia: Westminster, 1987), 77; Luke Timothy Johnson, *The Acts of the Apostles*, vol. 5, Sacra Pagina Series, ed. Daniel J. Harrington (Collegeville, Minn.: Liturgical, 1992), 3; David L. Balch, "Comments on the Genre and a Political Theme of Luke-Acts: A Preliminary Comparison of Two Hellenistic Historians," in *SBLSP* (Atlanta: Scholars, 1989), 343–61; *idem,* "The Genre of Luke-Acts: Individual Biography, Adventure Novel, or Political History?" *SWJT* 33 (Fall 1990) 11–19; Marion L. Soards, "The Speeches in Acts in Relation to Other Pertinent Ancient Literature," *ETL* 70 (1994): 89; Stefan Rebenich, "Historical Prose," in *Handbook of Classical Rhetoric in the Hellenistic Period: 330 B.C.–A.D. 400,* ed. Stanley E. Porter (Leiden: Brill, 1997), 306; Terrance Callan, "The Preface of Luke-Acts and Historiography," *NTS* 31 (1985) 580; Witherington, *Acts*, 32-9; and Chistoph Heil, "Arius Didymus and Luke-Acts," *NovT* 42 (2000) 392.
[9] Darryl W. Palmer, "Acts and the Ancient Historical Monograph," in *The Book of Acts in Its First Century Setting,*" vol. 1: *The Book of Acts in Its Ancient Literary Setting*, ed. Bruce W. Winter and Andrew D. Clarke (Grand Rapids: Eerdmans, 1993), 5.
[10] Martin Hengel, *Acts and the History of Earliest Christianity*, trans. John Bowden (Philadelphia: Fortress, 1979), 36; Kennedy, *New Testament Interpretation,* 114; Hans Conzelmann, *Acts of the Apostles: A Commentary on the Acts of the Apostles,* trans. James Limburg et al., Hermeneia (Philadelphia: Fortress, 1987), xi; Fitzmyer, *Acts*, 127; von Eckhard Plümacher, "*Terateia*: Fiktion und Wunder in der hellenistisch-römischen Geschichtsschreibung und in der Apostelgeschichte," *ZNW* 89 (1998) 66-90; and *idem,* "Cicero und Lukas: Bemerkungen zu Stil un Zweck der historischen Monographie," in *The Unity of Luke-Acts*, ed. J. Verheyden, BETL 142 (Leuven: Leuven Univ. Press, 1999), 770–73.

to the Old Testament as a model for Luke's construction of Acts. They contend that while Luke did write in the vein of Hellenistic historiography, he was heavily influenced by Deuteronomistic historical forms found in the LXX.[11] Gregory Sterling insisted that Luke-Acts belonged to a specific and narrowly defined category of history entitled apologetic historiography: ethnography. He claimed that Luke wrote his prose narrative as a member of the Christian movement to establish and explain the identity of the group to the world.[12] Hubert Cancik proposed that Acts represented a type of institutional history.[13] Finally, Kota Yamada posited that Luke wrote historical prose that was rhetorical in form and function.[14]

Clearly, interpreters have struggled to define and agree upon which type of history Acts represents. Much of the difficultly in locating Acts within the realm of Greco-Roman history exists because of the nature of such history. Hellenistic history represented a confluence of literary streams rather than a single literary tradition. Schmidt noted, "The consensus among historiographers seems to be that 'history' was not a narrowly defined genre in ancient Greek writing, but rather was on a wide spectrum of prose writing styles."[15] A second area of difficulty in identifying Acts firmly within the historical camp is Luke's literary style. David Mealand conducted in-depth analyses of the literary style of the Book of Acts using word samples and their functions. He determined that the style of Acts is

---

[11]Willam S. Kurz, "Luke-Acts and Historiography in the Greek Bible," in *SBLSP* (Atlanta: Scholars, 1980), 283–300; Daryl D. Schmidt, "The Historiography of Acts: Deuteronomistic or Hellenistic?" in *SBLSP* (Atlanta: Scholars, 1985), 417–27; and Brian S. Rosner, "Acts and Biblical History," in *The Book of Acts in Its First Century Setting*, vol. 1: *The Book of Acts in Its Ancient Literary Setting*, ed. Bruce W. Winter and Andrew D. Clarke (Grand Rapids: Eerdmans, 1993), 65–82.

[12]Gregory E. Sterling, "Luke-Acts and Apologetic Historiography," in *SBLSP* (Atlanta: Scholars , 1989), 326–42; and *idem*, *Historiography and Self-Definition: Josephus, Luke-Acts and Apologetic Historiography*, NovTSup 64 (Leiden: Brill, 1992), 17, 393.

[13]Hubert Cancik, "The History of Culture, Religion, and Institutions in Ancient Historiography: Philological Observations Concerning Luke's History," *JBL* 116 (1997) 673-95.

[14]Kota Yamada, "A Rhetorical History: The Literary Genre of the Acts of the Apostles," in *Rhetoric, Scripture and Theology: Essays from the 1994 Pretoria Conference*, JSNTSS 131 (Sheffield: Sheffield Academic, 1996), 230–50.

[15]Schmidt, "Rhetorical Influences," 51. See also Rebenich, "Historical Prose," 287.

somewhere between the LXX and that of Dionysios.[16] Luke's style is somewhat nebulous, neither purely historical nor purely biblical.

Exegetes such as Richard Pervo have seized upon the inability of scholars to locate Acts within the canons of Hellenistic history and argued that such inability is evidence that the genre of Acts is not history. Pervo has pointed to the genre of the Hellenistic novel as a possible setting for the literary form of Acts. He has referred to the presence of miracles and wonders, humor, shipwrecks, and a general entertaining nature as proof that Luke wrote Acts as a historical romance or novel.[17] Marianne Bonz agreed with Pervo's arguments but turned her attention from the romance novel to the Greco-Roman epic tradition. She theorized that Acts was a foundational epic much like Virgil's *Aeneid*. As an epic, Acts provided the ancient history and heritage of the Christian community.[18] James Dawsey noted that the stories in Acts bear a strong resemblance to folk epic but not historiography.[19]

While these interpreters have highlighted important aspects of the literary nature of Acts, they have not argued sufficiently that Acts should be categorized as a novel rather than history. Von Eckhard Plümacher has countered the arguments of Pervo. He contended that the presence of signs and wonders in the text of Acts are not sufficient evidence to locate Acts within the genre of the novel. He provided evidence that similar signs and wonders are present in Hellenistic histories.[20] Further, simply because a piece of literature is entertaining does not automatically mean that piece of literature was not intended to be history. Finally, the use of sources by Luke—a common assumption by most scholars—could have

---

[16]David L. Mealand, "Style, Genre, and Authorship in Acts, the Septuagint, and Hellenistic Historians," *Literary and Linguistic Computing* 14 (1999) 479–506. See also idem, "Hellenistic Historians and the Style of Acts," *ZNW* 82 (1991) 42–66.

[17]Richard I. Pervo, "Israel's Heritage and Claims upon the Genre(s) of Luke and Acts: The Problems of a History," in *Jesus and the Heritage of Israel: Luke's Narrative Claim upon Israel's Legacy*, ed. David P. Moessner and David L. Tiede, Luke the Interpreter of Israel 1 (Harrisburg: Trinity, 1999), 127–43.

[18]Marianne Palmer Bonz, "The Best of Times, the Worst of Times: Luke-Acts and Epic Tradition" (Ph.D. diss., Harvard Divinity School, 1996), revised as *The Past as Legacy: Luke-Acts and Ancient Epic Tradition* (Minneapolis: Fortress, 2000).

[19]James M. Dawsey, "Characteristics of Folk-Epic in Acts," in *SBLSP* (Atlanta: Scholars, 1989), 317–25.

[20]Plümacher, "*Terateia*," 66–90.

included certain folk stories handed down about the early disciples. However, the use of such sources does not automatically force one to classify Acts as folk epic.

A final literary genre to which interpreters have turned in an attempt to classify the genre of Acts is that of the biography. Charles Talbert was one of the first to make such a proposal. He argued that Luke-Acts was modeled on the form of the ancient biography genre such as found in the work of Diogenes Laertius's *Lives of the Eminent Philosophers*. Talbert insisted that Luke-Acts followed an "(a) life of founder + (b) succession narrative" format, which he identified in the work of Diogenes.[21] Later scholars noted that, while perhaps Talbert overstated the presence of an (a) + (b) pattern in the work of Diogenes Laertius, the genre of biography warranted further investigation. Loveday Alexander speculated that Acts, specifically the Pauline narrative in Acts, was modeled after the biographical tradition related to Socrates. She classified such a tradition as ancient intellectual biography.[22]

In response to the arguments marshaled for locating Acts within the biographical tradition, one must consider the comments of David Barr and Judith Wentling. They stated, "Luke-Acts does not fit neatly into any of the external organizational patterns we found in classical biographies. The existence of Acts prevents us from considering it a biography of one person."[23] Certainly, Luke and Acts have some biographical elements. The Gospel of Luke seems to emphasize the single character Jesus, and Acts spotlights numerous characters. Nonetheless, the two volumes are concerned with much more than just single characters. They include a multitude of minor characters and events which Luke interlaced to form a unified narrative.

Within which genre can one definitively place Acts? If one considers only the extant Greco-Roman genres, perhaps no answer exists. In a test

---

[21] Talbert, *Literary Patterns*, 134.
[22] Loveday C. A. Alexander, "Acts and Ancient Intellectual Biography," in *The Book of Acts in Its First Century Setting*, vol. 1: *The Book of Acts in Its Ancient Literary Setting*, ed. Bruce W. Winter and Andrew D. Clarke (Grand Rapids: Eerdmans, 1993), 31–63.
[23] David L. Barr and Judith L. Wentling, "The Conventions of Classical Biography and the Genre of Luke-Acts: A Preliminary Study," in *Luke Acts: New Perspectives from the Society of Biblical Literature Seminar*, ed. Charles H. Talbert (New York: Crossroad, 1984), 73.

of Cancik's suggestion concerning locating Acts within the historiography of philosophy or institutional history, Christoph Heil wrote, "However, the comparison of Luke-Acts with 'the historiography of philosophy' shows a typical dilemma of Form Criticism. If the net is cast widely and if a broad basis of texts is chosen, the number of parallels with Luke-Acts grows. If only one ancient text is compared with Luke-Acts, the formal parallels will be few (but possibly instructive nevertheless), and the discrepancies receive more attention."[24] While Heil was addressing Cancik's proposals, his comments have a bearing on all attempts to locate Luke-Acts within any existing Hellenistic literary genre. Both the Gospel of Luke and the companion volume Acts bear similarities to many different extant literary genres of the first century. However, neither the Gospel of Luke nor Acts exactly matches the organizational structure, themes, or style of any of these genres. Because the Gospel of Luke and Acts bear similarities to many Hellenistic genres, one should hesitate in asserting that the Gospel or Acts must fit within a specific genre. Larry McCormick stated:

> It is probable that Christian writers were influenced by their cultural environment and reflect its trends. However, the ancient world was a diverse cultural complex which we know only in a fragmentary way dependent on the chance survival of sources. The continual temptation is to draw direct lines of comparison or influence between surviving pieces without knowing their place in the larger context. We can find almost whatever we seek, and we can see significance in what we find. In such a case the study of literary forms is a task to be pursued with special caution, with a care not to use categories which arise out of imposed, rather than inherent classifications.[25]

In Acts one finds a narrative of the early beginnings—insomuch as Luke recorded them and in his understanding—of the Christian movement. Thus, one is pressured to assent to Cadbury's general conclusion

---

[24] Heil, "Arius Didymus," 360.
[25] Larry David McCormick, "Paul's Addresses to Jewish Audiences in the Acts of the Apostles: Luke's Model Witness and His Calling to Testify to 'The Hope of Israel'" (PhD diss., Fordham University, 1996), 9.

that "Luke's work is nearer to history than to any other familiar classification."[26] Acts appears to be the result of a confluence of several literary streams, the melding of various genres. However, the predominant or perhaps most prevailing and encompassing of these genres is that of history.

The downfall of labeling Acts as history—even as a default category—is that this classification does not satisfactorily address the issue of genre as related to the rhetorical situation of the work. Can one say anything further about the issue of genre? The answer to this question hinges upon the extent of the unity of the Gospel of Luke and Acts. Martin Hengel noted that Luke and Acts bear a striking historical and theological unity.[27] Tannehill also supported the thesis that the Gospel of Luke and Acts were unified, not only theologically but narratively. He proposed that the text of Acts carries forward narrative themes and agendas that Luke first raised in the text of the Gospel.[28] David Aune went a step beyond Hengel and Tannehill and argued that the issue of unity between Luke and Acts extends beyond narrative, historical, and theological themes to the issue of genre. He claimed that in addressing the issue of the genre of Acts one has to consider the genre of the Gospel of Luke, for the two could not be separated.[29]

Pervo and Mikeal Parsons have reacted strongly against Aune's suggestion of the generic unity of Luke and Acts. They do not doubt the historical unity of the two narratives but argue that the two do not have to be of one genre. They contended that "if the argument for generic unity is pressed vigorously, Luke must be regarded as nothing more than half of a work rather than as a Gospel. What then could be made of Matthew, Matthew [sic] Mark, and John?"[30] Perhaps with this statement Pervo and Parsons have unknowingly addressed the genre dilemma of Acts.

---

[26] Henry J. Cadbury, *The Making of Luke-Acts* (New York: Macmillan, 1927; reprint, London: S. P. C. K., 1968), 133.

[27] Hengel, *Acts,* 37.

[28] Tannehill, *Narrative Unity, passim.*

[29] Aune, *New Testament,* 77.

[30] Mikeal C. Parsons and Richard I. Pervo, *Rethinking the Unity of Luke and Acts* (Minneapolis: Fortress, 1993), 43. See also Richard I. Pervo, "Must Luke and Acts Belong to the Same Genre?" in *SBLSP* (Atlanta: Scholars, 1989), 309–16.

The thematic, narrative, and historical unity between the Gospel of Luke and Acts is plainly evident. The two are addressed to a single audience, Theophilus (Lk. 1:3; Acts 1:1). Further, Luke constructed the prologue of Acts to overlap key events and themes found in the conclusion of the Gospel, giving the narrative of Acts continuity with the narrative of Luke.[31] However, in spite of the overlapping elements the Gospel of Luke appears to have a different narrative flavor and agenda than Acts. Even Tannehill in his attempt to underline the narrative unity of Luke and Acts approached the two works differently. He approached the Gospel thematically, while his approach to Acts was more systematic. He stated that the different format of his two volumes was necessitated by the difference of narrative continuity between Luke and Acts.[32]

Pervo and Parsons appear to be correct in their assessment that Luke and Acts maintain narrative, thematic, and historical unity but fail to display generic unity. However, the presence of narrative, historical, and thematic unity force one to question why the two volumes appear to lack generic unity? Why would Luke choose to write two volumes that tell a single story, progress naturally through time, and develop the same themes, in two different genres? Why tell a single story two different ways? Perhaps Luke did not tell the same story two different ways, but through historical and literary constraints the two volumes only appear to follow two different genres.

In the opening prologue of the Gospel of Luke, one finds Luke's description of the narrative that is to follow. The narrative concerns the things that had been fulfilled. Luke was not the first to write down these events but, having investigated them himself, had chosen to write an orderly account for Theophilus, so that he might solidify what Theophilus had been taught (Luke 1:1-4). The mention of carefully investigating the events that had occurred, in addition to the mention of eyewitnesses and the handing down of stories, clearly indicates the use of sources in the construction of the Gospel

---

[31]In the prologue of Acts one finds at least six events which are present in the concluding words of the Gospel of Luke: (a) Post-resurrection appearances of Jesus (Luke 24 and Acts 1:3); (b) Meals with the disciples (Luke 24:40-43 and Acts 1:4); (c) Command to witness (Luke 24:42-49 and Acts 1:8); (d) Command to stay in Jerusalem (Luke 24:49 and Acts 1:6); (e) Ascension of Jesus (Luke 24:50-51 and Acts 1:9); (f) Return of disciples to Jerusalem (Luke 24:52-53 and Acts 1:12).

[32]Tannehill, *Narrative Unity*, 5–6.

and the subsequent volume of Acts. The most obvious of these sources for the Gospel of Luke is the Gospel of Mark. The sources for the Book of Acts are unknown and possibly will never be discovered. In considering the use of sources, specifically the use of Mark in the writing of the Gospel of Luke, could one envision the possibility that the Gospel of Luke looks like a Gospel for no other reason than the incorporation of this source? Could Luke appear to fit the Gospel genre because the themes and ideas of the Gospel of Mark constrained Luke's literary hand? Could the Gospel of Luke only appear to be a Gospel in genre while Luke actually intended the work to tell a single story using one genre in two volumes? If the Gospel of Luke is not fully a Gospel, and if the text of Acts is possibly the same genre as Luke, then how might one classify Luke-Acts? The possibility exists that classification within a single ancient literary class is impossible, for Luke may have engaged in a form of literary experimentation. Luke could have constructed a singled literary work by imitating not a single kind of literature but by manipulating and incorporating various literary streams in order to form a work that is an uneven mosaic with one element or repertoire at times dominating others. Such a suggestion would explain how the two works are a single literary genre in the mind of the author and yet defy later classification within specific literary streams.

How could one support the claim that Luke and Acts are actually unified as a single genre? The key is not to begin with the Gospel of Luke. Luke was constrained in the construction of his Gospel by his use of the Gospel of Mark. One should instead begin with the text of Acts and work backwards to the Gospel of Luke. One should determine what Luke was attempting to do within the text of Acts and then work backwards to the Gospel, seeking to find the same narrative agenda. In the text of Acts, Luke appears to have told the story of the triumphant gospel. The gospel is progressing to the ends of the earth through the witness of the disciples (Acts 1:8). Along the way—as the gospel progresses—resistance is encountered. As God is active, resistance is present. Sometimes the resistance comes from God's own people.[33] In each case of resistance, God overcomes the resistance set up against the gospel. The gospel continues to move triumphantly and without hindrance to the ends of the earth.[34]

---

[33] Stevens, "Luke's Perspective," 1–16.
[34] Stagg, *Acts*, 266.

The themes identified in Acts are the progression of the gospel, the meeting of resistance, and the overcoming of resistance by the power of God. In looking back to the Gospel of Luke, one finds the same themes, even in the prologue. In the prologue of the Gospel, Luke claims that what he is writing is a narrative of the things that have been fulfilled.[35] The participle is perfect passive. The question is therefore raised as to the referent of the participle. Who is the one by whom the events have been fulfilled? The most natural conclusion is to locate the participle as a divine passive participle, thus making God the referent.[36] God is the one who has accomplished the events that form the narrative Luke is about to relate. Therefore, in all that follows, the main character is not Jesus, Peter, Paul, or any of the other disciples or other minor characters. The main and central character of Luke's two-volume narrative is God himself. Therefore, the narrative is a story about what God has done. At the narrative level, this story is told through the use of the characters of Jesus and the disciples in Luke and through Peter and Paul as the main characters in Acts. In the Gospel of Luke, God, through Jesus and the disciples, proclaims the gospel with the ultimate design that all people hear this gospel message. The gospel is intended for the ends of the earth.[37] In the task of proclaiming the gospel, resistance is met time and again from Jews, the Pharisees, and even Jesus' own disciples.[38] The ultimate resistance encountered in the gospel is the crucifixion of Jesus. However, God overcame even this ultimate resistance through the resurrection of Jesus (Luke 23:26—24:53). With the ascension of Jesus, the task of proclaiming the gospel to the ends of the earth is handed over entirely to the disciples of Jesus and their followers. They are endowed with power and move forward through Jerusalem, Judea, and Samaria, and then towards the end of the earth by reaching Rome.

When Luke and Acts are considered together, Luke is not a Gospel, and Acts is not an independent historical monograph. Instead, the two works function together to tell a single story, the story of what God has done in moving the gospel to the ends of the earth. In this light, how

---

[35]Luke 1:1 (πεπληροφορημένων).
[36]Eduard Lohse, "Lukas als Theologe der Heilsgeschichte," *EvTh* 14 (1954) 261.
[37]Luke 2:29-32; 3:4-6; 4:18-19.
[38]For example see Luke 4:14-30; 6:1-5; 9:51-56; 11:14-26; 14:1-14; 20:1-40; 22:1-6; and 22:54-62.

should the two works be identified? Robert Maddox suggested that Luke was a "theological historian." Therefore, Luke-Acts would form a theological history.[39] In light of the above discussion, Maddox's suggestion is close to the mark, but greater clarity can be achieved. One might cautiously apply the term "theography." One could define a "theography" as a writing or history about God. Therefore, the two volumes of Luke and Acts work together to tell the history of God's movement. If such an identification is correct, then Luke has manipulated existing genres in order to tell his story in a new way. Luke's story is a historical work, but not one that would fit any Hellenistic category. His work is history only in the most general sense. In considering the genre of Luke and Acts, one must consider them as the history of God himself, how he has moved and what he has done. Perhaps, then, Luke-Acts should be considered a "theography" as a preliminary term to explain Luke's creative generic manipulation.

If Luke's story is that of the movement of God to advance the gospel, where and how does the identified rhetorical unit fit within this movement? The storyline of Acts begins as a continuation of the storyline of the Gospel of Luke. As noted above, six overlapping events are evident in the final chapter of Luke and the prologue of Acts. The story that seemed to conclude with the resurrection and ascension of Jesus has not ended. Those events were only the beginning.[40]

In the opening words of Acts, Jesus appears to his disciples and discusses the kingdom of God (Acts 1:3, 6-8). While the disciples are concerned with the restoration of the kingdom of God to Israel, their concern highlights a misunderstanding of Jesus' teaching. The kingdom of God has to do with the empowerment of the disciples by the Holy Spirit and their bearing of witness to the ends of the earth (Acts 1.8). Here one finds the rough narrative outline for the present work. The disciples will carry on the work of Jesus by bearing witness under the power of the Holy Spirit. The disciples will begin by bearing witness in Jerusalem (Acts 1:12—5:42). They will move to Judea and Samaria (Acts 6:1—12:25). They will

---

[39]Robert Maddox, *The Purpose of Luke-Acts*, FRLANT 126 (Göttingen: Vandenhoeck & Ruprecht, 1982).
[40]Gerald L. Stevens, personal conversation, April 14, 2003.

continue to advance toward the ends of the earth (Acts 13:1—28:31). The primary theme of the book will be the outward expansion of the kingdom of God, but as noted above, this theme will work in concert with two other themes identified in the Stephen Speech. God is active, and when God is active, he is resisted.[41]

After the ascension of Jesus, the disciples go back to Jerusalem and complete the number of disciples so that their witness to the resurrection of Jesus can be borne (Acts 1:15-26). Once the number of disciples is again twelve, Pentecost occurs and the believers are empowered as Jesus promised. Having received the power of the Holy Spirit, the believers begin to bear witness in Jerusalem (2:1-41). The immediate result of the event is the acceptance of the message and the subsequent baptism of three thousand people (2:41). The larger effects that result from the empowering and bearing of witness are a unity among the believers, caring for the needs among the community, fellowship, and an awe of God (2:42-47). The immediate effects come in a summary statement found after an intense moving of the Holy Spirit and subsequent bearing of witness in Jerusalem.

Soon after the gospel begins to advance in Jerusalem, this progress experiences resistance (Acts 3:1—4:35). The antagonism to the gospel is external to the movement of the disciples and is found after the healing and subsequent preaching by Peter and John in the temple precincts. Peter and John are hauled before the Sanhedrin for bearing witness, and the disciples are put in jail until the next day (4:1-3). The resistance is quickly overcome. The efforts of the priests, the captain of the temple guard, and the Sadducess are not enough to stop the gospel. Many people who hear the message believe, and the number of believers grows (4:4). Further, when the Jewish rulers tell Peter and John to stop speaking or teaching in the name of Jesus, the apostles refuse, even after repeated threats. The threats have no effect on the people, for they are praising God (4:16, 18, 21). The believers meet with Peter and John, and, after hearing of the threats of the Sanhedrin, pray to God. Their prayer receives a response as the place where they are meeting is shaken. Again, all are filled with the Holy Spirit and speak the word of God boldly (4:31).

---

[41] Stevens, "Luke's Perspective," 1–16.

Saul, the Overcome and Empowered Enemy

To this point in the narrative, the outward progression of the gospel in Jerusalem has experienced only one source of resistance. The resistance is external to the movement and consists of imprisonment and threats. However—in spite of the resistance—people believe, the Holy Spirit continues to empower the believers, and they continue to bear witness. One should note that after this story of resistance Luke placed a short summary section (Acts 4:32-37). In this short pericope, Luke noted the results of the gospel movement after resistance had been overcome. Interestingly, the results are similar to those found in the previous summary section (2:42-47). Unity and fellowship exist among the believers. Further, needs are met and the bearing of witness to the resurrection continues (4:32-47).

The gospel has short respite, for resistance is again faced. This time the resistance is internal to the gospel movement (Acts 4:36—5:16). Joseph, a Levite, brings money to the disciples as part of the meeting of the needs of the believers. Ananias and Sapphira, fellow believers, sell a field but withhold part of the money they receive. In so doing they resist the Holy Spirit. They resist by hindering the effects of the gospel, which to this point have been the caring and meeting of needs. The resistance is quickly and dramatically overcome as both Ananias and Sapphira are struck dead (5:5, 10).

One may now characterize the types of resistance that the gospel encounters. The gospel may face external resistance in attempts to stop the bearing of witness. The gospel may encounter internal resistance in attempts to limit or hinder the work of God but not stop the bearing of witness. The result of the overcoming of the resistance by Ananias and Sapphira is great fear among the believers. The apostles keep bearing witness, and the number of believers grows. Finally, many are healed in miraculous ways (5:11-16). Significantly, after the resistance is overcome, the spread of the gospel continues.

Once again, the overcoming of resistance provides the gospel movement little rest. Opposition arises that is external to the movement (5:17-42). The Jewish rulers attempt to stop the bearing of witness by arresting the apostles and putting them in jail. The external pressure is an attempt to put an end to the bearing of witness. The resistance is soon overcome. An angel appears and opens the doors of the prison, and the apostles enter the temple and begin to teach the people (5:21). When the

Sanhedrin convenes, the apostles are not found in the jail but in the temple teaching, the very practice the Jewish leaders had tried to curtail. The leaders bring the disciples before the Sanhedrin and remind them of the orders they had been given not to teach or speak in the name of Jesus. The disciples refuse to obey; therefore, the Sanhedrin wants to put the apostles to death. However, Gamaliel warns them to leave the apostles alone lest they be found fighting against God (5:35-39).

Gamaliel's speech is of prime importance in the context. His words are the last words found concerning external attempts to resist the gospel in the first major narrative section of Acts (1:12—5:42). His words provide the narrative point that external pressure to stop the bearing of witness will fail because those bearing witness represent God's interests. Fighting against God is pointless. The speech of Gamaliel is Luke's narrative comment about the resistance faced by the gospel to this point. Resistance to the gospel will be overcome. Such is the case in the present setting. The apostles leave the Sanhedrin and continue to teach and bear witness to Jesus (5:41-42).

In the first narrative block of Acts—the gospel advancing in Jerusalem—the story is one of progress and resistance. Each time resistance is faced—external or internal—that resistance is overcome. Fellowship, unity, a meeting of physical needs, and continued growth of the gospel movement are the outcome. Rounding out this section is the speech by Gamaliel, in which he notes what is already apparent to the reader. All resistance to the gospel is pointless, for such resistance is fighting against God.

With the appointment of the seven—a move that meets physical needs and results in continued growth among the believers—and the preaching of Stephen, the second major narrative section of Acts begins (6:1—12:25). As Stephen preaches, opposition arises from the members of the synagogue of the Freemen (6:8—8:3). Those resisting Stephen are Hellenistic Jews. They are opposed to Stephen, who also is linked to the Hellenists. These Hellenistic Jews try to argue against Stephen but are not able to stand up against his wisdom. Therefore, they persuade men to accuse Stephen falsely of blasphemy, which leads to his arrest. These actions amount to external resistance, an attempt to stop the bearing of witness.

A mob drags Stephen before the Sanhedrin, where he must answer to the charges brought against him. Out of his speech come two important themes for the text of Acts: (1) God is always active, even outside the land of promise; and (2) God's people have always resisted him.[42] These themes can be observed in the first narrative movement of Acts and play out in the Stephen episode.

The mob stones Stephen after his speech. The resistance seems to have overcome the gospel (7:54-56). The matter is further complicated when a larger persecution breaks out on the Jerusalem church as a result of the stoning of Stephen. At the fore of this persecution is a man by the name of Saul (8:1-3).

Saul's character is important, for he is identified with the Hellenistic Jews. He is in agreement with their actions and at one with their persecution. Saul participates in their attempt to end the bearing of witness by ravaging the Jerusalem church. He goes from house to house dragging off people in order to put them in prison (8:1-3). Saul replaces the mob as the preeminent external threat to the progress of the gospel. He is ferocious and persistent. He is an antagonist who is part of an external resistance—the stoning of Stephen—that is not yet overcome. One should note that while the Hellenists stone Stephen and Saul persecutes the church, the bearing of witness does not stop but expands. The persecution has an unintended effect. Those who bear witness scatter to Judea and Samaria, the next region of witness expansion (1:8; 8:4).

One of those scattered is Philip, one of the seven Hellenists appointed by the church in Jerusalem. He goes forth with others fleeing Jerusalem on account of the persecution. Philip travels to Samaria and there sees the gospel progress. The Holy Spirit falls upon the believers in Samaria as they accept his message (8:5-17). The expansion of the gospel is soon met with internal resistance. Simon, who is part of the gospel movement in Samaria, resists. His resistance is his request to receive the ability to give the Holy Spirit to those upon whom he might lay hands. Simon's request amounts to a limiting of the Holy Spirit. He wishes to give the Holy Spirit only to those upon whom he lays hands (8:18-19). His request is a limiting of witness, not a stopping of witness. Peter rebukes Simon, and the resistance is overcome (8:20-25). From this point, Philip goes forward and bears witness to an Ethiopian eunuch, a foreshadowing of the ends of the earth (8:26-40).

---

[42]Ibid., 1–16.

Philip the Hellenist bears witness, and thus the gospel progresses. Curiously, Luke then returned to the story of Saul, who is also identified with the Hellenists. Luke constructed the Saul narrative so that the plot continued through the Philip narrative. When Saul is again seen he is still breathing threats, something he began in Acts 8:3. In effect, Luke has encircled the narrative about Philip with the narrative about Saul. The effect is a contrasting of two Hellenists and their two opposing responses to the gospel. Philip is a Hellenist who heeds the gospel and bears witness. Saul resists and tries to stop the bearing of witness. Narratively, Philip represents the proper response of a Hellenistic Jew to the gospel. Saul must either be overthrown or become like Philip.

The trajectory of the narrative to this point has been the conflict between the expanding gospel proclamation and resistance. In each encounter God overcomes resistance, and the gospel progresses. Thus, in the selected narrative about Saul, the resistance should be overcome and the gospel should progress. Here lies the rhetorical situation behind the present rhetorical unit. The designated narrative is one of conflict between Saul and the progressing gospel to Judea and Samaria. This conflict sets up an inevitable collision between God and Saul, the persecutor and enemy of the gospel. In this conflict, God—the chief actor in the "theography" that is Acts—must somehow overcome the resistance of Saul and once again advance the gospel in Judea and Samaria. How God overcomes Saul's resistance is the essence and substance of the ensuing narrative.

The Analysis of Acts 9:1-26

Within the rhetorical unit of Acts 9:1-26a, Luke transformed the character of Saul by showing Saul overpowered in his resistance as the persecutor and enemy of the church and then by portraying him as empowered in his bearing of witness for the gospel. Luke accomplished this process of transformation in four narrative panels. That is, Luke constructed the larger narrative from four shorter narratives. Each shorter narrative represents a stage in the process of the transformation of the character of Saul. By analyzing these different component narratives, one can discover Luke's outline of character transformation.

Saul, the Overcome and Empowered Enemy

Because the present unit of study consists of narrative and not direct speech, one should not use the Hellenistic rhetorical handbooks as interpretive tools. Due to the literary nature of the text, the *progymnasmata* should be probed for interpretive handles in analyzing the text. The present text of study is a narrative of Saul's experience on the road to Damascus and the subsequent results of that experience. Turning to the *progymnasmata* of Theon, one does find instructions for the construction of a proper narrative. Theon defined narrative as "an explanatory account of matters which have occurred or as if they had occurred."[43] Accordingly, each properly constructed narration was to consist of six elements: (1) character(s); (2) the actions of the character(s); (3) the place of activity; (4) the time of activity; (5) the manner in which the activity was done; and (6) the reason for the actions.[44] The following analysis will trace these elements of narrative in the present rhetorical unit. A table then will be presented in order to provide a summary of the analysis of these elements within the rhetorical unit.

Saul the Overcome Enemy (Acts 9:1-9)

In the opening narration of the Damascus Road event, Saul the persecutor collides with Jesus the persecuted and is totally overcome. The narrative scene is bounded by an *inclusio* of leading. In Acts v. 2, Saul sets out to "lead" the members of "The Way" back to Jerusalem, and in v. 8, Saul is himself "led by the hand" into Damascus. A journeying motif is also predominant in the text as the narrative setting shifts from Jerusalem, to the road, to Damascus, while the narrative time seems to remain constant or indefinite. The event transpires sometime during the day on the journey (v. 3). In this journeying narration, Luke employed three characters: Saul, Jesus, and Saul's traveling companions, who act as one person. Luke's characterization of Jesus and the companions remains constant throughout the narrative. Luke portrayed Jesus as one who is a persecuted, heavenly judge who has the right to indict and overcome Saul. This heavenly judge knows Saul, has plans for Saul, and has the authority to command him

---

[43] Theon 5.1.
[44] Ibid., 5.4-11.

(vv. 4-6). Luke depicted the traveling companions as helpful fellow travelers of Saul who remain somewhat ignorant and amazed at the events that transpire. They hear but do not see (vv. 7-8).

The character of Saul, on the other hand, does not remain constant. Two opposing characterizations of Saul arise in the narrative. The first characterization of Saul is that of the enemy and arch-persecutor of the church. The narrative begins with Saul portrayed "still breathing threats and murder against the disciples of the Lord." Saul threatens the disciples and is willing even to murder them. Saul has an attitude that is hostile to the members of the Way. In the narrative, Saul is willing to act upon his attitude or view of the disciples. He is willing to persecute the Way by going to the High Priest and asking for letters that would grant him the authority to bind and lead those he finds in the Damascus synagogues back to Jerusalem.[45] This action of asking for the letters and his willingness to travel to Damascus demonstrate that Saul is highly motivated in his persecution efforts.[46] Saul is the archenemy of the disciples, completely hostile, and willing to act upon his hostility (vv. 1-3).

Luke first characterized Saul as the enemy of the disciples of the Lord. However, Luke did not allow this characterization to continue, for within the narrative Saul is transformed through an encounter with Jesus on the road to Damascus. After Saul's encounter with Jesus, a new character of Saul the overcome emerges. The character of Saul is no longer one of hostility and persecution but one of brokenness and helplessness. Saul encounters Jesus and is overcome by a light. Saul comes under heavenly judgment as Jesus indicts him as a persecutor. Further, the Saul who encounters Jesus is ignorant of what is happening to him and ignorant of the one who overcomes and indicts him. Saul's authority from the high

---

[45]The asking for letters is more than likely an attempt by Saul to legitimize and empower his persecuting actions. Saul asks for letters "for himself" so that he "might find" and "might lead" any he found back to Jerusalem. Clearly, Saul is acting out his agenda through his own power. He wishes to have the letters for the High Priest to legitimize his actions.

[46]These character traits are simply developments of traits first depicted in Acts 8:1-3. In 8:1-3 Luke described Saul as one who was hostile to Stephen and the church in Jerusalem. Further, this Saul was willing to act upon his hostility by going house to house and imprisoning men and women who were members of the Jerusalem church. The present narrative is simply a continuation of the persecuting efforts of Saul. Saul is still hostile to the disciples and is willing to act upon his hostility.

priest and personal agenda of persecution are stripped and replaced by the commands of Jesus to rise and enter the city. Curiously, Saul is in such a pitiful state that he is not able to obey. He has to be raised from the ground and led by the hand into Damascus, where he sits for three days blind, refusing food and drink. In Luke's narrative, the one who once breathed threats and murder is reduced to one who is helpless, weak, humbled, and blind.[47]

The Lukan characterization of Saul is that of radical reversal. Saul the persecutor and enemy of the disciples of the Lord is overcome. However, in keeping with Theon's pattern, the complete characterization of Saul cannot be understood apart from his actions and the manner and reasons that stand behind his actions and those of the other characters within the narrative.

According to Theon, Act, Manner, and Reason were three aspects of every narrative that were inseparable from Character.[48] While "Act" is self-explanatory, "Manner" and "Reason" are not. In Theon's understanding, "Manner" and "Reason" lay behind the "Act" of characters in the narrative. Theon instructed his readers that "inseparably connected with 'manner' is whether the act occurred unintentionally or intentionally. Each is divided into three: the unintentional into ignorance, chance and necessity; the intentional has occurred either with force or secretly or with deceit."[49] He also taught that "with 'reason' for the activities belong: whether it has occurred for the sake of acquiring benefits, or for removing evil; or because account

---

[47]Acts 9:4-6, 8-9. This new characterization of Saul is one of irony. While he went to Damascus to lead, he in turn is led. While Saul's eyes are open, he cannot see. While he was persecuting the disciples on his own power, he can now no longer rise, eat, or even drink.

[48]Theon 5.4-14.

[49]Ibid., 5.32-34. Theon employed the lexeme Βιά to speak of force. The word can imply the use of violence or power. However, Theon seems to have had a larger semantic range in mind. With Βιά Theon certainly included the use of violence or might in the action of the character. Nonetheless, since there are only three categories of intentional action, actions performed openly—volitionally—also are, by default, intentionally forceful actions. Therefore, to state that the actions of a character occur "intentionally with force" can simply mean that the character acted openly and with willful volition. The locating of volitional action within Βιά becomes apparent when one follows the suggestion of Butts and interprets Theon's comments in light of Cicero or Aristotle. See Butts, "Progymnasmata," 369.

of friendship, or because of a wife, or for the sake of children, or because of emotions (love, hate, envy, pity, drunkenness, and passions similar to these)."[50]

In the opening of the narrative, Luke portrayed Saul as one who threatened the disciples, asked for letters, made plans to bind the disciples, and then traveled to Damascus (vv. 1-3). Saul undertakes each of these actions intentionally and with force. Saul intentionally acts upon his hostile attitudes against the members of the Way. No one forced him to engage in his persecution activities. Saul acts intentionally for at least three reasons. First, Saul acts out of probable emotions of hatred and anger. His hostile views of the disciples are plainly seen in the threats and promises of murder that he uttered. Second, he more than likely acts for the purpose of removing evil. He wishes to destroy the members of the Way. Finally, Saul acts for the sake of his religious faith. Saul views the members of the Way as direct threats to his religious faith who need to be punished.

Interestingly, while Jesus' actions are different from those of Saul, some of the manner and reasons for his actions are the same. Jesus speaks to Saul indicting him of persecution on the road to Damascus. In appearing to Saul, he overpowers him and subsequently commands him to rise and enter the city (vv. 4-6). Jesus acts, just like Saul, intentionally and with force. He is not forced to act upon Saul but does so openly. Jesus acts for at least two reasons. First, Jesus acts for the sake of removing evil. Ironically, Saul the persecutor and archenemy of the disciples happens to be the evil receiving Jesus' actions in this case. Second, Jesus acts for the sake of his disciples. By overcoming Saul, Jesus spares them harm and humiliation.

Both Jesus and Saul act intentionally with force for the sake of removing evil and for the members of their religious groups. When these two characters collide, Jesus is victorious, and Saul is overcome. As a result of his encounter with Jesus, Saul's actions cease. Saul first falls to the ground. He speaks to Jesus and opens his eyes, but no further action is seen from the character Saul (vv. 4-6). Saul is not able to obey the commands that he receives from Jesus. The actions that Luke did describe were no longer those of one who acted intentionally with force. After the encounter with Jesus, instead of acting intentionally, Saul is only able to act unintentionally out of necessity. He falls to the ground because of the brightness of the

---

[50]Ibid., 5.35-38.

light. He is forced to question Jesus, because he is unaware of Jesus' identity. Saul opens his eyes only because the light forced him to close them. Saul completes his limited actions for two reasons. First, Saul acts out of his emotion of fear. Saul has been overcome by a light and encounters a voice he does not know. He is blind and unable to rise from the ground due to the experience. Finally, Saul acts to acquire benefits for himself. He questions Jesus to obtain the identity of the one who has overcome him. Even here, Luke displayed the tragic reversal of Saul as the identifying reply comes in the form of a divine judgment.

The final characters in the narrative are Saul's traveling companions. Luke sketched the actions of these characters in brief strokes. However, the actions of these characters highlight the dramatic reversal of Saul from persecutor to one who is helpless and broken. The companions hear the voice that indicts Saul but fail to see anyone. Because of the overwhelming events, they are forced to raise Saul from the earth and lead him into Damascus (vv. 7-8). The companions' actions are accomplished unintentionally through chance and necessity. By their chance presence on the road with Saul, they hear the voice of Jesus. Because of the inability of Saul to rise and walk, they are forced to raise Saul and lead him into the city of Damascus. Their actions are accomplished for two reasons. First, they act on the account of friendship or perhaps pity of Saul. They do not leave him on the road in his helpless estate. Second, they act for the possible reason of the emotion of fear. Hearing the voice and seeing its effect upon Saul, the companions act by caring for Saul in his time of need.

The characterization of Saul in this first narrative panel is now complete. Saul is openly hostile to the members of the Way and is willing to act intentionally and with force against these members. He seeks to persecute them because of his severe hatred and attempts to remove what he considers evil. However, this intentional actor encounters another intentional actor on the road to Damascus. Saul encounters Jesus, who also is acting to remove evil. The evil is Saul in this case. In the ensuing conflict, Jesus emerges as the victor and Saul the vanquished. No longer is Saul the intentional actor who persecutes the disciples of the Lord, but he is instead broken and blind, unable to resist the unintentional actions of his fellow travelers. Saul, the one who threatens and hates, is transformed into Saul, the one who fears. After his encounter with Jesus, Saul is a man under divine judgment, unable to rise, unable to see, unable to eat, and unable to drink. Saul is overcome.

Table 1. The Overcome Saul (Acts 9:1-9)

Character	(A) Saul (before encounter): threatens disciples; willing to murder; self-motivated; persecutor; travels to Damascus; empowered by letters; empowered to bind
(B) Saul (after encounter): overcome by light; persecutor; ignorant of voice; commanded by Jesus; unable to rise; blind; unable to go to Damascus; unable to obey Jesus; not eating or drinking
(C) Jesus: persecuted; authority to command; overcomes Saul; knows Saul; has plans for Saul; heavenly judge
(D) Travelers: amazed; speechless; hearing but not seeing; helpers of Saul
Act	(A) Saul (before encounter): threatens disciples; asks for letters; plans to bind; purposes to travel to Damascus
(B) Saul (after encounter): falls to ground; speaks to Jesus; opens eyes
(C) Jesus: speaks to Saul; indicts of persecution; commands Saul
(D) Travelers: hear; raise Saul; lead Saul
Time	Time is technically indefinite, sometime during the journey to Damascus.
Place	Journey Motif: Jerusalem→Road to Damascus→Damascus
Manner	(A) Saul (before encounter): intentional: force
(B) Saul (after encounter): unintentional: necessity; unintentional: ignorance
(C) Jesus: intentional: force
(D) Travelers: unintentional: chance; unintentional: necessity
Reason	(A) Saul (before encounter): emotion-hatred; removing of evil; for sake of religious faith
(B) Saul (after encounter): for sake of acquiring benefits; emotion: fear
(C) Jesus: removing of evil; for sake of disciples
(D) Travelers: on account of friendship/pity; emotion: fear

Ananias the Resistant Disciple (Acts 9:10-16)

The second narrative panel consists of a dialogue between two main characters, Ananias and the Lord. Luke marked the bounds of the narrative with shifts in location and character. Beginning in Acts 9.10, the characters shift from Saul and his companions to Ananias and the Lord. The place of the subsequent dialogue is some undisclosed location in Damascus, possibly the residence of Ananias. The time could be anytime during the three days that Saul sat waiting in Damascus. The narrative ends with the final words of the Lord to Ananias in Acts 9.16 and the subsequent shift in narrative location and characters in Acts 9:17.

Saul, the Overcome and Empowered Enemy

The present section is a wonderful example of a complex narrative within a narrative, that is a complete story told within an encompassing story.[51] In this embedded story, Saul's character recedes to the background, while the characters of Ananias and the Lord come to the fore. Luke's suppressing of the character of Saul has an interesting effect in the narrative context. As noted above, in the previous narrative panel Saul the persecutor was overcome and left in a state of helplessness and brokenness. By restraining Saul's character in the present narrative, Luke continued the sense of helplessness and brokenness from the previous episode. In the current narrative Saul is not allowed to act or speak. Instead, Saul is only discussed, viewed passively by the current actors who dispute the true nature of Saul's character.

As stated above, the two primary characters in the present narrative are the Lord and Ananias. Luke characterized the Lord as one who knew Ananias and appeared to him in order to commission him. The Lord speaks with authority, reveals his plans for Ananias, and overcomes the resistance offered by Ananias. The Lord has plans for Saul and is the only one who knows Saul's true state (9:10-12, 15-16). Luke portrayed Ananias as a disciple of the Lord and a resident of Damascus. Ananias is commissioned by God and yet is resistant to the Lord's guidance. Ananias is ignorant of Saul's true state and thus terrified of who he thinks Saul still is (9:10-11, 13-15).

The entire scene that takes place between Ananias and the Lord hinges upon a discussion of Saul's true character and state. Saul is viewed passively, never allowed to act or speak. Ananias views Saul as one who does evil against the saints. Saul is empowered by the high priests and is intent on binding those who call on the name of the Lord (vv. 13-14). The Lord observes Saul praying while in a helpless state. Saul is blind, waiting, and in need. Saul's character is in tension. He can see a vision but remains physically blind (vv. 11-12). What Saul currently represents is not what the Lord intends for Saul. According to Luke, Saul has been chosen by God to be the bearer of the name of the Lord. Saul is to be one who suffers for the name of the Lord (vv. 15-16). The Lord intends that Saul be the very opposite of the person Ananias thinks he is. Instead of a persecutor, the Lord intends Saul to be persecuted. Instead of one who

---

[51]Ibid., 5.427-428.

does evil to the saints, the Lord intends that Saul be one who bears the name of the Lord. In place of the authority of the high priest, the Lord intends that Saul be his chosen vessel.

Luke portrayed the Lord as one who is an all-knowing authority, while Ananias is an ignorant, resistant disciple. In these roles Luke had the Lord appear to Ananias and communicate a commission to the disciple. When the Lord encounters the resistance of Ananias, he overrules the resistance and reveals his plans for the former persecutor. The Lord acts intentionally with force at all times in the present panel. He chooses to appear to Ananias. He speaks and commands obedience from Ananias. His reasons for acting are singular. The Lord acts to acquire benefits for his name. He appears to Ananias and commissions him so that Saul might become the one whom the Lord intends him to be. Ananias acts by listening to the Lord and then resisting his commission. His actions display a lack of intentionality. He listens out of necessity as the Lord appears to him. He resists, not intentionally, but unintentionally because of his ignorance of who Saul now is. His actions are the result of his emotion of fear.

Luke's portrait of Saul is characterized by tension. Through Ananias's eyes, Luke depicted Saul as one who harms the saints and had intended to arrive in Damascus to bind them. Saul acts intentionally with force out of his desire to remove evil, out of his hatred, and for the sake of his religious faith. Ananias's view of Saul at one time was correct but is so no longer, because the Lord has overcome Saul. Through the Lord, Luke corrected Ananias's view of Saul. Saul is one who sees a vision, prays, and waits for transformation. Saul acts unintentionally out of necessity. In his state of blindness and brokenness after his encounter with Jesus, he has no choice but to wait and pray. He waits to acquire the benefit of receiving his sight and waits out of the emotion of fear as a result of encountering Jesus.

With the above analysis in view, the characterization of Saul in the present narrative panel is complete. Luke depicted Saul as one who is still overcome. The Lord is the most powerful actor in the panel. The Lord is the only one who acts intentionally and with force. Saul is not allowed to be an active character, but one who is viewed passively. Saul is also in the process of transformation. Some confusion still exists as to who Saul really is. Because of the confusion, Luke has yet to reveal the person Saul is to become. The Lord intends Saul's character to be stripped of his former identity and remade. Saul's identity is to be transformed from persecutor to persecuted, from one who does evil to one who is a chosen vessel, and from one who binds to one who bears the name of the Lord.[52]

Table 2. God and Ananias (Acts 9:10-16)

Character	(A) Lord: knows Ananias; commissions Ananias; speaks with authority; has plan for Ananias; rejects resistance; has plan for Saul; knows truth about Saul (B) Ananias: disciple of the Lord; resident of Damascus; commissioned by the Lord; resistant to God; ignorant of Saul; afraid of Saul (C) Saul (Ananias): evil doer to saints; empowered by High Priest; intent on binding (D) Saul (Lord): praying; blind; waiting; in need; chosen by God; bearer of name; suffer for name
Act	(A) Lord: appears to Ananias; commissions Ananias; overcomes resistance; reveals plans for Saul (B) Ananias: listens to God; rejects commission (C) Saul (Ananias): harms saints; arrives in Damascus (D) Saul (Lord): sees vision; prays; waits for Ananias
Time	Sometime during or at end of three days in Damascus
Place	Damascus—possibly the residence of Ananias
Manner	(A) Lord: intentional: force (B) Ananias: unintentional: necessity; unintentional: necessity (C) Saul (Ananias): intentional: force (D) Saul (Lord): unintentional: necessity
Reason	(A) Lord: for sake of acquiring benefits (B) Ananias: emotion: fear (C) Saul (Ananias): removing evil; emotion: hatred; for sake of religious faith (D) Saul (Lord): emotion: fear; acquiring benefits

The Partially Restored Saul (Acts 9:17-19a)

This narrative panel contains Luke's depiction of the beginnings of the process of restoring Saul after his encounter with Jesus on the road. It is demarcated from the larger narrative by place, characters, and time. The narrative occurs in the house of Judas on Straight Street (9:11, 17). The main characters are Saul and Ananias, and the time is sometime after the

---

[52]Luke depicted Ananias as resisting the command and commission of the Lord. This resistance is internal to the movement of the progressing gospel. As such, the resistance is an attempt to limit the bearing of witness. Ananias does not deny the bearing of witness in general but the bearing of witness in particular to the one to whom the Lord sends him.

dialogue between Ananias and God and at the end of the three days of fasting by Saul. In v. 19b, the shifts in characters, setting, and time mark the end of the narrative panel.

The most important feature of the unit in view is Luke's portrayal of Saul. Luke characterized Saul as one whose identity has changed. Luke reversed some of the effects of Saul's encounter with Jesus on the road. Saul regains his strength and his sight. Thus the narrative tension of the previous panel is removed. Saul also enjoys a new relationship with the members of the Way. He is no longer their persecutor but their brother. Further, Saul identifies with the disciples as he is baptized. As his identity and relationships have changed, Saul ends his period of fasting, takes food, and grows physically strong (vv. 17-19a).

However, Luke did not reverse all of the effects of the encounter with Jesus, nor did he include all of the intended results. Luke brought Saul back to the foreground but did not yet portray him as an active character. Saul is still acted upon, and thus the essence of Saul's overcome nature remains intact. Saul, while regaining strength, and enjoying a new identity, does not act. He does not utilize his regained strength nor does he take advantage of his new relationship to the disciples. Further, notably absent in the description of Saul's identity is the Lord's revealed identity for Saul. Saul is physically restored but he is not yet one who bears the name of the Lord. Saul is not yet suffering for the name of the Lord. In the present panel, Luke included elements of restoration in Saul's character. However, Saul is not yet fully restored.

In Luke's rendering, the character of Ananias undergoes changes similar to those seen in Saul. Ananias is now obedient to God's commission. His change in obedience renders a change in his identity. He is now the brother of Saul. Just like Saul, Ananias has seen Jesus and has been commissioned by him. As such, Ananias is the instrument of God by which Saul regains his sight.

Further insight into the characters of Saul and Ananias may be gained through an analysis of their actions, including the manner and reason for their actions. Luke plainly depicted Saul as a passive actor in the text. Saul listens to Ananias. He has hands laid upon him. He is baptized.[53] He receives food and sees only after he is healed through the actions of another.

---

[53] Note the passive voice.

All of Saul's actions take place unintentionally through necessity. Out of necessity—blindness—Saul listens to Ananias and has hands laid upon him. The reception of his sight and the vision of Jesus lead Saul to the necessity of receiving baptism, while the practice of fasting necessitates the receiving of food. Saul acts in this manner for at least two reasons. First, Saul allows himself to be acted upon so that he may acquire benefits. He wishes to receive his sight and gain understanding of the events that have transpired. Saul also acts for the sake of the Lord. In response to the encounter with Jesus and to the healing that has come by the Lord's commission, Saul allows himself to be baptized.

Ananias acts for the same reasons as Saul. Ananias enters the house of Judas and lays hands on Saul, revealing God's will for Saul. He does so unintentionally out of necessity. Ananias did not wish to go to Saul but does so out of obedience to the Lord. God forced him to go to Saul. Thus, Ananias' actions are accomplished for the sake of the Lord.

One should note that Luke did not yet characterize Saul as an intentional actor. Saul begins the larger narrative as a person who acts intentionally with force. Through his intentional actions Saul is identified as a persecutor of Jesus and the disciples, one who is hostile to the members of the Way. Through the ensuing narrative, Luke removed this identity from Saul. Saul is no longer a persecutor and one hostile to the members of the Way, but he is instead a brother, one who is baptized. Further, after his encounter with Jesus, Saul was left physically broken and helpless. Saul has now regained his physical strength, but he does nothing with this strength. He receives healing and a new commission, but he does not act upon them. Saul remains passive. Luke allowed tension to remain in the narrative panel. Saul is only partially restored. The story is not yet over. For complete restoration to occur, Saul must intentionally act with force in his new role and identity.

Table 3. The Restored Saul (Acts 9:17-19a)

Character	(A) Saul: brother of Ananias; one who has seen Jesus; one who sees; baptized; physically strong; no longer fasting
	(B) Ananias: obedient to commission; brother of Saul; knows Jesus; instrument of healing
Act	(A) Saul: listens to Ananias; has hands laid on; baptized; receives food; sees
	(B) Ananias: enters house; lays hands on Saul; speaks to Saul
Time	After three days of fasting and praying; after vision of Ananias
Place	House of Judas on Straight Street
Manner	(A) Saul: unintentional: necessity
	(B) Ananias: unintentional: necessity
Reason	(A) Saul: acquiring of benefits; for the sake of the Lord; emotion: joy
	(B) Ananias: for the sake of the Lord

Saul the Empowered Witness (Acts 9:19b-26a)

The final narrative panel includes the climax of Luke's transformation of Saul from his role as a persecutor to his role as one who bears the name of the Lord. The panel is distinguished from the larger narrative by an *inclusio* of reference to the disciples in Damascus. In v. 19b, Saul remains with the disciples in Damascus for some days. In v. 25, the Damascus disciples help Saul escape a plot on his life. The time of the present narrative is the period following the dialogue between Ananias and Saul, though the exact number of days is indefinite. The events in the narrative take place within the city of Damascus, in the synagogues and at the city wall. Other exact location markers are absent from the narrative.

Luke completed his transformation of Saul in this final Damascus narrative, bringing to completion the effects brought about by the encounter with Jesus on the road. Luke brought Saul to the foreground as the main actor, depicting him as one who now associates with the disciples. Saul preaches that Jesus is the Son of God and grows more powerful in his proclamation. He engages in debate with the Jews and overpowers them, proving that Jesus is the Christ. Further, his actions amaze the crowds, who marvel at the transformation of the one who once sought to destroy those who called upon the name Saul now proclaims. Saul's transformation leads to a plot on his life. However, Saul becomes aware of the plot, and those he once sought to destroy now protect and rescue him (vv. 19-20, 22-25).

Luke has transformed Saul into the image of what Saul once sought to destroy. The radical reversal of Saul's character is complete. Saul is no longer the persecutor of the disciples but a disciple himself. Saul does not attempt to stop the bearing of witness but himself bears witness in a powerful manner. His actions fulfill his intended role prescribed by the Lord. He is persecuted as he bears the name of the Lord.

Saul's actions include his staying with the disciples and preaching in the synagogue. He debates with the Jews and then escapes their persecuting efforts. Saul acts intentionally with force and secretly. Saul intentionally preaches, stays in Damascus, and engages in debates with his fellow Jews concerning the identity of Jesus. When he discovers that the Jews have plotted against his life he intentionally but secretly leaves Damascus. Saul acts for at least two reasons. He acts for the sake of the Lord and for the sake of his religious faith. Saul's preaching and related efforts in Damascus arise out of his encounter with Jesus and his new understanding of his past actions. He engages his fellow Jews—remarkably resembling the former character of Saul—so that they might understand the true identity of Jesus.

Luke has completed the radical transformation of Saul's character. He achieved the transformation by allowing Saul to act intentionally once again. Luke even returned to the reasons for Saul's actions. Luke changed only the emotion of hatred and desire to remove evil. Primarily, Saul still acts for the sake of his religious faith. However, his actions have changed in response to his encounter with Jesus. Saul returns to the same manner and reasons for action, but his actions change because of his understanding of the identity of Jesus and of his own identity change.

Additional insight is gained by analyzing the other characters in the narrative. Three other characters interact with Saul in the narrative: the disciples, the crowd, and the Jews. Luke characterized the disciples as those who reside in Damascus, and those who protect Saul (vv. 19, 25). The disciples act by associating with Saul and rescuing him from death. They act unintentionally out of chance and necessity. By chance, Saul is transformed while in Damascus. Thus, they associate with him. Out of necessity they help Saul escape the plot of the Jews. They act out of friendship and possibly love for Saul.

Saul amazes the crowd because they are ignorant of the transformation that has occurred (v. 21). They question Saul's actions unintentionally out of their ignorance. They question the events, because they wish to acquire benefits. They wish to understand how the Saul who once persecuted the ones who called upon the name of the Lord now proclaims this same name.

Finally, Luke illustrated the Jews as residents of Damascus who are confounded and overcome by Saul. They are potential murderers and persecutors of Saul. They engage in debate with Saul and subsequently plot to kill him, watching the gate for their opportunity (vv. 22-24). They act intentionally with force and with deceit, engaging in debate and plotting to kill Saul. They act for the sake of removing evil and for the sake of their religious faith out of their emotion of hatred for Saul. Ironically, the Jews resemble Saul's previous characterization in action, manner, and reason. They offer resistance much as did Saul, and their efforts, just like Saul's, are frustrated.

Throughout this final scene, Luke restored and empowered a transformed Saul. Luke restored Saul to a position in which he acts intentionally and with force for his religious faith and for the sake of the Lord. These actions in their manner and reason resemble who Saul once was. However, Saul's actions as an intentional actor have changed. He no longer persecutes but proclaims. Saul does not offer threats and murder but is himself the recipient of threats and attempted murder. Saul's source of authority and empowerment was once that of the high priest, but now he possesses the authority and empowerment of God and is able to overcome resistance that he meets in debate and a plot. Saul is restored as an intentional actor and empowered as a witness. Ironically, resistance still remains among the Jews, setting up a narrative tension in the plot to this point. Two outcomes of Jewish resistance exist. Jewish resistance can be overcome completely and set aside—as seen in the first narrative block of Acts—or Jewish resistance can be transformed to Jewish support of the progression of the gospel.

Table 4. Saul the Empowered Witness (Acts 9:19b-26a)

Character	(A) Saul: associated with disciples; preacher in Damascus; powerful; able to confound; can prove Jesus is the Christ; knows of threat; protected by disciples; persecuted by Jews (B) Disciples: residents of Damascus; protectors of Saul (C) Crowd: amazed by Saul; ignorant of transformation (D) Jews: overcome by Saul; residents of Damascus; potential murderers; persecutors
Act	(A) Saul: stays with disciples; preaches in synagogue; debates with Jews; escapes persecution (B) Disciples: associate with Saul; rescue Saul (C) Crowd: question Saul (D) Jews: debate with Saul; plot to kill Saul; watch gates
Time	Days following episode with Ananias and Saul
Place	Damascus
Manner	(A) Saul: intentional: force; intentional: secrecy (B) Disciples: unintentional: chance; unintentional: necessity (C) Crowd: unintentional: ignorance (D) Jews: intentional: force; intentional: deceit
Reason	(A) Saul: for sake of the Lord; for the sake of religious faith (B) Disciples: for sake of friendship; emotion: love (C) Crowd: acquiring benefits (D) Jews: removing of evil; for sake of religious faith; emotion: hatred

Summary

This analysis of the rhetorical unit in light of Theon's six elements of a complete narration now makes concluding comments possible. The rhetorical unit is Luke's paradigmatic portrayal of the radical transformation of external resistance to the progression of the gospel. Saul was the arch-persecutor of the church, who breathed threats and murder against the disciples of the Lord. He acted intentionally and with force for the sake of his religious faith in order to remove evil. Saul stood in the way of the progression of the gospel to the ends of the earth. Therefore, Saul's resistance had to be overcome.

On a journey to Damascus to further his persecuting actions, Saul encountered another intentional actor. Saul collided with Jesus and was overcome. The overcoming of Saul was complete. Luke portrayed the aftermath of the encounter between Saul and Jesus in terms of Saul's helplessness and brokenness. Saul was unable to see, act, or resist action. Jesus, however, emerged victorious and remained an intentional actor who commissioned Ananias to go to Saul. With the Lord's commission to Ananias, Luke provided a trajectory of transformation for Saul's character.

However, Luke did not immediately accomplish this transformation. Instead, Saul remained in the background, a character of tension, caught between his past identity as a persecutor and his future identity as the chosen vessel of God. Through the healing by Ananias, Luke portrayed Saul as physically restored, but nothing more. Saul's restoration and transformation only was partial. He understood who had appeared to him and was physically strengthened, but he did not act. Only in the final scene did Luke portray Saul as one who was transformed fully and restored. Saul returned to the fore of the narrative as one who was able to act intentionally and did so for his religious faith and for the Lord. However, Saul's actions had changed. Saul had a new identity. He was identical to those he once sought to destroy, but in this new identity Saul had great power to confound the Jews as he bore witness, proving the identity of Jesus. This powerful confounding ability was the conclusion of Luke's transformation of Saul. The story of Saul is a story of resistance that is met, overcome, and transformed. Saul represents one possible outcome of resisting the progression of the gospel. God overcomes all resistance, but resistance to the gospel is not final. The prospect exists of resistance being transformed through a changed identity leading to a subsequent empowering and restoration. The present rhetorical unit can be portrayed pictorially as a U-shaped plot. In this plot, Saul moves from a position of acting intentionally and with force under the power and authority of the high priest through a period of helplessness to a position of acting intentionally and with force under the power and authority of the Lord.

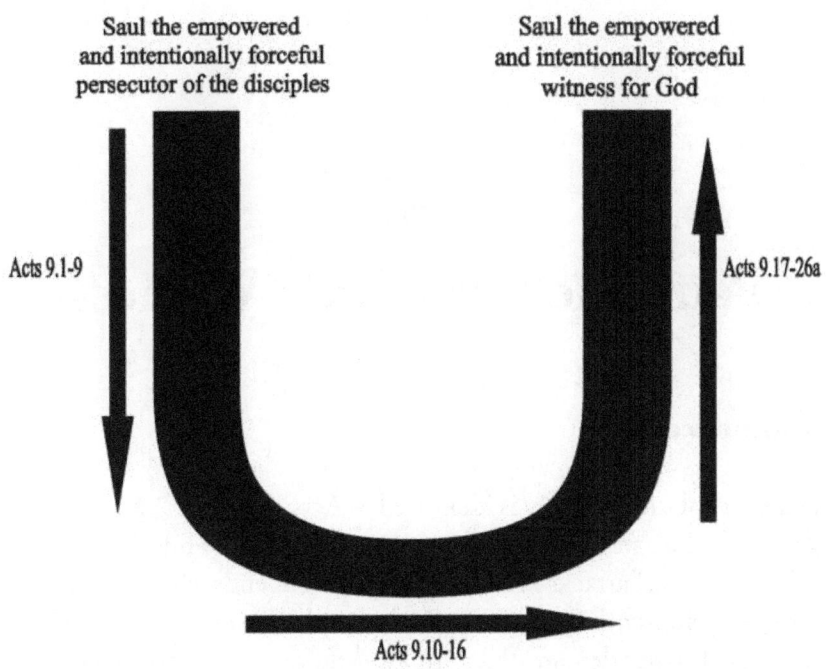

Fig. 1. The Lukan Paradigm for Saul's Character Transformation

3
Paul, the Overcome Witness

The Rhetorical Unit

The rhetorical unit of study is identified as Acts 21:33—22:24a. The unit begins with the arrival of the Chiliarch in Acts 21:33 and his attempt to lead Paul into the barracks in Acts 21:34. The unit ends when the Chiliarch completes his intention of taking Paul into the barracks in Acts 22:24a. The unit is further demarcated with an *inclusio* formed by the cry of the crowd for Paul's death in Acts 21:26 and 22:22. The present unit consists of a speech embedded within an encircling narrative of Paul's binding and arrest. Luke placed the present narrative/speech unit within the last narrative block of Acts, the progression of the gospel to the ends of the earth (Acts 13-28). The unit also forms the beginning of the *Paulusbild* in Acts (Acts 21:33—26.32).

The Rhetorical Situation

In determining the rhetorical situation of the present unit, one must determine the placement of the unit within the larger narrative setting. Second, an investigation of the genre and possible *stasis* of the speech should be undertaken and combined with the overall narrative placement. Through these investigations, the rhetorical situation should become evident.

The narrative movement of Acts 1:12-9.26a has been surveyed in the previous chapter. In this movement, one notices that the story of Acts is that of the progression of the gospel to the ends of the earth. As the gospel progresses, resistance is met and subsequently overcome. Two types of resistance oppose the advancing gospel. First, external resistance confronts the expanding gospel in an attempt to stop the bearing of witness. Second, internal resistance challenges the growing gospel in an attempt to limit the bearing of witness. In each and every case, the resistance is overcome and, in the case of Saul, transformed. When resistance is overcome, growth, unity, fellowship, provision of needs, and the continual bearing of witness are the results.

After the transformation of Saul and his subsequent departure from Damascus, Saul attempts to join the disciples whom he once persecuted in Jerusalem. The effect of this former persecutor uniting with those he once persecuted is growth of the gospel, even though resistance, both internal and external to the movement is encountered (Acts 9:31). The gospel continues to expand in Judea and Samaria as Peter ministers in Lydda and Joppa (Acts 9:32-43). During this time of growth an angel of God appears to a God-fearing Roman centurion named Cornelius, telling him to send for Peter (Acts 10:1-7). God also appears to Peter telling him to go to Cornelius when requested. Nevertheless, Peter resists, much like Ananias had resisted God. Peter does not want to go to the one whom God had specified. However, God overcomes the resistance of Peter with a triple vision (Acts 10:9-22). Peter does go to Cornelius and the gospel expands in a Pentecost-like moment (Acts 10:23-48).

The apostles and brothers in Judea hear of Peter's actions, therefore necessitating Peter's return to Jerusalem to explain the events that have unfolded. Some disciples in Jerusalem have some objections to Peter's actions. Once again, internal resistance to the progression of the gospel appears. The attempt is to limit the bearing of witness by those sent by God. Peter explains the circumstances of the event using a key phrase. He could not oppose God (Acts 10:17). For Peter, to act in any manner other than he did would have been to oppose God. Hearing Peter's report culminating in the conclusion that limiting witness is tantamount to opposing God, those in Jerusalem relent (Acts 11:1-18). Resistance is overcome.

After the overcoming of resistance—that of Peter and those brothers and apostles in Jerusalem—growth and unity are present among the believers (Acts 11:19-30). The gospel advances beyond Judea and Samaria to Phonecia, Cypress, and Antioch, but at first only to Jews. However, a great number of Greeks hear the message of the gospel in Antioch and believe (Acts 11:21). Further, the needs of the believers are met. Saul and Barnabas are sent by the disciples in Antioch—now called Christians—with an offering for those living in Judea facing famine (Act 11:25-30).

The gospel does not advance far without again encountering resistance. This time external resistance through Herod confronts the gospel movement (Acts 12:1-23). Herod arrests some of the church and has James the brother of John put to death. Seeing that his actions please the Jews, he continues his persecution by imprisoning Peter (Acts 12:1-4). The intended purpose of this external resistance is to stop the bearing of witness and outward growth of God's kingdom. God overcomes the resistance by sending an angel to free Peter from prison (Acts 12:6-18). Yet the freeing of Peter does nothing about the larger problem of Herod as a source of resistance. God eventually does deal with Herod in an extreme manner by striking him down and allowing him to be eaten with worms, thus terminating the external resistance (Acts 12:19-23).

Following the outcome of Herod's resistance—the overcoming by God—is a short summary statement. The result of the overcoming of Herod's resistance is a growth of the word of God, which continues to spread (Acts 12.24). Barnabas and Saul return to Antioch after finishing their mission. The mention of their mission echoes a sense of unity and meeting of needs.

This last summary scene ends the second major narrative block of Acts (Acts 6:1—12:25). The gospel has overcome all resistance and continues to spread. The internal resistance of limiting witness has been identified as opposing God. The external resistance has been overcome by removal or transformation. The scene is now set for the last major narrative block, the progression of the gospel to the ends of the earth (Acts 13–28).

The present rhetorical unit of study falls within the last narrative movement of Acts. By now the thematic progress of the gospel is clear. (1) The gospel progresses. (2) The gospel meets resistance (internal or external).

(3) The gospel triumphs over the resistance. (4) Church growth, unity, and the provision of needs are the result as the gospel continues to advance.

The third narrative block of Acts is somewhat different, literarily, from the first two blocks. The final movement focuses on a central character, Saul/Paul, instead of focusing on numerous characters and events. However, the storyline is the same. Although all other major institutions and characters recede to the background, the gospel continues to move forward in a triumphant manner through the person and character of Saul/Paul.

The movement of the gospel toward the ends of the earth begins with the setting apart of Saul and Barnabas by the Holy Spirit and the church at Antioch. The two men are appointed to continue the work the Lord has for them. Their subsequent journey broadens the boundaries of the gospel. Yet as the gospel expands, resistance is still met (Acts 13:1—14:28).

Saul and Barnabas go forth under the guidance of the Holy Spirit and proclaim the word of God.[1] On their journey the two men meet continued resistance to their bearing of witness.[2] In each case, the opposition is overcome, and the result is continued growth of the gospel.[3] Many believe, and the preaching of the two men is not stopped.

Paul and Barnabas return to Antioch, only to find that the resistance they continually faced on their journey also must be faced in Antioch and subsequently in Jerusalem (Acts 15:1-35). Some men from Judea arrive claiming that Gentiles who believe must first be circumcised, or they cannot be saved. This claim is a type of internal resistance that threatens to limit the outward movement of the kingdom of God. Paul and Barnabas disagree with the men from Judea, but the church in Antioch is unable to settle the dispute. Therefore, the Antioch church sends Paul and Barnabas to confront the issue in Jerusalem. In Jerusalem, the believers who are resisting by limiting the bearing of witness are identified as Pharisees (Acts 15:5). The apostles and the elders consider the question. As they deliberate, Peter speaks as he did before in Acts 11 and likens the resistance to a testing of God. Peter's language here is similar to his words to Ananias and Sapphira (Acts 5:9). The apostles and elders settle the issue with a

---

[1] Acts 13:4-6, 13-41, 46; 14:1-3, 8-18, 21-25.
[2] Acts 13:6-8, 45, 50; 14:4-5, 19.
[3] Acts 13:9-12, 48-52; 14:6-7, 27.

letter calling for basic purity standards among the believing Gentiles. The resistance is overcome, and the church in Jerusalem and all churches that receive the report are encouraged. The word of the Lord continues to be preached as in Antioch (Acts 15:30-35).

After the apostles and elders settled the significant internal threat to the progression of the gospel, the expansion of the gospel is dealt another blow. Paul and Barnabas split as a mission team. Paul and Barnabas had planned to journey forth again to continue the expansion of the gospel. However, their relationship falls into schism and turmoil. Stevens has argued that the turmoil created is due to Paul's resistance to the Holy Spirit.[4] In response to the strife, Paul sets out on his own, but soon is stopped by the Holy Spirit and then the Spirit of Jesus (Acts 16:6-7). Stevens contends that Luke intended to echo the Damascus road event with the mentioning of the Spirit of Jesus.[5] Thus, the character who sets out in a different direction from Barnabas is more like the Saul who resisted God than the Paul who is a bearer of witness. According to Stevens, after Paul's encounter with the Spirit of Jesus, he receives a correcting vision—which he obeys—and journeys to Macedonia.[6] According to Stevens's assessment of the passage, Paul himself becomes a source of resistance to the outward progression of the gospel. Paul's resistance would be internal and thus an attempt to limit the bearing of witness. Following Stevens's argument, the limiting of witness would be Paul's refusal to follow the Holy Spirit's leading in his journeys to bear witness.

Having received guidance from God to travel to Macedonia, Paul journeys to Philippi where he continues his task of proclaiming the gospel message. From this point of the journey—and not before!—one begins to see the gospel expand and encounter resistance. Paul proclaims the message of God. As he does he encounters resistance.[7] In each account, resistance is overcome and the gospel advances, and the proclamation of the gospel message continues.[8]

---

[4]Stevens, "Luke's Perspective," 12–16. See chapter 1 for a detailed review of Stevens's argument.
[5]Ibid., 15.
[6]Ibid., 16; and Acts 16:9-10.
[7]Acts 16:19-24; 17:13; 18:12-13.
[8]Acts 16:25-40; 17:10-14; 18:14-17.

Growth and resistance continue as common themes to this point in the text. Interestingly, Paul himself now could possibly be a source of internal resistance. This possibility should not surprise the reader. All other characters internal to the gospel movement have faded from view. Both the Jerusalem and Antioch church disappear in the narrative, as do all other characters central to the outward expansion of the gospel. Paul is the only main character who remains. If internal resistance should arise, then such resistance only can come from the single remaining main character. The reader has seen resistance from members internal to the movement before in the characters of the Jerusalem church, Ananias, and even Peter. Therefore, resistance from Paul would only be in keeping with the narrative flow of the text and in keeping with his character history.

After briefly returning from his journey, Paul sets out again, this time to Ephesus (Acts 18:24—19:20). The Ephesian narrative functions thematically like the previous summary statements in Acts that follow the overcoming of resistance. In Ephesus, after the resistance to Paul has been overcome, the gospel experiences great success. The name of the Lord is held in high honor. Many believe and scrolls about sorcery are burned. The final statement in the narrative provides an excellent summary. The word of the Lord spreads and grows in power (Acts 19:20).

The final outward movement of the gospel to the ends of the earth in the text of Acts is to be to Rome (Acts 19:21). However, as Stevens has noted, Paul decides that he must first go to Jerusalem instead of following the leading of the Holy Spirit to Rome.[9] The setting is similar to that of the beginning of Paul's second mission journey when he abandoned Barnabas in order to set out on his own, following his own agenda. According to Stevens, Paul's decision to go to Jerusalem first is tantamount to resisting the Holy Spirit.[10] Paul's resistance is therefore an internal resistance that limits the bearing of witness by refusing to follow the leading of the Holy Spirit.

Once Paul decides to go to Jerusalem instead of Rome, the Ephesian ministry collapses in a riot (Acts 19:23-41). Paul leaves Ephesus and begins

---

[9] Stevens, "Luke's Perspective," 18–20.
[10] Stevens supports his argument with six key texts: Acts 19:21; 20:22-33; 21:4, 11-12; 22:17-21; and 23:11. For the purposes of this study, Stevens's theory will be assumed correct in order to trace possible trajectories in the ensuing narratives.

his journey back to Jerusalem. Prior to arriving, he hears repeated warnings not to go to Jerusalem. Thus, when Paul arrives in Jerusalem he is in direct opposition to his friends and the Holy Spirit. Paul is an immediate problem for the Jerusalem church leaders, who are worried about the Jews who have been misinformed about Paul's teaching (Acts 21:17-26). In an attempt to assuage the Jerusalem church, Paul engages in a temple ritual that results in his arrest. Paul in Roman custody provides the larger rhetorical situation for the second Damascus road narrative. The second Damascus road narrative, a paradigmatic story of Saul's resistance to God, appears in the context of Paul's present resistance to the Holy Spirit. At the climax of his resistance—Paul's presence in Jerusalem and the subsequent binding, which occurs in fulfillment of the prophecy of Agabus—Luke retold the story of Saul, the archenemy of the church, who encountered God and was overcome, through the mouth of Paul himself (Acts 21:10-13).

The immediate rhetorical setting of the present unit is somewhat more complex. Upon Paul's arrival in Jerusalem, he and his companions go and greet James and the elders in order to tell them of the ministry among the Gentiles (Acts 21:17-19). James and the elders are pleased, but Paul's arrival has created a dilemma for the Jerusalem church. James relates that Jews have been informed that Paul teaches Jews to turn from the Law of Moses. This charge includes accusations that Paul teaches Jews to turn from the customs of their people and not to have their children circumcised (Acts 21:21). Note that the problem for the Jerusalem church is not Paul's ministry among the Gentiles but what Paul is accused of teaching the Jews.

James urges Paul to participate in purification rites with four other men. His participation, according to James, will demonstrate that Paul does not teach the Jews to abandon the Law of Moses. Paul's practice is meant to vindicate his teaching (Acts 21:22-25). Once in the temple—in obedience to James—Paul is seen by Jews from Asia. These Jews rally a crowd and raise two charges against Paul. First, the Jews accuse Paul of teaching all men everywhere against the Law, against the people, and against the temple (Acts 21:28). Their charge and subsequent reaction demonstrate an underestimation on the part of James of Jerusalem's reaction to Paul. The charge consists of Paul's teaching, but not what he is teaching the Jews. The charge concerns what Paul is teaching all people. Gentiles are included in the accusation. The basic substance of the ascribed charge is that Paul is teaching all people not to be Jews. That is, Paul has effectively broken down barriers between Jews and Gentiles. Second, the Asian Jews accuse Paul of defiling the temple. The Asian Jews accuse Paul of acting upon his teaching by breaking down the barriers between Jews and Gentiles by bringing a Gentile into the temple (Acts 21:28-29).

The crowd responds with rioting and chaos. They drag Paul out of the temple and begin to beat him in an attempt to take his life (Acts 21:30-32). The crowd would have succeeded if the Roman Chiliarch had not arrived on the scene on account of the commotion. After a brief conversation with the Chiliarch, Paul then speaks to the crowd. In this speech, Luke presented the Damascus road event from Paul's perspective. The immediate setting is of prime importance. Paul's arrival in Jerusalem is marked by fear and controversy over a report that has come to Jerusalem about Paul's teaching. Once in the temple to allay the fear and controversy, Paul is charged with breaking down barriers between Jews and Gentiles and of acting on his teaching by bringing Trophimus into the temple. Instead of allaying fears, Paul's actions have engendered greater fear and controversy, which explode into rioting, the closing of the temple, and the beating of Paul. Thus, when Luke began the scene of Paul's arrest and defense, the situation in Jerusalem was one of rioting, beating, and chaos. The rhetorical situation for both the narrative and the speech is that of confusion and violence.

The genre of the chosen rhetorical unit is a mixture of speech and narrative.[11] The enveloping narrative is that of Paul's arrest by the Chiliarch.[12] The speech is Paul's defense before the Jewish crowd that has

---

[11] At this stage the question arises as to the ability to analyze speech and narrative at the same time. Certainly, the two are different genres, but Luke incorporated the speeches into the narrative as part of the fabric of the story. The problem of interpreting speech and narrative at the same time is deciding which is the primary bearer of meaning. One must decide whether the speech intent equals narrative intent and vice versa. More than likely, two separate levels are functioning within the text at the same time. The speech may have an intent and message if considered alone, but this isolated message is not necessarily the intent of the longer narrative. The possibility exists that the narrative may have a different intent that is accentuated by the differing intent and meaning apparent in the speech. In the following analysis, care will be taken not to equate the speech intent and meaning with narrative intent. Instead, the interaction between the two will be discussed.

[12] Acts 21:33-40; 22:2, 22-24a.

just attempted to kill him.[13] Paul's speech is judicial in flavor.[14] The speech does not take place in an official courtroom, but Luke included adequate markers to equate the present speech with a typical judicial speech. Charges are brought against Paul in Acts 21:28. The crowd—functioning as a jury—has already rendered their decision in Acts 21:36. Paul uses the legal term ἀπολογίας in Acts 22:1. Finally, although the setting is not officially a trial, Paul clearly is speaking in defense of his life.

The case against Paul is highly disreputable and difficult.[15] Paul is accused of defiling the temple. The horrific nature of the charge is seen in the response by the crowd. Further, the crowd believes the charge and has arrived at a verdict. The prescribed method of addressing such an audience, according to Hellenistic rhetorical theory, was to use insinuation.[16] Insinuation was an attempt to use dissimulation and misdirection to bring the audience to a state of good-will.[17]

The *stasis* or main issue of conflict addressed in the speech should concern Paul's teaching since Paul's teaching is the source of the conflict at hand.[18] The *stasis* of the speech should follow with the crowd charging, "You have taught incorrectly." Paul's reply could come from one of three angles. First, Paul could respond with a simple denial, "I have not taught incorrectly." In so doing, Paul would have relied upon the *stasis* of conjecture.[19] Paul also could have answered, "I have not taught incorrectly as seen in the correct interpretation of the Mosaic Law." If this had been Paul's reply, he would have relied upon the legal *stasis*.[20] Finally, Paul could

---

[13]Although Paul is arrested by the Roman Chiliarch, the audience of Paul's speech is the Jewish crowd. Jacob Jervell, *Die Apostelgeschichte*, KEKNT 17 (Göttingen: Vandenhoeck & Ruprecht, 1998), 541.

[14]Kennedy, *New Testament*, 134; William R. Long, "The Paulusbild in the Trial of Paul in Acts," in *SBLSP* (Chico, Calif.: Scholars, 1983), 97; Soards, *Speeches*, 111; Veltman, "Defense Speeches," 253; Jerome H. Neyrey, "The Forensic Defense Speech and Paul's Trial Speeches in Acts 22–26: Form and Function," in *Luke-Acts: New Perspectives from the Society of Biblical Literature Seminar*, ed. Charles H. Talbert (New York: Crossroad, 1984), 210; and McCormick, "Paul's Addresses," 212.

[15][Cic.] *Rhet. Her.*1.3.5; and Cic. *Inv. Rhet.* 1.15.20.

[16][Cic.] *Rhet. Her.* 1.6.9; Quint. *Inst.* 4.1.42; and Cic. *Inv. Rhet.* 1.15.20.

[17]Cic. *Inv. Rhet.* 1.15.20-21.

[18]Quint. *Inst.* 3.6.4.

[19][Cic.] *Rhet. Her.* 1.11.18.

[20]Ibid., 1.11.19.

have retorted, "I do not deny what I have taught. However, allow me to explain the reasons for my teaching and their correctness." In this manner, Paul would have built his case upon the juridical *stasis*.[21]

In a quick overview of Paul's speech, one observes that Paul does not address the obvious issue at hand. Paul's speech addresses a different *stasis* question. The speech begins by addressing the nebulous charge "You are not a good Jew." To this charge Paul replies, "I am a good Jew." The *stasis* appears to be that of conjecture. However, such an approach does not match the actual charges of the crowd. Why would Luke have Paul begin his speech by addressing an issue other than the one at hand? The answer lies in the need to use insinuation. As stated above, the case at hand concerns a dishonorable charge. The crowd is already angered and has given their verdict. Paul must therefore win the crowd over before he can address the true issue at hand. Thus, he begins by addressing the issue of being a good Jew through his *exordium* and *narratio*. This procedure is a strategy to win the favor of the audience. Once the audience's good will is achieved, Paul could move to the true issue at hand, "You have taught incorrectly." When Paul does finally address the issue at hand, his approach follows that of the juridical stasis. He does not deny his actions but places the blame upon another. This process is termed *metastasis*.[22] In his speech, Paul moves to shift the blame to God. God made him do that of which he is charged.[23]

In light of this consideration of the immediate rhetorical situation, including the *stasis* and genre of the embedded speech, the following conclusions are now offered. The immediate rhetorical setting for the present unit is a scene of rioting, chaos, and beating. Paul has arrived in Jerusalem in direct conflict with the Holy Spirit, thus creating a problem for himself and for the church in Jerusalem. Seizing Paul in the temple, the Asian Jews charge Paul with teaching incorrectly as a Jew. Hearing the charge, the crowd responds violently, supposing the charge to be true. The crowd is so firmly decided against Paul and the charge so dishonorable

---

[21]Ibid., 1.14.24.
[22]Contra Long, "Paulusbild," 100. [Cic] *Rhet. Her.* 1.15.25; and Quint. *Inst.* 7.4.14. See also McCormick, "Paul's Addresses," 212; Kennedy, *New Testament Interpretaton*, 134; and Soards, *Speeches*, 111.
[23]Acts 22:17-21; Harrisville, "Acts 22:6-21," 182.

that Paul must speak in defense of his actions through insinuation. At this point of violence and rioting, Luke included the story of Paul's Damascus road experience as Saul. It is important to note the similar rhetorical situations that surround the two Damascus narratives that have appeared in the text of Acts to this point. The current setting—just like the setting in Acts 9—occurs at a moment of resistance against the progress of the gospel. Also, the rhetorical situations of both occur amidst violence, beating, and attempted murder. In Acts 9, Saul was breathing violence and murder and taking action upon his threats. Now the crowd is breathing similar threats and taking action upon them. What were Luke's reasons for including the paradigmatic story of Saul's resistance overcome and transformed in the current setting? Could the story bear elements central to current resistance that must be overcome and transformed in Paul? Could the character of Paul in the present narrative resemble more the former Saul that must be overcome rather than the later Paul who is the empowered witness?

The Analysis of Acts 21:33—22:24a

In the arrest and trial narrative of Acts 21:33—22:24a, Luke portrayed Paul occupying a state of powerlessness and helplessness. In this portrayal—consisting of two narrative panels and a judicial speech—Luke incorporated a slightly modified form of the Damascus event. Using this event, Luke intensified the portrait of a feeble and ineffective Paul who had not accepted his role as God's empowered witness to Rome.

Paul in Chains (Acts 21:33-40; 22:2)

In the midst of the chaos and rioting by the crowd, a new narrative panel begins with the arrival of the Roman Chiliarch (Acts 21:33). The entrance of the Chiliarch signals the end of the beating of Paul by the crowd, but Paul's situation does not improve. The Chiliarch arrests Paul and has him put in chains. The narrative panel ends with the beginning of Paul's address to the crowd (22:1). The entire narrative takes place in the area surrounding the temple and on the steps leading into the Roman barracks (21:28).

The narrative occurs during the moment of unrest in the temple after the end of Paul's seven days of purification (21:27).

Luke utilized four main characters in this first narrative panel: the Roman Chiliarch, Paul, the soldiers, and the crowd. Luke portrayed the Roman Chiliarch as a man of authority. The Chiliarch has the authority to arrest and chain Paul (21:33). He exercises authority over his soldiers by ordering them to bind Paul (21:33). The Chiliarch expresses his authority by questioning the crowd and having Paul taken to the barracks (21:33-34). Finally, the Chilarch has authority over Paul's ability to speak (21:37, 39-40). While the Chiliarch is a man of authority, Luke portrayed him wielding his authority in ignorance. The Chiliarch is ignorant of the cause of the riot and ignorant of Paul's identity (21:33-34, 37-38).

The character of Paul stands in stark contrast to the Roman Chiliarch. The Chiliarch is a man of authority, but Paul is a man who is powerless and vulnerable. In the text, Paul is a man of high standing, a citizen of Tarsus (21:39). Ironically, Luke characterized this man of high standing as one who is arrested and chained as a criminal (21:33). He is condemned by the crowd and confused with a rebel (21:36, 38). He is helpless against the attacks of the crowd and must be protected by the soldiers (21:35). Finally, Paul has no authority to speak. He must ask permission to speak to both the Chiliarch and the crowd (21:37, 39).

Luke represented the crowd as a violent mob. The crowd is confused as to the nature of the gathering but is unified in resorting to violence (21:34, 36). Tragically, this confused and violent crowd sits in judgment over Paul, much like a jury rendering their condemnation (21:36; 22:2).

Finally, Luke employed the soldiers as characters exemplifying those who act out of necessity and obedience. The soldiers bind Paul in obedience to their Chiliarch. They are forced to carry Paul in order to protect him from the violence of the crowd.

As a man of authority, the Chiliarch acts by arresting Paul and ordering him chained (21:33). He questions the cause of the riot and orders Paul to the barracks, permitting him to speak on the steps (21:34, 40). The Chiliarch acts unintentionally out of necessity. The actions and violence of the crowd force him to move and arrest the person he deems to be the source of the present conflict. He acts for the sake of peace and for acquiring benefits. He wishes to find the cause of the riot. Finally, the Chiliarch acts to remove evil. Paul happens to be the evil the Chiliarch acts to remove.

In the scene, Luke did not present Paul as an active character. Instead of acting, Paul is acted upon as a passive character. He is overcome by the crowd, the Chiliarch, and the soldiers. Paul speaks to the Chiliarch on the barracks steps and addresses the crowd in the Hebrew dialect, but only with the permission of the Chiliarch (21:37, 39-40). Paul's actions occur unintentionally out of necessity. Paul is forced to speak to the Chiliarch because of his arrest and binding. Further, he is forced to address the crowd in an attempt to defend himself against their charges. Paul's conduct is accomplished for the acquiring of benefits, his release, and for the sake of justice.

Luke presented the crowd as condemning Paul and rioting (21:36). However, when Paul addresses them, the crowd listens like a jury to his defense (22:2). The crowd acts intentionally and with force. They choose to riot and condemn Paul. Further, they choose of their own accord to listen to Paul's defense. They act out of emotion. They have hatred and anger toward Paul. They also act in order to acquire benefits. They wish to understand the reason for Paul's actions. Finally, the soldiers act by binding Paul and carrying him up the steps of the barracks. They do so unintentionally out of necessity. They are obeying the orders of the Roman Chiliarch.

In this narrative panel, Luke portrayed Paul as one subjugated and humiliated. Paul does not act but others act upon him. He is treated as a common criminal and put in chains by a man of authority who acts out of ignorance. Paul is evil, a rebel who must be dealt with in a severe and decisive manner by both the Chiliarch and the crowd. Paul is condemned by a rioting crowd, which does not understand the reasons for rioting. Finally, Paul is helpless to defend himself physically but has to be protected by those acting upon the orders of another. In this situation, he is unable to speak without first obtaining permission. At this point, Luke provides the reader with a Paul who is overcome. Paul's arrival in Jerusalem has resulted in only rioting, chaos, and the overthrowing of Paul.

Table 5. Paul in Chains (Acts 21:33-40; 22:2)

Character	(A) *Chiliarch:* man with authority to bind, arrest, order, and question; ignorant of cause of riot; ignorant of Paul's identity (B) *Paul:* arrested; chained; carried by soldiers; condemned by crowd; identified as rebel; citizen of Tarsus; unable to speak on own accord (C) *Crowd:* confused; violent; condemn Paul; sit as jury (D) *Soldiers:* bind Paul; carry Paul; obedient to Chiliarch
Act	(A) *Chiliarch:* arrests Paul; chains Paul; questions crowd; orders soldiers; permits Paul to speak (B) *Paul:* speaks to Chiliarch; motions to crowd; addresses crowd (C) *Crowd:* condemn Paul, riot; listen to Paul (D) *Soldiers:* bind Paul; carry Paul
Time	End of seven days of purification
Place	Temple area; steps of barracks
Manner	(A) *Chiliarch:* unintentional: necessity (B) *Paul:* unintentional: necessity (C) *Crowd:* intentional: force (D) *Soldiers:* unintentional: necessity
Reason	(A) *Chiliarch:* for sake of peace; acquiring of benefits; removing evil (B) *Paul:* acquiring benefits; for sake of justice (C) *Crowd:* emotion: hatred and anger; acquiring of benefits (D) *Soldiers:* for sake of obedience

Paul Remains in Chains (Acts 22:22-24a)

The final narrative panel of the scene begins with the interruption of Paul's speech by the crowd.[24] The panel concludes with the successful completion of the Chiliarch's desire to have Paul taken into the barracks (22:24a). The narrative time and place do not differ from the previously investigated narrative panel. The narrative time is still at the end of seven days of purification, though now the time has shifted to the end of Paul's defense speech. The narrative occurs on the steps of the Roman barracks. In this scene which concludes and encases the first defense speech of Paul, Luke maintained the suppression and overcoming of Paul first illustrated in 21:22-40 and 22:2.

Luke employed three characters: the crowd, the Chiliarch, and Paul. He portrayed the crowd as an enraged group that passes final judgment

---

[24] Acts 22:22. The encircling narrative of Paul's binding and arrest is interpreted separately from the Pauline defense speech so that the themes of the narrative might be distinguished from, and then compared to, the themes of the Pauline defense speech. The encircling narrative and embedded defense speech are investigated separately in order to understand each individually and how the two function together corporately.

upon Paul, calling for his death (22:22-23). The Chiliarch is still a man of authority who uses his authority to have Paul taken into the barracks (22:24). Luke characterized Paul as one who is interrupted and not allowed to finish (22:22). Paul is the agitator of the crowd, who deem him worthy of death, and he is taken by force into the barracks (22:23-24).

The crowd acts by calling for Paul's life, tearing their garments, and throwing dust into the air (22:22-23). They act intentionally with force in response to Paul's defense speech. They act out of their emotion of anger with Paul for his statements. They condemn Paul in order to remove evil and for the sake of their religious faith. The Chiliarch acts by taking Paul into the barracks. He does so unintentionally out of necessity. The actions of the crowd and speech of Paul do not permit the Chiliarch any insight into the cause of the riot. Therefore, he must complete his intention of taking Paul into the barracks for interrogation. He acts for the sake of peace and for the sake of acquiring benefits. He is attempting to find out the cause of the riot. Luke did not allow Paul to act or speak at all. He portrayed Paul only as one upon whom others act.

In this narrative panel, Luke's portrayal of Paul as one who is overcome and helpless intensifies. Paul is not permitted to continue his defense. The crowd condemns him to death, and the Chiliarch takes him into the barracks. Luke allowed no action from Paul at all. Instead, Paul is at the mercy of the Roman Chiliarch and unable to respond to those who call for his life.

Table 6. Paul Remains in Chains (Acts 22:22-24a)

Character	(A) *Crowd:* pass judgment; enraged (B) *Chiliarch:* completes plan (C) *Paul:* interrupted; condemned; agitator; under arrest in barracks
Act	(A) *Crowd:* call for Paul's life; tear garments; throw dust (B) *Chiliarch:* takes Paul into barracks (C) *Paul:* no action
Time	End of Pauline defense speech
Place	Steps of barracks
Manner	(A) *Crowd:* intentional: force (B) *Chiliarch:* unintentional: necessity (C) *Paul:* no action
Reason	(A) *Crowd:* emotion: anger, hatred; removing evil; for sake of religious faith (B) *Chiliarch:* acquiring of benefits; for the sake of peace (C) *Paul:* no action

Luke surrounded the first defense speech with narrative panels that portray a Paul who is anything but an empowered witness. Paul's speech—whatever the content—fails to change the verdict of the crowd or the intended action of the Chiliarch. Instead of changing the decision of the crowd, Paul's speech seems only to have deepened their resolve to call for his death. With his speech Paul does not achieve the ability to act intentionally but finds even his ability to act unintentionally removed. Luke rendered Paul completely passive within the narrative. Regardless of the content of the speech, Paul remains helpless and humiliated.

Paul's First Defense (Acts 22:1, 3-21)

Paul's address in defense to the crowd begins in Acts 22:1. As noted above, the genre of the speech is judicial. Before any investigation of the speech, two questions concerning the speech must be addressed. First, is the speech, as written by Luke, complete? Second, what is the structure of the speech?

In considering the completeness of the Pauline defense speech, one is not considering whether Luke accurately and completely recorded a speech by Paul to a crowd from the steps of the barracks. The issue of completeness is an issue of the comparative wholeness of the speech in light of Hellenistic rhetorical conventions and canons. Is Paul's speech which begins in 22:1 and ends on account of a recorded interruption in 22:21 a complete judicial speech in light of Greco-Roman rhetorical conventions? When the speech is considered, one may see that the speech is not a complete judicial speech for two reasons.[25]

First, the speech as presented by Luke does not contain all the integral parts of a judicial speech. According to the rhetorical handbooks, the typical judicial speech contained six parts: *exordium, narratio, divisio, confirmatio, refutatio,* and *conclusio.*[26] Nevertheless, not every part was needed nor included in a judicial speech. An orator varied the construction of his speech depending upon the situation at hand. He could lengthen or even excise complete parts of a judicial speech due to the great flexibility

---

[25] For additional arguments regarding the incomplete nature of this first Pauline defense speech, see Soards, *Speeches*, 111; and Witherington, *Acts*, 667.
[26] [Cic.] *Rhet. Her.* 1.3.4; Quint. *Inst.* 3.9.1; and Cic. *Inv. Rhet.* 1.14.19.

of Hellenistic rhetoric.[27] However, at least three parts seem to have been present in some form in every judicial speech: the *exordium, confirmatio,* and *conclusio.* Every judicial speech contained some type of introduction, a series of proofs or evidence, and some sort of conclusion. The present speech in Acts 22 is missing two of these integral parts: proofs and a conclusion.

A quick survey of the present speech reveals that much of the speech reads as a narrative of Paul's previous life.[28] The speech contains a continuous narrative of Paul's previous behavior as Saul in his persecution of the members of the Way. In relating the details of his previous life, the character Paul does not put forth any arguments nor offer proofs, artificial or inartificial, to back up his claims. The speech consists solely of Paul's narrative of his previous life. Therefore, one should not equate this narration of previous actions with proofs.[29] In Hellenistic rhetoric the *narratio* did resemble some types of proofs. However, Quintilian stated that in spite of their similarity, the *narratio* was different because such was found in a continuous form.[30] In the Pauline speech of Acts 22, the relating of past actions is in a continuous form until the interruption by the crowd. Therefore, the relating of past actions should be identified as narrative and not with a series of formal proofs.

Further, at the point of interruption, as Barrett has noted, the trajectory of the speech may be traced. "The speaker might have well continued: My mission to the Gentiles was undertaken only on God's command, not at my desire."[31] Such a possible trajectory indicates that the *stasis* of the speech is *metastasis.* Following this trajectory, one could see how the speech could include proofs from Scripture as well as artificial and inartificial proofs to support the argument that Paul had gone to the Gentiles only because God had forced him to go.

---

[27]Quint. *Inst.* 2.13.1-2, 7, 16.

[28]See also Stanley E. Porter, *The Paul of Acts: Essays in Literary Criticism, Rhetoric, and Theology,* WUNT 115 (Tübingen: Mohr/Siebeck, 1999), 134; and Talbert, *Reading Acts,* 198.

[29]Long identified this narrative as a series of proofs. See Long, "Paulusbild," 98; and idem, "Trial of Paul," 219.

[30]Quint. *Inst.* 4.2.78-79.

[31]C. K. Barrett, *A Critical and Exegetical Commentary on the Acts of the Apostles,* vol. 2, ICC (Edinburgh: T. & T. Clark, 1998), 1032.

The second section that is missing from the present speech is any form of *conclusio*. The speech does not end because Luke had the crowd interrupt (22:22). A normal *conclusio* would include some sort of recapitulation of points as well as a call for a judgment from the audience.[32] However, no such recapitulation or call for judgment is present.

A second reason to consider the speech as incomplete is the ability of the reader to understand how the speech could have continued. As noted above, the probable trajectory of the speech can be inferred. Luke portrayed Paul as obtaining the goodwill of the audience by addressing the issue of his Jewishness. Yet Paul's Jewishness is not the issue at hand. Paul's teaching and actions based upon his teachings are the issue at hand. With the temple vision narrative Luke brought up the basis for the issue at hand for the first time (22:17-21). God had sent Paul to the Gentiles. However, Luke records the crowd interrupting Paul before this issue can be addressed any further. That Paul never addresses the issue at hand but could have done so if the speech had continued indicates that the speech is not complete.

If the present embedded speech is not complete, then what is the structure of the extant portion? Interpreters have not reached any firm agreement as to the outline of the speech. Long and McCormick outlined the speech as follows: *exordium* (Acts 22:1-2); *narratio* (Acts 22:3); and proofs (22:4-21).[33] The identification of proofs is somewhat misguided, as noted above. Therefore, this outline may be set aside. Witherington has provided a second outline dividing the speech into two parts, *exordium* (22:1-2), and *narratio* (22:3-21). Witherington has rightly noted the absence of proofs in the present speech but has included a portion of narrative that is not part of the Pauline speech (22:2). Neyrey provided some rhetorical analysis of the speech. However, his outline is somewhat convoluted and inconsistent.[34] Finally, Talbert identified 22:6-21 as a *narratio* but did not identify any further parts of the speech. Yet, his identification of a *narratio* is simply the determination of the beginning of the Damascus narrative which is based upon and literarily dependent upon the previous narrative in 22:4-5. Having no adequate rhetorical

---

[32] Quint. *Inst.* 6.1.1-2; Cic. *Inv. Rhet.* 1.70.98; and [Cic.] *Rhet. Her.* 2.30.47.
[33] Long, "Paulusbild," 98; idem, "Trial of Paul," 219; and McCormick, "Paul's Addresses," 210–11.
[34] Neyrey, "Forensic Defense Speech," 221.

outline of the present Pauline defense speech, one may suggest the following outline. Luke constructed the Pauline defense speech in two parts, *exordium* and *narratio*. The *exordium* is short (22:1, 3). The *narratio* extends until the point of interruption (22:4-21).

The *Exordium* (Acts 22:1, 3)

Paul's speech to the crowd from the steps of the barracks begins in Acts 22:1, signaling the beginning of the *exordium*. In Hellenistic rhetoric the *exordium* was used by orators to prepare the audience for the rest of the speech.[35] The preparing of the audience by the orator usually involved two tasks: the introduction of the subject and the winning of the goodwill of the audience.[36] Hellenistic rhetoricians instructed their students that two types of introductions could be used in the opening of a speech. One could use a direct opening or the subtle approach, also called insinuation.[37]

The direct opening was an introduction in which the orator used plain language and attempted to bring the audience to a receptive and attentive state.[38] With insinuation, the orator was facing a case that involved a dishonorable or doubtful cause that had produced a prejudicial attitude among the judge or audience.[39] Pseudo-Cicero stated that three events necessitated the use of the indirect approach: when a discreditable cause had alienated the audience, when the hearer had been won over by previous speeches, and when the hearer had been wearied by previous speeches.[40] In these instances, the orator was to "insinuate himself little by little into the minds of the judges" so that they might be won over to the orator's side.[41] One common way for the orator to insinuate himself was to substitute a favored topic for the ill-favored topic, person, or action currently at hand.[42] Once the orator had obtained the goodwill and favor

---

[35] [Cic.] *Rhet. Her.* 1.3.4.
[36] Quint. *Inst.* 4.1.1, 5.
[37] Quint. *Inst.* 4.1.42; [Cic.] *Rhet. Her.* 1.4.6; and Cic. *Inv. Rhet.* 1.15.20-21.
[38] Cic. *Inv. Rhet.* 1.15.20; and [Cic.] *Rhet. Her.* 1.4.6.
[39] [Cic.] *Rhet. Her.* 1.4.6.
[40] Ibid., 1.6.9.
[41] Quint. *Inst.* 4.1.42.
[42] Cic. *Inv. Rhet.* 1.17.24.

of the audience through the substituted discussion, the speaker could gradually turn the speech to address the true issue at hand, which he had concealed from the beginning of his speech.[43]

Which type of opening did Luke employ in the *exordium* of Paul's first defense speech, and how far does this introduction stretch? One must note that at the beginning of the speech, Paul is at a rhetorical disadvantage. The Asian Jews have won over the crowd with their previous speech (21:28). When he addresses the crowd, Paul is in chains and thus humiliated before them. He appears to be guilty (v. 33). The crowd has already decided Paul's guilt and his punishment (v. 36). Finally, Paul's case is highly dishonorable. The Asian Jews have accused him of breaking down the boundaries between Jew and Gentile and of acting upon his teaching by defiling the temple (v. 28).

Rhetorically, Paul is facing a difficult defense. According to the instructions of the Hellenistic rhetoricians, the proper course of action for one in Paul's situation was to use insinuation to begin his speech.[44] If Luke chose to follow this rhetorical procedure, then the *exordium* should contain two marks. First, the *exordium* should include an attempt to gain the goodwill of the audience, possibly by substituting something favored for the currently dishonorable issue at hand.[45] Second, Luke should have concealed the true issue at hand throughout the *exordium* and addressed the issue at a later point in the speech.[46]

Analyzing the speech, one finds an intense effort by Luke through the character of Paul to obtain the goodwill of the audience. Luke had Paul stress the bond between himself and the audience by highlighting that they are fellow Jews using familial terms (22:1). The bond between Paul and the audience is strengthened with the use of the common language of the people in Paul's address (21:40; 22:2). Luke worked to gain the goodwill of the audience through Paul by preparing them for a lengthy defense in the exordium, encouraging them to listen.[47] Luke allowed Paul to substitute a favored topic for the ill-favored topic at hand, Paul's teaching. Paul's

---

[43]Ibid.
[44][Cic.] *Rhet. Her.* 1.4.6; Quint. *Inst.* 4.1.42; and Cic. *Inv. Rhet.* 1.15.20-21.
[45]Cic. 1.17.24.
[46]Ibid.
[47]Acts 22:1; and [Cic.] *Rhet. Her.* 1.4.7.

speech centers upon the premise that he is a good Jew (22:3). Using a rhetorical technique of gaining goodwill, Luke enumerated the points which he would discuss concerning Paul's Jewishness.[48] Paul's Jewishness would include a discussion of his birth in Tarsus, his upbringing in the present city—Tarsus or Jerusalem?—his training under Gamaliel, and his common zeal for God (22:3). In the enumeration of points, Luke made one final plea for goodwill by praising the zealous character of the audience.[49] With the enumeration of points in support of the premise that Paul is a good Jew, the *exordium* ends and the *narratio* begins. The *narratio* begins in 22:4 with a discussion of Paul's zeal which is one of the four attributes offered in support of the main premise.

Luke began the Pauline defense speech by obtaining the goodwill of the audience. Paul is a good Jew who holds to correct practice. The effort is an attempt to ingratiate Paul with the audience. Every indication is that Paul is making a direct opening in which he promises to discuss his own person and character.[50] However, the opening of the speech does not include any mention of Paul's teaching, which is the issue at hand. The premise concerning Paul's Jewishness is an attempt to switch the topic to one that is favored. The practice in view is insinuation. The style of the *exordium* is simple. Paul speaks in the common idiom of the people and does not use complex thought or phrasing.[51]

In the *exordium,* Paul is in trouble. The Asian Jews have charged Paul with a dishonorable offence, and the crowd is prejudiced against him. Therefore, Paul's course of action is to use insinuation to win the goodwill of his audience—substituting something favored for that which is ill favored—before he can address the issue at hand. If Paul is successful in this quest, then the audience will follow along and change their minds concerning their condemnation.

---

[48][Cic.] *Rhet. Her.* 1.4.7.
[49]Ibid., 1.5.8.
[50]Ibid., 1.5.8; Quint. *Inst.* 4.1.35; and Cic. *Inst.* 1.16.22.
[51][Cic.] 4.8.11.

The *Narratio* (Acts 22:4-21)

The *narratio* of Paul's defense begins in 22:4 with an expansion of Paul's zeal, which was the last proffered aspect of his Jewishness. The presentation of Paul's zealous behavior for God reveals a choice to deal with the four supporting aspects of Paul's Jewishness out of order. Two reasons could lie behind the presentation of Paul's zeal first. Often, Hellenistic rhetoricians offered the strongest arguments of a case first and last so that they would be remembered by the audience.[52] The possibility also exists that Luke suppressed the first three aspects of Paul's Jewishness, choosing only to narrate Paul's zeal.[53]

The purpose of a *narratio* was to persuade the judge or audience of the correctness of the orator's speech by offering facts concerning the case in view.[54] In building a *narratio* for a judicial speech, an orator could choose one of two paths. First, one could build a *narratio* that expounded the facts of the case. Second, the orator could construct a *narratio* that set forth all the facts that had a bearing on the case.[55] The current *narratio* is an example of the second path. The *narratio* was to be brief, but long narrations were permissible if the present case required one.[56] The present narration is not incredibly long but sufficiently discusses the background of events necessary to illustrate Paul's zeal for God.

Before further analysis can be accomplished, one must consider what type of interpretive scheme to use for the *narratio* of this judicial speech. In light of the similar definitions, explanations, and forms of the *narratio* as described in the Hellenistic rhetorical handbooks and Theon's *progymnasmata*, Theon's six elements of narrative will be used as the interpretive tool for the following analysis.[57]

One may divide the *narratio* of Paul's defense speech into three narrative panels (22:4-11, 12-16, and 17-21). In these narrative panels, the character of Paul fades and the character of Saul comes to the fore. The portrait of

---

[52][Cic.] *Rhet. Her.* 3.10.18.
[53]Quint. *Inst.* 4.2.101.
[54]Ibid., 4.2.21.
[55]Ibid., 4.2.11.
[56]Quint. *Inst.* 4.2.31, 47; and [Cic.] *Rhet. Her.* 1.7.14.
[57]Theon 5.1, 39-40; Cic. *Inv. Rhet.* 1.19.27; 1.20.28; and Quint. *Inst.* 4.2.31.

Saul that emerges is that of Saul the intentionally forceful persecutor of the disciples of the Lord. This Saul is overcome and overpowered in an encounter with Jesus on the road to Damascus. The portrait of Saul is that of Saul in Acts 9. However, the transformation that results from Saul's encounter with Jesus in Acts 9 is not found in Acts 22. Instead of transformation, in the present rendering of the Damascus narrative Saul remains resistant to God's guidance, even after his overpowering by Jesus on the Damascus road and healing by Ananias.[58]

Saul the Persecutor (Acts 22:4-11)

The present narrative panel begins with Saul persecuting the members of the Way to the point of death (v. 4). In his persecution efforts, Saul undertakes a journey to Damascus (v. 5). His arrival in Damascus signals the end of this narrative panel (v. 11). The narrative takes place sometime in the past during the middle of the day. The narrative incorporates a journeying motif with most of the narrative taking place on the road near the city of Damascus (v. 6).

Luke developed the narrative using three main characters: Saul, Saul's companions, and Jesus. Luke characterized Saul in two opposing ways. First, Luke characterized Saul before his encounter with Jesus on the road to Damascus. Before his encounter, Saul is a murderous persecutor of the Way (v. 4). He is empowered by the religious authorities to bind the members of the Way and bring them to Jerusalem for punishment. He travels to Damascus to carry out his persecuting efforts. However, Saul encounters Jesus on the road to Damascus. Through his encounter with Jesus, Saul is indicted as a persecutor (vv. 7-8). Saul is stripped of his authority and given a new command by Jesus (v. 10). However, Saul is ignorant of this Jesus who speaks to him and because of this encounter is blind and unable to obey (vv. 6-11). Saul is helpless and unable to complete his journey and thus must be led into Damascus by the hand. The Lukan characterization of Saul is that of reversal. Saul begins as an empowered persecutor of the members of the Way. Nevertheless, after encountering

---

[58] After analyzing the three narrative panels of the *narratio*, the overall movement of the defense speech will be compared to the movement of the encircling narrative.

Jesus, he is blind, under indictment, and unable to obey the new orders he has received.

Jesus is the second character in the narrative. Jesus is the heavenly judge who is persecuted (vv. 7-8). This persecuted judge confronts his persecutor and overcomes him (vv. 6-7). After overcoming the one who persecutes him, Jesus replaces Saul's commission and reveals a new path for Saul (v. 10).

The fellow travelers of Saul are the final character within the narrative. These companions are the ignorant helpers of Saul. They see the light that overcomes Saul but do not hear the voice that addresses him (v. 9). In response to the events that transpire, the companions are forced into the role of caring for Saul by leading him into the city of Damascus (v. 11).

Further insight into the characters might be gained though an investigation of their actions with accompanying reasons and manner of action. Saul acts by killing members of the Way (v. 4). He persecutes them by imprisoning them and traveling to Damascus to execute plans for punishing them (vv. 4-6). Saul acts intentionally with force. He acts on his own accord in his persecution efforts. His actions are accomplished as an outgrowth of his emotion of hatred of the members of the Way. Further, Saul persecutes these people for the sake of removing evil and for his religious faith. After Saul encounters Jesus on the road to Damascus, he falls to the ground and questions the identity and purposes of the one who has overcome him. Saul's actions arise unintentionally out of necessity and ignorance. The power of the light forces Saul to the ground, and his ignorance of Jesus gives rise to his questions. The reasons behind Saul's actions are the emotion of fear of what is occurring and the attempt to acquire benefits. Saul wishes to understand what is happening.

Luke portrayed Jesus as an intentional actor. Jesus overcomes Saul, indicts him, and replaces the commission of the priests and elders with his own commands (vv. 6-8, 10). Jesus acts intentionally and with force for the sake of removing evil. He overpowers Saul for the sake of the Way and to acquire benefits. God has appointed tasks for Saul.

The traveling companions do very little within the narrative. They see the light and lead Saul by the hand into Damascus (vv. 9, 11). Their actions are performed unintentionally out of chance and necessity. They see the light simply because they are traveling with Saul. They lead Saul by the hand because he is unable to continue his journey to Damascus on account of his blindness. They lead Saul for the sake of pity or friendship.

The first narrative panel is a story of radical and complete reversal of Saul in his role as a persecutor of the Way. Saul attempts to punish and kill the members of the Way in an intentionally forceful manner under the authority of the priests and elders. He does so for his religious faith and in order to remove evil. However, in his persecuting attempts he meets Jesus, who is another intentionally forceful actor. Jesus also is acting to remove evil and for the sake of his religious group. When these two forceful characters meet, Saul is overcome. His commission is stripped, and his plans are changed. Paul's emotion of anger becomes fear. His attempts to remove evil result in the removal of his sight and authority. Saul is powerless to obey the new commission of Jesus by going into Damascus. He must rely upon the pity of those traveling with him to enter the city of Damascus. Saul is reduced to a state of weakness and humility.

Table 7. Saul the Persecutor (Acts 22:4-11)

Character	(A) *Saul (before):* murderer; persecutor; empowered by religious authorities; travels to Damascus; desires to punish "The Way"
	(B) *Saul (after):* overcome by light; ignorant of Jesus; indicted as a persecutor; ignorant of Jesus' designs; blind; unable to obey; led by others
	(C) *Jesus:* heavenly judge; persecuted; overcomes Saul; commands Saul; has plans for Saul
	(D) *Companions:* see light; do not hear voice; helpers of Saul
Act	(A) *Saul (before):* kills "The Way"; persecutes "The Way"; imprisons "The Way"; travels to Damascus
	(B) *Saul (after):* falls to ground; questions identity; questions purpose
	(C) *Jesus:* overcomes Saul; indicts Saul; commands Saul
	(D) *Companions:* see light; lead Saul
Time	Middle of the day
Place	Near Damascus on the road
Manner	(A) *Saul (before):* intentional: force
	(B) *Saul (after):* unintentional: necessity; unintentional: ignorance
	(C) *Jesus:* intentional: force
	(D) *Companions:* unintentional: chance; unintentional: necessity
Reason	(A) *Saul (before):* emotion: hatred; removing evil; for sake of religious faith
	(B) *Saul (after):* emotion: fear; acquiring benefits
	(C) *Jesus:* removing evil; for sake of "The Way"; acquiring benefits
	(D) *Companions:* for sake of friendship or pity

Saul and Ananias: Acts 22:12-16

The second narrative panel of the *narratio* begins with the introduction of the new character Ananias who is a godly man.[59] The scene ends with the commissioning of Saul by Ananias and the subsequent shift in narrative time and location to Jerusalem (v. 16). The scene takes place somewhere in the city of Damascus, sometime after Saul entered the city. Luke used the scene to identify the trajectory of Saul's future course. However, he left Saul overcome and powerless. Saul does not act upon the commission he receives.

Luke employed only two characters in this narrative panel, Saul and Ananias. He characterized Ananias as a godly man who resided in Damascus (v. 12). This godly man is a man of good report among his fellow Jews in Damascus (v. 12). Further, Ananias is an instrument of healing and one who reveals God's will and commission for Saul (vv. 13-16). Luke depicted Saul as one who once again physically sees (v. 13). Saul also understands his new purpose. He has been appointed to know God's will, to see his character, hear his voice, and bear witness of these things to all people (vv. 14-16). However, Saul does not yet fulfill his new purpose.

Ananias acts by healing Saul and commissioning him with God's new purposes. He acts intentionally and with force. Ananias comes to Saul on his own accord in order to heal and commission Saul. Luke portrayed Ananias as acting for the sake of God and Saul, and to acquire benefits. Saul is to be a witness to all people, but Luke portrayed him as completely passive. He is acted upon by Ananias. He sees only after Ananias places his hands upon him. He hears the commission of God through Ananias but does not act upon this new commission.

In the present panel, some of the effects of Saul's encounter with Jesus are reversed. Saul does regain his sight, and he receives a new purpose and commission. Saul is one who has been chosen to be a witness to all people. Ironically, Luke does not allow Saul to act upon this commission. Saul does not act at all. This lack of action forms a tension in the narrative between what Saul is and what he is supposed to be. Saul is supposed to

---

[59]Acts 22:12. Interestingly, even here, the attempt to stress Paul's Jewishness is observed. Ananias is called a godly man rather than identified as a member of the Way.

be a witness, chosen and empowered by God. However, Luke leaves him helpless.

Table 8. Saul and Ananias (Acts 22:12-16)

Character	(A) *Ananias:* resident of Damascus; godly man; well thought of by Jews; reveals God's will; healer of Saul (B) *Saul:* physically seeing; appointed to know God's will, and character, and hear God's voice; appointed as a witness to all people
Act	(A) *Ananias:* heals Saul; reveals God's will; commissions Saul (B) *Saul:* no actions
Time	Sometime after Saul arrives in Damascus
Place	Somewhere in Damascus
Manner	(A) *Ananias:* intentional: force (B) *Saul:* no actions
Reason	(A) *Ananias:* for the sake of God; acquiring benefits; for the sake of Saul (B) *Saul:* no actions

Saul the Resistant Witness (Acts 22:17-21)

The final narrative panel of the *narratio* of Paul's defense speech begins in v. 17 with Saul's return to Jerusalem. The scene ends with the interruption by the crowd in v. 22. The narrative takes place in the Jerusalem temple sometime after Saul's encounter with Jesus and his commissioning by Ananias. Interestingly, although Luke has commissioned Saul through Ananias as a witness to all people, he did not portray Saul as such. Saul is still resisting God. Now, however, his resistance to God is not persecution, but a refusal to fulfill his commission as a witness according to God's specific directions. Saul wishes to stay in Jerusalem to witness to the Jews who are present. The Lord, however, must instruct Saul twice to leave Jerusalem. The irony of this narrative's placement is strong. Luke suppressed the telling of this narrative in chronological narrative time, that is sometime soon after Acts 9. However, now he brings this narrative to the fore.[60] At the very moment that Saul is in Jerusalem—in direct conflict with the Holy Spirit—Luke related a narrative in which God forbids Saul's presence in Jerusalem.

Luke employed two characters in the present narrative panel: Saul and the Lord. He portrayed Saul as one who is religious. Saul is praying to

---

[60]Stevens, "Luke's Perspective," 31–32.

God and worshiping in the temple (Acts 22:17). Saul sees God and knows his identity (22:17). However, Saul is not welcome in Jerusalem as a witness. He receives a commission from God to go to the Gentiles, but Saul resists this commission until overcome by God (vv. 18-20). Luke characterized the Lord as one who appears to Saul in a vision (v. 18). The Lord is also one of authority who orders Saul to leave Jerusalem and rejects Saul's arguments to remain in Jerusalem (vv. 18, 21).

In the narrative, Saul acts by praying and telling God that he knows more about the acceptance of his witness in Jerusalem than God (vv. 17, 19-20). Saul's actions are executed intentionally and with force. He returns to Jerusalem to the temple after his Damascus experience and forcefully rejects God's command. Saul continues to act for the sake of his religious faith, specifically those Jews in Jerusalem. Possibly his actions are motivated by love or attachment. God acts in the narrative by ordering Saul to leave Jerusalem and revealing that Jerusalem will never accept Saul's witness (vv. 18, 21). God, just like Saul, acts intentionally and with force. He acts to acquire benefits. He wishes to move his new witness outward to those who will accept his witness.

In the present narrative, one finds a scene much like the first narrative panel of the *narratio*. Saul is an intentionally forceful actor who meets God, who is another intentionally forceful actor. In their encounter, Saul resists God and is overcome. He is ordered out of Jerusalem. Note that up to this point Saul still has not fulfilled his commissioned role as a witness. Instead, he is resisting the location of fulfilling this appointed role. The panel forms the foundation for a later argument based upon *metastasis*. Yet, the crowd interrupts Paul before he can continue. By allowing the crowd to interrupt, Luke permitted the last portrait of the speech to be that of Saul, still resisting his role as a witness to the gospel. He is still helpless, only having regained his sight. Instead of powerfully bearing witness, Saul's witness is rejected. In the previous Damascus narrative in Acts 9, the encounter with Jesus on the road to Damascus left Saul helpless and defeated. However, he was transformed, empowered, and became a witness for the gospel. No such transformation is present in this telling of the Damascus event. Saul is left helpless, resisting his divinely appointed role.

Table 9. Saul the Resistant Witness (Acts 22:17-21)

Character	(A) *Saul:* praying; worshiping; seeing God; not welcome in Jerusalem; resistant to God's plans; commanded by God; commissioned to Gentiles (B) *Lord:* appears in vision; orders Saul; rejects Saul's resistance
Act	(A) *Saul:* prays; tells God no (B) *Lord:* orders Saul to leave; reveals rejection of Jerusalem Jews
Time	Sometime after returning to Jerusalem
Place	Jerusalem temple
Manner	(A) *Saul:* intentional: force (B) *Lord:* intentional: force
Reason	(A) *Saul:* for sake of religious faith; emotion: love, attachment (B) *Lord:* acquiring benefits

The Resistant Saul Is the Resistant Paul

What was Luke's purpose for including the Damascus narrative in this first defense speech of Paul before the Jerusalem crowd? According to Stevens, Paul's arrival in Jerusalem is an example of Paul's resistance to the guidance and direction of the Holy Spirit.[61] Paul's entrance into Jerusalem results in his beating, arrest, and chaining. Luke reduced Paul to a state of helplessness and humiliation by overcoming him with the crowd and the Chiliarch. One could assume the events of the narrative result from Paul's arrival in Jerusalem as he follows the Holy Spirit. Paul's overpowering and arrest could be read as part of the Holy Spirit's plan. However, within this narrative of Paul, Luke embedded the narrative of Saul by means of a defense speech to the crowd. The story of Saul was familiar to the reader. Saul's story was one of resistance to God. This resistant Saul was subsequently overcome and transformed into a witness. In the present rendering of the narrative, Luke made a brilliant editorial decision. He added a short narrative of a discussion between Saul and the Lord in the Jerusalem temple. This narrative highlighted Saul's resistance to his divinely appointed role as a witness.[62] Luke then interrupted the *narratio* at this point leaving the image of Saul resisting his role as a divine witness standing. He did not complete the transformation of Saul from empowered persecutor to empowered witness. The Lord had overcome Saul on the road, removed his commission, restored Saul's sight, and given him a new

---

[61] Ibid., 17-37.
[62] Ibid., 28, 31.

commission as a witness. Yet Saul does not act upon this commission. Instead he argues with God over how he should fulfill his role as a witness.

Stopping the speech at this point, Luke then returned to the story of Paul. Paul also is powerless and resisting his role as divinely appointed witness. Thus, Luke inserted the Damascus event to highlight and illustrate the present actions of Paul. The character of Paul the witness has become like the character of Saul the persecutor, as he has intentionally resisted God. Therefore, God again has acted intentionally and with force to overcome Paul, bringing him to a state of powerlessness. God has begun to transform Paul just as he transformed Saul. However, the transformation of Paul is incomplete just as that of Saul is left incomplete in the narrative. Paul—just as did Saul—is currently resisting his role as a divinely appointed witness. Therefore, following the Lukan paradigm of transformation portrayed in Acts 9, Paul will remain powerless and overcome until he accepts his divine role as a witness. Paul's acceptance of his commission location should then result in his subsequent empowerment.

The same character plot used to chart Saul's transformation in Acts 9 may now be used to plot Paul's present transformation. Paul headed toward Jerusalem as an intentionally resistant witness. In response to this resistance God has overcome Paul, stripping him of power and authority. God must transform Paul, bringing him to accept his commissioned location as a divinely appointed witness. Yet, in the present scene Paul continues to resist this role. The transformation of Paul into an empowered witness remains incomplete due to this continued resistance.

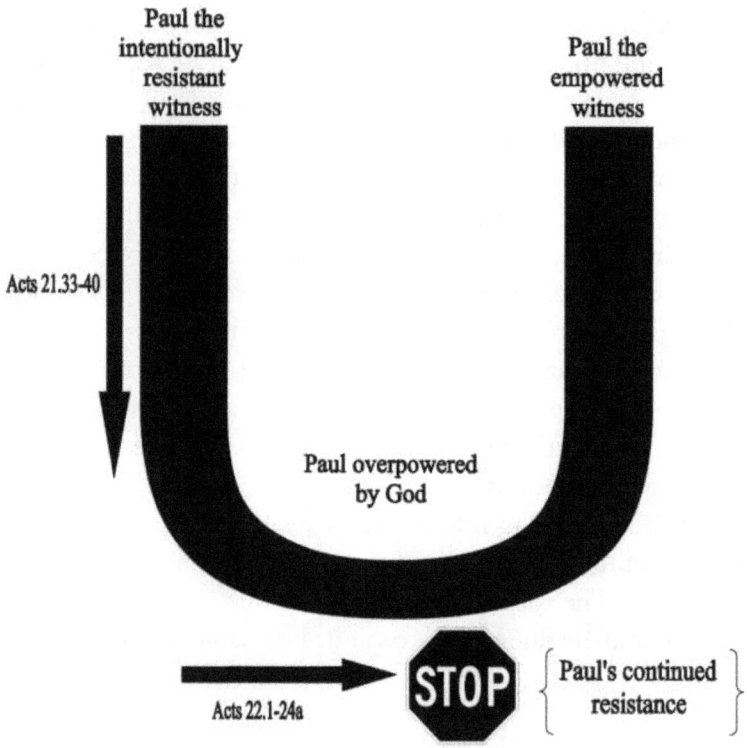

Fig. 2. The Interrupted Transformation of Paul's Character

4
Paul the Witness

The Rhetorical Unit

The next unit of study is Acts 25:23—26:32. The unit is a mixture of narrative and speech that Luke delimited with two *inclusios*. The first enclosing bracket is the double declaration of Paul's innocence (Acts 25:25; 26:31-32). The second is the entering and exiting of the characters Agrippa, Festus, Bernice, the tribunes, and the leading men (Acts 25:23; 26:30-31). The physical movement of these characters marks the beginning and ending of the scene.

Luke placed this narrative and embedded speech scene at the end of the *Paulusbild* just before the journey to Rome, which marks the conclusion of the last programmatic unit of Acts, the movement of the gospel to the ends of the earth (13:1—28:31). The unit also forms a closing bracket of the larger trial narrative (21:33—26:32) and functions as the final scene in the narrative of Pauline resistance to the divine necessity of Roman witness (19:21—26:32).

The Rhetorical Situation

Paul's speech before a mixed audience at Caesarea is a direct result of the failure of Paul's earlier speech (Acts 22) to convince the crowd in the Jerusalem temple. Paul spoke to the crowd outside the temple in hopes of defending himself against their charges and judgment. However, his speech was a complete failure. The crowd refused to vindicate Paul. Instead of acquittal, the crowd continued to call for Paul's death (22:22). Unable to ascertain the nature of the riot, the chiliarch has no choice but to interrogate his prisoner (vv. 24-25). Paul thwarts the attempts to interrogate him by force when he claims his Roman citizenship (vv. 25-29).

The chiliarch, still at a loss as to the cause of the riot, holds a hearing with Paul and the Sanhedrin. Paul speaks before this group, but the result is again rioting and chaos, just as in the temple (Acts 23:9). Because of the violence, the chiliarch once again orders Paul taken into the barracks (Acts 23:10). Paul makes no positive impact in Jerusalem. He is a prisoner of the Romans, and each time he speaks he brings about violence among the Jerusalem Jews. At this point, the Lord appears to Paul in a vision informing Paul that he must testify in Rome as he has in Jerusalem. The vision is ironic for if Paul speaks in Rome as—in the same manner—he has spoken in Jerusalem, then the result will only be rioting and chaos.[1] Paul would be totally ineffective in Rome. Further, the statement is ironic because Paul has not borne witness in Jerusalem. He has spoken in defense of his actions, but at no point has he spoken of Jesus or the gospel, or made a call for repentance. Stevens has identified this vision as a "word of grace."[2] The purpose of the vision is to set Paul back on course with God's will. Paul might be in Jerusalem, but he *must* go to Rome.

The reception of the vision creates a narrative dilemma. The Lord has instructed Paul that the proper venue for his witness is Rome. However, Paul is currently unable to go to Rome due to his imprisonment. The Lord will have to free Paul from prison if he is to go to Rome. In the preceding narrative, when Paul was imprisoned, God freed him (Acts 16:25-28). When the apostles Peter and John were in prison, God freed them (5:17-20; 12:5-11). A narrative precedent exists for God to free

---

[1] Stevens, "Luke's Perspective," 34.
[2] Ibid., 33–34.

Paul now from prison. No such deliverance occurs. Yet, the absence of deliverance does not indicate an absence of God's movement. The Jews make a plot on Paul's life, but the plot surfaces and Paul is spared (23:12-35). The chiliarch transfers Paul to a safer venue for trial. Paul is tried again in Caesarea. However, through a miscarriage of justice, Paul languishes in prison for two years (24:1-27). External resistance meets the bearing of witness to the ends of the earth. The resistance is overcome with the appointment of Festus as the new procurator.

Festus decides to retry Paul, but another plot is made upon Paul's life. Paul calls upon Caesar in an effort to spare himself from the plot. Curiously, with his appeal, Paul seals his own fate. Paul will go to Rome, but he will remain in chains. The narrative precedent of deliverance from prison is not achieved because of Paul's own appeal to Caesar.

At this point in the narrative, Luke inserted the third and final Damascus narrative. Paul will be going to Rome but will do so in chains. The Jerusalem episode and trial of Paul come to a close. At the end of this episode, once again the reader encounters a story of Pauline resistance to God, evoking memory of Saul the persecutor. Notably, the larger trial narrative begins and ends with this story of Pauline resistance. In the middle of these two narratives Luke placed the word of grace from God to Paul (Acts 23:11). Has this vision changed the characterization of Paul within the narrative? Is the character of Paul still that of Saul the overcome persecutor, or has the vision of grace completed the transformation left unfinished in Acts 22 so that he is once again Paul the empowered witness? What tensions are created by Paul's remaining in chains and his new direction of travel to Rome?

The immediate situation of the present rhetorical unit is that of a hearing before Festus. Because of Paul's appeal to the emperor, Festus must send Paul to Rome. However, he must send some type of legal brief concerning the case and is at a loss as to what to write. Agrippa and Bernice arrive to pay their respects to the new governor. During their visit, Festus relates to Agrippa the difficulty of Paul's case. Agrippa expresses interest in hearing the case. Festus seizes the opportunity, perhaps hoping the hearing would provide the details needed to construct the legal brief for the emperor (25:13-22).

The text of Paul's appearance is a mixture of speech and narrative. The narrative encircles the speech in much the same way as narrative surrounded Paul's speech in Acts 22. This scene, however, is somewhat different. In the present narrative, Luke portrayed an audience that was calm and receptive. This audience is unable to charge or convict Paul, while the audience in Acts 22 called for Paul's death. The current audience is gathered for the sole purpose of discovering whether Paul has done anything wrong (25:25-27).

When Paul speaks, he does so before people of standing instead of a mob (25:23). His speech is judicial in flavor.[3] The narrative setting does not permit one officially to label the proceedings as a trial. Neither Festus nor Agrippa can offer a ruling because Paul is destined for the emperor. Nevertheless, sufficient markers are present within the text denoting a judicial setting even if the outcome of the scene is not official. First, Festus mentions that he has investigated the background of the charges (25:25). The text contains the mention of a legal brief (25:26). Paul is a prisoner who has been accused (25:24, 27). Paul is commanded to speak on his behalf, implying a defense (26:1). Three forms of the word ἀπολογέω are present in the text (26:1, 24). In Paul's speech, he indicates that he understands his situation as one in which he has been accused (26:2). Finally, judgment by the audience is issued concerning the innocence of Paul (26:31-32).

A judicial theme runs throughout the entire rhetorical unit. Therefore, the embedded speech should adhere to a judicial speech structure. Because the audience is not hostile, the scene is a fact-finding hearing, and no disgraceful action is in view other than Festus's experience of Jews calling for Paul's death, a direct opening could be made in the speech.[4] In constructing the speech, Luke could have allowed Paul to argue from one of three *stases*. First, Paul could deny the charges made against him by the Jews. Such a defense would rely upon the conjectural *stasis*.[5] Such denials are not present in the speech. Second, Paul could qualify his actions by choosing to discuss the correct interpretation of the law. This defense would be built upon the legal *stasis*.[6] Such a *stasis* is a possibility for the

---

[3]Abraham J. Malherbe, "'Not in a Corner': Early Christian Apologetic in Acts 26:26," *SecCent* 5 (1985–86) 201; McCormick, "Paul's Addresses," 294; Winter, "Official Proceedings," 333; Veltman, "Defense Speeches," 255; Fitzmyer, *Acts*, 754.
[4][Cic.] *Rhet. Her.* 1.4.6.
[5]Ibid. 1.11.18.
[6]Ibid. 1.11.19.

speech, as Paul does discuss Moses and the prophets (Acts 26:22). However, Paul is standing before a Roman court, which would not accept the legal standing of the Law of Moses and the prophets. Further, Paul uses this phrase to describe what he taught and not the reasons for his teaching and actions. Thus, the *stasis* of the speech is not legal. Finally, Paul could agree to the content of the charges but deny the nature of such charges. Such a speech would be based upon the juridical *stasis*.[7] In the speech, Paul does not deny the charges but justifies his actions with his obedience to an encounter with God (26:19-21). Paul places the responsibility for his actions upon God. This process is termed *metastasis*, a sub-genre of the juridical *stasis*.[8]

The present rhetorical unit is a combination of narrative and judicial speech. The immediate rhetorical setting for the narrative is the need to discover the truth behind the events surrounding Paul's arrest and imprisonment. What had Paul done wrong? Thus, Paul once again must defend himself and his actions. He does so by placing the responsibility for his actions upon God. Interestingly, in the setting of discovering what really happened, Luke included the Damascus road narrative. Somehow, the story of Saul resisting God by persecuting the disciples interprets what has happened in Jerusalem.

The Analysis of Acts 25:23—26:32

The present rhetorical unit consists of a forensic defense speech encompassed by two narrative panels (25:23—26:1 and 26:24-32). In the defense speech, Luke incorporated a slightly modified version of the Damascus event. By combining this past event with the encircling narrative, Luke was able to characterize Paul as the once empowered witness of God who has been overpowered because of his resistance. Yet this witness is not totally helpless but is in the process of becoming empowered once again.

---

[7][Cic.] *Rhet. Her.* 1.11.19.
[8][Cic.] *Rhet. Her.* 1.15.25; and Quint. *Inst.* 7.4.13-14. See also Soards, *Speeches*, 122; and Kennedy, *New Testament Interpretation*, 137.

Paul before Agrippa (Acts 25:23—26:1)

Luke began the present scene with the entrance of Agrippa and his entourage of Bernice, Festus, the tribunes, and leading men of the city. The setting is that of a trial or formal hearing in which Paul is declared innocent even before he speaks. The hearing is necessary because the Jews have asked Festus to condemn Paul. However, before Festus could hold an actual trial, Paul called upon Caesar. Because Festus still is not sure of the proper charges that he must send to Caesar, he asks Agrippa to advise him after hearing Paul, a role Agrippa is willing to play.

The scene that Luke constructed is much more complex than the first trial scene (21:33—22:24). He employed four main characters: Agrippa, Paul, Festus, and the remaining audience.[9] The narrative panel begins with the entrance of Agrippa and his entourage into the hall and ends with the beginning of Paul's speech (25:23; 26:1). The place is the audience hall of Festus in Caesarea a day after Festus first informed Agrippa of his legal dilemma involving Paul (25:22-23).

In the scene, Luke portrayed Agrippa as a man of pomp and authority. Agrippa has the authority to sit as a judge, and he is one whose guidance is sought in the present case (25:23, 26; 26:1). Festus is the other authority in the scene, having the ability to call for Paul; but, unlike Agrippa, he sits as a judge who is ignorant in the current proceedings (25:23, 25-26). Festus's authority in the narrative is under pressure and constraint. Although Festus currently has power over Paul, he is under pressure by the Jews to condemn Paul and constrained by his position to send Paul to the emperor (25:24-25, 27). Luke characterized Paul as a man who is a prisoner and condemned by the Jews (25:23-24). Paul is innocent of all charges, but this innocent man must be sent to the emperor for trial (25:25). Paul is powerless in the present situation. He has no authority to speak and no ability to go and come as he wishes (25:23; 26:1). Luke characterized the audience as playing a minor background role in the scene. The audience sits as a jury so they might come to some decision concerning Paul's actions (25:23-24, 26).

---

[9]The audience consists of Bernice, the leading men, and the tribunes. However, in the narrative Luke collapsed these into a single character in the background, for none play any distinctive role as the proceedings take place.

Paul the Witness

As the scene transpires, Agrippa enters the hall, listens to Festus, and commands Paul to speak (25:23—26:1). His actions are accomplished intentionally and with force. He sits as a judge over Paul, attempting to discern the facts of the case. He intentionally acts out of emotion, his curiosity, and for the sake of friendship with Festus. Festus, just like Agrippa, enters the hall, orders Paul brought forward, and speaks to the gathered audience (25:23-27). He acts intentionally and with force as he enters the hall and orders Paul brought forward. He is the commanding official in the present setting. However, he speaks to the audience unintentionally out of necessity. Festus has gathered the audience to fulfill his duty of constructing a legal brief, which he is unable to complete. The audience plays a minor role in the narrative. They enter the hall and listen to Festus. Their actions are accomplished intentionally and with force. They sit as a jury determining the facts of the case for Festus. They are gathered for the sake of friendship with Festus.

The character of Paul stands in stark contrast to the previous three characters. While Agrippa, Festus, and the audience act intentionally and with force, Luke did not allow Paul to act at all in the narrative. Others act upon Paul. Paul is condemned, brought, and ordered to speak. He has no choice in the timing of the scene or in the content of his speech. He is commanded to defend himself (26:1).

In this scene Paul is totally helpless at the mercy and under the control of others. Paul's status has not changed since the failure of his speech in Acts 22. He is still a prisoner and ordered about by Roman authorities. The Jews still call for Paul's death, and the Roman authorities are inept in their attempts to grasp the situation. Paul remains overcome, but now he is overcome and heading to Rome to stand trial. The vision in 23:11 has not changed Paul's station. He remains powerless and overcome, although he is now headed to Rome.

Table 10. Paul before Agrippa (Acts 25:23—26:1)

Character	(A) *Agrippa:* judge; pomp; guidance sought; authority (B) *Paul:* brought, condemned; prisoner, bound for emperor, speaks with permission (C) *Festus:* authority; pressured; ignorant of facts; constrained by office (D) *Audience:* jury
Act	(A) *Agrippa:* enters hall; listens to Festus; commands Paul to speak (B) *Paul:* no action (C) *Festus:* enters hall; orders Paul brought; speaks to audience (D) *Audience:* enters hall; listens to Festus
Time	The day after Festus related Paul's case to Agrippa and Bernice
Place	Audience hall of Festus
Manner	(A) *Agrippa:* intentional: force (B) *Paul:* no action (C) *Festus:* intentional: force; unintentional: necessity (D) *Audience:* intentional: force
Reason	(A) *Agrippa:* emotion: curiosity; for sake of friendship (B) *Paul:* no action (C) *Festus:* for sake of duty (D) *Audience:* for sake of friendship

Paul the Ineffective Witness (Acts 26:24-32)

After the speech by Paul, Luke returned to the narrative of Paul before Agrippa in the audience hall of Festus. The scene begins with Festus interrupting Paul, thus ending the speech in Acts 26:24. The scene ends with the retreat of the audience from the audience hall in vv. 30-32. In the scene, Luke characterized Paul's speech as a failure. Paul's situation does not change, and the audience rejects the *stasis* of his speech. Paul remains helpless and overcome with a new twist of irony added. Paul is heading to Rome in chains because of his own actions.

Luke began the present narrative panel as an interruption of Paul's speech.[10] Luke employed four characters in this panel: Festus, Agrippa, Paul, and the audience. He portrayed Festus as stopping Paul in mid-speech. Festus interrupts because he has reached a decision concerning the case: Paul is innocent but crazy (vv. 24, 31). Agrippa also interrupts Paul, rejecting the basis of Paul's arguments. Just like Festus, Agrippa assents to Paul's innocence (vv. 28, 31-32). The audience rejects Paul's speech by leaving the hall, but they too declare Paul's innocence (vv. 30-31).

---

[10]Note the genitive absolute of v. 24. Paul has not yet finished speaking when Festus interrupts.

The primary characterization of Paul in the present panel is that of innocence (vv. 31-32). Paul has done nothing worthy of death or imprisonment. This characterization of innocence is in tension with the rest of Luke's characterization of Paul. An innocent man who has done nothing wrong is interrupted, labeled as mad, left in chains, and ignored as he attempts to continue to speak (vv. 24, 26, 28-32). Paul's innocence has no effect on his standing or ability to gain acceptance for his claims.

As the scene develops, Festus acts by interrupting Paul, labels him as mad, leaves the hall, and declares Paul innocent (vv. 24, 30-31). His actions are all accomplished intentionally and with force. As the official authority of the scene, Festus has reached his own verdict concerning Paul. He acts intentionally out of emotion, perhaps his shock at Paul's statements. Further, he acts for the sake of justice. He declares Paul innocent but leaves the hall not accepting the basis of Paul's arguments. Agrippa also rejects Paul's arguments, leaves the hall, and declares Paul's innocence (vv. 28, 30-31). He acts intentionally and with force. He cannot accept Paul's arguments but acknowledges that Paul has done no wrong. He issues his declaration of innocence for the sake of justice. The audience acts in the same manner and for the same reasons as Agrippa. They leave the hall with Agrippa and Festus and declare Paul's innocence.

All the characters that surround Paul act intentionally and with force. They do so for justice but reject Paul's arguments. However, justice is not accomplished because of Paul's own actions. Luke characterized Paul as disputing the statements of Festus and Agrippa with no effect (vv. 25-27, 29). Paul's rebuttals are given unintentionally out of necessity. The interruptions of Festus and Agrippa forced Paul to reply rather than continue with his speech. Paul counters the statements of his judges in order to acquire benefits. He wishes to gain his freedom. Paul cannot achieve the benefits he desires because by his own actions—his calling upon the emperor—he remains in chains (v. 32).

In the present narrative panel, Luke vindicated Paul but left two complications in the narrative. First, Paul is unable to convince those with whom he speaks. His arguments are ineffective and incomplete as the audience retreats from the hall.[11] Second, Paul remains in chains as a result of his own

---

[11] Perhaps Luke intended here to allude to a bearing of witness, but one is unable to determine with any certainty this intention. No full discussion of the kerygma or full

doing. At the end of the scene, in spite of the declaration of Paul's innocence, he is still helpless and ineffective. Paul remains a prisoner, unable to act on his own power and unable to bear an effective witness. Luke left Paul an unintentional actor. With this scene the trial narrative ends. Interestingly, this scene highlights Paul's helpless state and is the last image of Paul the reader views before Paul heads to Rome. Paul is heading to Rome, but not exactly in the freedom intended by God. Paul could have traveled to Rome as a free man, but because of his own actions he will travel in a helpless state in chains.

Table 11. Paul the Ineffective Witness (Acts 26:24-32)

Character	(A) *Paul:* sound mind; bold; believes prophets; interrupted; prisoner; innocent (B) *Festus:* ignorant; judge; disregards arguments (C) *Agrippa:* disregards arguments; believes prophets; knowledgeable; judge (D) *Audience:* judges; disregard arguments
Act	(A) *Paul:* answers Festus; redirects to Agrippa (B) *Festus:* interrupts; judges Paul; leaves; discusses case (C) *Agrippa:* interrupts; leaves; discusses case; declares Paul innocent (D) *Audience:* listen; leave
Time	End of Paul's speech
Place	Audience hall of Festus
Manner	(A) *Paul:* unintentional: necessity; intentional: force (B) *Festus:* intentional: force (C) *Agrippa:* intentional: force (D) *Audience:* intentional: force
Reason	(A) *Paul:* acquire benefits; for sake of Jesus (B) *Festus:* rejection of arguments (C) *Agrippa:* for sake of justice; rejection of arguments (D) *Audience:* rejection of arguments

Paul's Defense Before Agrippa (Acts 26:2-23)

Paul's address to Agrippa begins in Acts 26:2 at the urging of Agrippa. As discussed above, the genre of the speech is judicial. Before any investigation of the speech, as with 22:1, 3-21, two questions must be addressed. First, is the speech as composed by Luke, complete in light of Hellenistic rhetorical standards? Second, what is the rhetorical structure of the speech?

A surprising number of interpreters have considered Paul's speech before Agrippa to be complete.[12] However, when considered in light of

---

call to repentance is present. If presented, then the gospel is presented only in the starkest terms. Paul has spoken in keeping with Moses and the prophets.

[12] See Crouch, "Persuasive Moment," 334; Witherington, *Acts*, 737–38; Long, "Trial of Paul," 238–39; and Winter, "Official Proceedings," 329–30.

Hellenistic rhetoric, Paul's speech before Agrippa is not complete. One may marshal three arguments against those who consider the speech as complete. First, key elements necessary for a complete judicial speech are absent. As noted in the discussion of Paul's first defense speech, a judicial speech was to consist of six elements: *exordium, narratio, divisio, confirmatio, refutatio,* and *conclusio*.[13] Due to the flexibility of Hellenistic rhetoric, all that was needed to construct a defense speech were the *exordium, confirmatio,* and the *conclusio*. In the present speech, the *confirmatio* and *conclusio* are noticeably absent.

In an overview of the speech, one can determine that no sustained arguments are provided by Paul. Luke constructed no proofs, artificial or inartificial. The majority of the speech (vv. 10-21) is a continuous narrative concerning Paul's previous life and behavior. Quintilian equated the continuous narrative with the *narratio* and not the *confirmatio*.[14] Second, any form of *peroratio* or *conclusio* is absent from Paul's speech. Paul made no effort to recapitulate or call his audience to make a judgment.[15]

A second reason to consider the speech as incomplete is the presence of Festus's interruption of Paul (v. 24). Of special interest is the grammar of the interruption. Luke described the interruption using a genitive absolute. This Greek structure focuses on the simultaneous nature of the interruption with Paul's speech. Paul was not through speaking when Festus interrupted.

Finally, Paul's speech should not be viewed as complete because one is able to trace the probable trajectory the speech would have followed had Luke allowed Paul to continue. Paul declared that he had said nothing in contradiction to the prophets or Moses (v. 22). Proofs supporting this claim would have followed. Paul should have developed what the prophets and Moses had said to support his claim. Paul made no such development. Instead of speaking, Paul is interrupted and forced to contest statements by Festus and Agrippa. Before he can return to his proofs and then conclude his speech, the audience leaves.

As it stands, the speech of Paul before Agrippa is not complete. Therefore, what is the rhetorical structure of the extant speech? In light of

---

[13][Cic.] *Rhet. Her.* 1.3.4; and Cic. *Inv. Rhet.* 1.14.19.
[14]Quint. *Inst.* 4.2.78-79.
[15]Ibid. 6.1-2; and Cic. *Inv. Rhet.* 1.70.98.

the above discussion, one may eliminate rhetorical outlines that provide complete structures for the defense speech. After rejecting these outlines, only two proposed outlines remain. The first, that of Neyrey, is too convoluted to be of any assistance.[16] Kennedy provided the second outline. He diagrammed Paul's speech into three elements: *proem* (vv. 2-3), *narratio* (vv. 4-18), and proof (vv. 19-23).[17] Kennedy's assessment of the rhetorical structure of this speech has three drawbacks. First, Kennedy identified the *narratio* as beginning in v. 4. His division appears to be obvious with the mentioning of Paul's former life. However, the point of the statement by Paul is not to illuminate his life so much as to humiliate his accusers through the use of a rhetorical device.[18] Second, Kennedy posited that a proof begins in v. 19. Yet Paul's discussion of his former life does not end but continues in successive narrative form. Finally, Paul's statements in vv. 19-21 have no direct connection to what follows in vv. 22-23. Paul ends his narrative with his arrest in the temple and then begins a new section of his speech. In light of these difficulties with Kennedy's proposed structure, a new rhetorical structure is now submitted. For analytical purposes, the following rhetorical structure will be followed: *exordium* (vv. 2-8); *narratio* (vv. 9-21); and *propositio* (vv. 22-23).

The Exordium (Acts 26:2-8)

Paul begins his speech, as any good rhetorician would, with the motioning of his hand.[19] Paul then speaks. His first few words comprise an *exordium* that is aimed at gaining Agrippa's favor, the proper tactic in a direct opening.[20] Paul considers himself blessed because he stands before one who is an expert in the matter he is about to discuss. An expert such as Agrippa is needed, Paul argues, because the nature of the case concerns sectarian issues of the Jews. The mentioning of the need for expertise

---

[16]Neyrey, "Forensic Defense Speech," 221. Neyrey's forensic outlines display a misunderstanding of Hellenistic rhetoric resulting in a chaotic and overlapping outline in which portions of the speech function as different parts simultaneously.
[17]Kennedy, *New Testament Interpretation*, 137.
[18]See discussion below.
[19]Quint. *Inst.* 11.3.92.
[20]Ibid., 4.1.42.

concerning religious matters classifies the case as difficult or obscure.[21] A normal judge cannot grasp the arguments—a fact that has necessitated the present hearing.

The Hellenistic rhetorical handbooks provided guidelines for one in Paul's situation, trying to gain the favor of the judge and jury using a direct opening. One could make use of any combination of four approaches. An orator could capture the goodwill of the audience by discussing his own person, the person of his adversaries, the person of his hearers, and the facts of the case themselves.[22] Luke made use of all four of these approaches.

First, Luke portrayed Paul as discussing the nature of the case and the judge's ability to render a good judgment. Only Agrippa has the proper knowledge to serve as a good judge.[23] Second, in vv. 4-5 Paul turns upon his accusers and singles them out. Their testimony concerning Paul's life will not match their charges if they are willing to testify. Thus, they are false accusers.[24] This evidence shames his accusers. Third, Paul implies that his own person is above reproach (vv. 4-5). Paul is a good Jew who has lived as a Pharisee.[25] Finally, Paul discusses the nature and facts of the case. In vv. 6-9, Paul lays forth the important point that he would discuss in the following speech. The basis of his case is his belief in the basic hope of his religious faith, the resurrection of the dead.[26]

The Narratio (Acts 26:9-21)

Having identified the point that has direct bearing upon his case—the resurrection—Paul moves to present a narration of facts that have bearing upon the case.[27] His narration begins with a description of his persecuting

---

[21]Cic. *Inv. Rhet.* 1.15.20.
[22][Cic.] *Rhet. Her.* 1.4.7.
[23]Ibid., 1.5.8.; and Quint. *Inst.* 4.1.16.
[24][Cic.] *Rhet. Her.* 1.5.8. Goodwill from the judge could be attained by showing an accuser to be treacherous or cruel.
[25]Acts 26:4-5; Cic. *Inv. Rhet.* 1.16.22.
[26]Identifying the points of the case was one manner of gaining the goodwill of the judge. See Quint. *Inst.* 4.1.35.
[27]Two types of narrations existed: the facts of the case and the facts that had bearing upon the case. See Quint. *Inst.* 4.2.11.

activities as a Jew in Jerusalem. This narration must provide the evidence that brought Paul to act as he has, *metastasis*, and to hold firmly to the resurrection of the dead.

Saul, the Overcome Persecutor (Acts 26:9-18)

In the opening panel of the *narratio*, Luke portrayed Paul as Saul, the vicious persecutor of the saints who was overcome and transformed by God. The scene begins in v. 9 with Paul's statement of his persecution attempts and concludes in v. 19 with the shift in address to Agrippa. The setting of the panel is sometime in the past in Jerusalem and Damascus.

Luke employed four characters in his construction of this first narrative panel: Saul, Jesus, the companions of Saul, and the saints. The character of Saul does not remain constant throughout the narrative. Luke first characterized Saul as one who does everything he can against Jesus (v. 9). Saul punishes and violently persecutes the saints, forcing them to blaspheme. Under the power and authority of the priests, Saul rages against the saints and pursues them wherever he might find them outside of Jerusalem (vv. 10-12). Saul does not remain this violent persecutor but is overcome through an encounter with Jesus. After his encounter with Jesus, Saul is overcome, indicted as a persecutor and one who resisted God (vv. 13-14). Saul is ignorant of Jesus' identity, but after Jesus' appearance Saul receives a new commission as a servant and witness, one chosen by God for a special mission of turning people to God through Jesus (Acts vv. 15-17, 19). The Lukan characterization of Saul was that of radical reversal and transformation. Jesus stops Saul's activity as a violent persecutor and transforms him into one who turns people to God.

In the panel, Luke depicted Jesus as a persecuted heavenly judge who overcomes Saul and subsequently empowers him as a servant and witness (vv. 14-19). He portrayed the companions as those overcome by the light (v. 14). The saints are persecuted by Saul, just as Saul persecuted Jesus (vv. 10-12).

Before his encounter with Jesus, Saul seeks to imprison the saints. He votes for their death, forces them to blaspheme, and pursues the saints to Damascus. He acts intentionally and with force. Under the authority of the priests, Saul seeks to punish the saints harshly. He seeks to punish the saints out of his emotion of hatred and out of the desire to remove evil. However, after his encounter with Jesus on the road to Damascus, Saul is changed. Saul falls to the ground, questions Jesus, and listens. He acts unintentionally out of necessity. He has no choice but is overcome by the brilliance of the light. Saul acts in response to the light out of the emotion of fear and to acquire benefits. He wishes to know who has confronted him.

In the text, Jesus acts by overpowering Saul, indicting him as a persecutor, and recommissioning Saul. He acts intentionally and with force. He maneuvers to remove the persecutor of the saints. Jesus acts to remove evil and to acquire benefits. Jesus encounters Saul to gain a servant and witness to turn people to God.

The companions and the saints are minor characters in the narrative. The companions fall to the ground unintentionally out of necessity. The brilliance of the light overcomes them. They fall possibly on account of the emotion of fear. The saints do not act but are acted upon by Saul in his persecution efforts.

The present Damascus narrative bears a strong resemblance to the previous two tellings of the story. Saul, the intentionally forceful persecutor of the church acting to remove evil, met another intentionally forceful actor acting to remove evil. In this encounter Saul is overcome. The scene differs in that Luke deleted explicit references to Saul's blindness and powerlessness. Saul is overcome by the light but immediately given a new commission and purpose by Jesus himself. Some indications of powerlessness remain in the narrative, as Saul does not act upon the new commission in the present scene. Such an implication is minor, however, and in the background. The editorial maneuverings of Luke lead to a portrait of Saul overcome but immediately transformed. Saul is no longer the violent persecutor but the commissioned servant and witness.

Table 12. Saul, the Overcome Persecutor (Acts 26:9-18)

Character	(A) *Saul (before)*: persecutor; empowered by priests; votes against saints; punishes saints; forces blasphemy; rages against saints; pursues saints; travels to Damascus (B) *Saul (after)*: overcome by light; indicted as persecutor; resisting God; ignorant of Jesus; commissioned by Jesus; servant; witness; chosen by God; appointed for special mission (C) *Jesus*: heavenly judge; persecuted; overcomes Saul; commissions Saul (D) *Companions*: overcome by light (E) *Saints*: persecuted by Saul
Act	(A) *Saul (before)*: imprisons saints; votes for death; forces blasphemy; pursues saints; journeys to Damascus (B) *Saul (after)*: falls to ground; questions Jesus; listens to Jesus (C) *Jesus*: overpowers Saul; indicts Saul; recommissions Saul (D) *Companions*: fall to ground (E) *Saints*: no action
Time	Past
Place	Jerusalem and road to Damascus
Manner	(A) *Saul (before)*: intentional: force (B) *Saul (after)*: unintentional: necessity (C) *Jesus*: intentional: force (D) *Companions*: unintentional: necessity (E) *Saints*: no actions
Reason	(A) *Saul (before)*: emotion: hatred; removing evil (B) *Saul (after)*: emotion: fear; acquiring benefits (C) *Jesus*: removing evil; acquiring benefits (D) *Companions*: emotion: fear (E) *Saints*: no actions

Saul, the Obedient Witness (Acts 26:19-21)

The concluding narrative panel of the *narratio* begins in v. 19 with Paul's address to Agrippa. The panel concludes with the mention of Paul's arrest in the temple (v. 21). Luke used this scene to complete Saul's transformation from empowered persecutor to empowered witness, but in different terms than in Acts 9. The narrative occurs sometime in the past in Damascus, Jerusalem, the country of the Jews, among the Gentiles, and in the temple.

In the narrative, Luke utilized two characters: Saul and the Jews. He characterized Saul as one who is obedient to the vision he received from Jesus. He is a witness for God to all people and has called people to repentance (vv. 19-20). As a result of his obedience to God—fulfilling his divinely appointed role—the Jews seize Paul and try to kill him (v. 21) Luke characterized these particular Jews as those who seize and attempt to kill (v. 21).

Paul the Witness

Saul acts in obedience to his vision by bearing witness (vv. 19-21). He bears witness intentionally and with force, going to both Jews and Gentiles. He bears witness for the sake of obedience to God. The Jews, on the other hand, seize Paul and attempt to kill him. They too are acting intentionally and with force, but to remove evil.

With this short narrative panel, Luke returned Saul/Paul to the status of an intentional actor who obeys God. The transformation from resistant persecutor is complete. Saul fulfills his divinely appointed role and in so doing is persecuted.[28] Ironically, Saul is not delivered from his persecution. The last words of the *narratio* create an unusual tension. Saul is transformed and obedient, and yet he remains overcome. The Jews have seized him and attempted to kill him. This tension does not fit the thematic movement of Acts. When God moves, he is resisted. However, God overcomes all resistance. In the current narrative setting, God has not overcome the resistance. Saul remains in custody as a result of the seizure by the Jews. What resistance remains to be overcome? Does Paul remain in custody because of the resistance of the Jews or because of his own resistance?

Table 13. Saul, the Obedient Witness (Acts 26:19-21)

Character	(A) *Saul:* obedient; witness for God to all people; turns people to repentance; seized by Jews
	(B) *Jews:* seize Paul; attempt to kill Paul
Act	(A) *Saul:* obeys vision; bears witness
	(B) *Jews:* seize Paul; attempt to kill him
Time	Past
Place	Damascus; Jerusalem; area of Jews and Gentiles; Temple
Manner	(A) *Saul:* intentional: force
	(B) *Jews:* intentional: force
Reason	(A) *Saul:* for sake of obedience
	(B) *Jews:* removing of evil

The Propositio and Concluding Analysis (Acts 26:22-23)

In a judicial speech, following the conclusion of the *narratio* an orator could choose to place a *propositio*. In this section the speaker would provide

---

[28] See the discussion of the transformation of Saul in chapter 3.

the divisions of his proofs based upon his narration for his audience.[29] Luke already has alluded to the basis of the case in Acts 26:6-8. Paul holds to the hope of the resurrection as a tenet of his religious faith. Paul returns to this point here in his *propositio*.

Paul claims to have received help up to this day. He has faced resistance and persecution as he has fulfilled his divinely appointed role but has overcome. However, he currently is still in chains. He stands before all and bears witness. Paul has spoken nothing outside of the prophets or Moses. The Christ first had to suffer and then rise from the dead. Paul returns to the resurrection of the dead, which is the basis of his case. Scriptural proofs should follow as well as arguments based upon Paul's own past life to support this statement.

Luke did not allow Paul to continue. He had Festus interrupt and declare Paul insane. Festus cannot accept the premise of Paul's case. With the interruption the speech effectively is over. Paul does respond to Festus, claiming that he is not mad but speaks true and reasonable words. He turns to King Agrippa for support (vv. 25-26). Paul's answer has the appearance of a *refutatio,* but the spontaneity of Festus's interruption and Paul's response preclude the formal identification as such.[30] Paul then attempts to return to his speech by returning to the prophets as the basis of his *propositio* (v. 27). By refusing to become a Christian Agrippa does not allow Paul to return to his speech. Paul's last words are telling. His last words speak of his chains, thus highlighting his state of powerlessness and helplessness. Paul would have Agrippa believe and be just like him except for the chains. Agrippa and the rest of the audience leave the hall and comment that Paul was innocent but must be sent to the emperor. Because of his own words, Paul will remain in chains.

Saul the Witness Is Not Paul the Witness

The Lukan characterization of Paul in Acts 25:23—26-32 is one of tension. Luke allowed Paul to portray himself as a divinely empowered, obedient witness with the retelling of the Damascus narrative. In so doing, Luke

---

[29]Quint. *Inst.* 4.4.1.
[30]Cic. *Inv. Rhet.* 1.62.78.

emphasized the second half of the first Damascus narrative, the transformation and empowerment of Saul into a witness. Saul was once the violent persecutor of the saints, but through an encounter with Jesus he became the obedient witness to all people. However, the Saul of Paul's speech is not the Paul of Luke's narrative. In the encompassing narrative, Paul is not Saul the empowered witness but Paul the overcome witness. Paul is still a prisoner. He remains under the control of the authorities, unable even to speak without permission. His attempts to bear witness are rejected. Finally and most telling, Paul will remain in this situation—in chains, overpowered, and helpless—because of his own actions. Paul chose to call upon the emperor. Nevertheless all is not hopeless. Paul is headed to Rome, his divinely appointed destination. Further, echoes of who Paul once was and is intended to be once again surface in the retelling of the Damascus narrative. The result of Luke's insertion of the Damascus narrative contrasts the character of the transformed Saul with the overpowered Saul.

In short, the portrait of Paul in this final rhetorical unit is mixed. He is both "Saul the empowered" and "Paul the overpowered." The mixed character of Paul could be due to Luke's current narrative agenda. According to Stevens, in Acts 19:21 Paul decided that he should head to Jerusalem when the divine necessity was for Paul to bear witness in Rome.[31] As seen in the preceding chapter's analysis, when Paul chose to go to Jerusalem instead of Rome, the result was disastrous. Paul was overpowered and his witness vacated. Using the Damascus narrative, Luke illustrated that the character of Paul functionally was identical to that of Saul the resistant persecutor. However, Paul experienced another encounter with God, the word of grace in 23:11. This vision begins to set Paul once again on track. Thus, one can understand the present mixed portrait of Paul if the Lukan paradigm of transformation of Saul from Acts 9 is functioning. God is currently transforming Paul from his state of disobedience and resistance to a state of obedience and empowerment. The indication of the transformation of resistance is found in the suppression of details and the emphasis of the obedience to the divine appointment of bearing witness in the third telling of the Damascus experience. However, at the present time in the narrative, the transformation is not complete. Paul is headed

---

[31] Stevens, "Luke's Perspective," 17–37.

to Rome, and there he will bear witness as mandated by God. However, because of his own actions he is going in chains as one who cannot yet act intentionally and with force. Further transformation is needed before Paul is once again the divinely empowered witness for the gospel. Luke began the process of transformation and allowed the reader to anticipate further transformation. Perhaps Luke will complete the transformation of Paul as he travels to Rome so that when Paul arrives he can powerfully and effectively bear witness. The current text only allows one to project or anticipate this further transformation following the Lukan paradigm of Saul's transformation in Acts 9.

Considering the larger setting, Luke used the entire *Paulusbild* narrative as an illustration of overpowering and transforming Paul from resistance to obedience. In the present rhetorical unit, the reader observes the use of the Damascus narrative with the emphases upon the empowering and bearing of witness by Saul to highlight the current transformation of Paul into an empowered witness. In Acts 26, in contrast with the previous Damascus narrative of Acts 22, Luke emphasized the overpowering and vacating of Paul's witness. Thus, the current rhetorical unit is a continuation of the transformation process begun in the previous telling of the Damascus narrative and may be plotted following the U-shaped character plot.

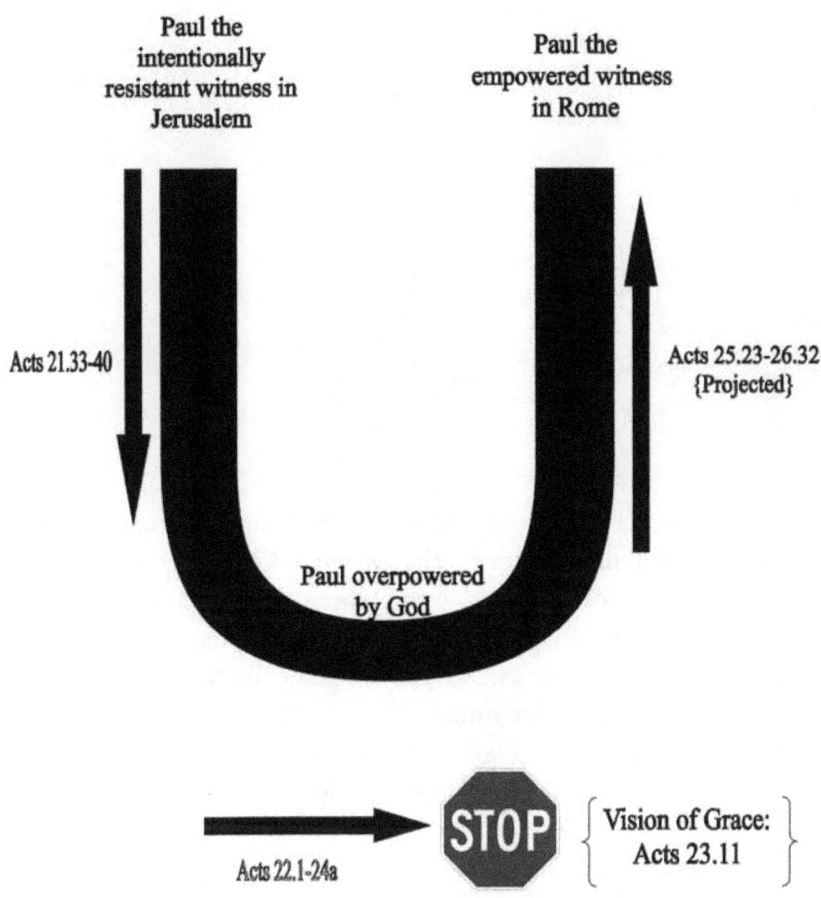

Fig. 3. The Projected Transformation of Paul's Character

5
Conclusion

Why did Luke include the narrative of Saul's Damascus road experience three times in the text of Acts? What was his literary agenda? Recently, few scholars have gone beyond von Dobschütz's conclusion that Luke employed the repetitions of the narratives for emphasis. In light of the above study, however, one can see that such a conclusion addresses only the surface of Luke's literary intent.

One might consider Luke's narrative of Luke-Acts a "theography," that is, a history of what God has done. Specifically, Luke composed a story of the history of God's actions as he moved to advance the gospel. God worked to widen the bearing of witness so the gospel might reach the ends of the earth. As God moved to advance the gospel, people resisted. The gospel faced external pressure, which attempted to stop the bearing of witness, and internal pressure, which threatened to limit the bearing of witness. However, in each instance, God overcame the resistance to the gospel. The gospel continued forward with fellowship, unity, a meeting of needs, and continued growth as the results. In general, God removed or destroyed gospel resistance. Yet in the case of Saul, Luke portrayed not an overcoming through removal but an overcoming through transformation.

Conclusion

Saul emerged within the storyline of Acts as the arch-persecutor of the disciples of Jesus. Saul was a Hellenistic Jew resisting the expansion of the gospel. He acted in an intentionally forceful manner to stop the bearing of witness. However in Acts 9:1-26a, through an encounter with Jesus, who also was an intentionally forceful actor, Saul was overcome. Saul found himself helpless and broken. The Lord did not allow Saul to remain in this helpless state. Through Ananias, Saul was physically restored. Once physically restored, Saul once again began to act in an intentionally forceful manner. This time he acted by bearing a powerful witness that confounded all who heard him. In 9:1-26a, Luke provided the reader with a paradigm of resistance transformed: (1) Saul acted in an intentionally forceful manner resisting the expansion of the gospel; (2) the Lord overcame Saul, leaving him broken, helpless, and powerless; and (3) the Lord restored and empowered Saul to act in an intentionally forceful manner by bearing witness and thus facilitating the expansion of the gospel.

The story of Saul resisting the progression of the gospel appears again in Acts 21:33—22:24a within a different narrative context. Saul the persecutor had become Paul the missionary and church planter. However, the narrative ethos of the resistant Saul constantly lurked in the background of Paul's character and surfaced at key points in the narrative. As Stevens argues, Paul arrived in Jerusalem, not in compliance with, but in defiance of the Holy Spirit. In spite of repeated warnings and direct commands from the Spirit to travel to Rome, Paul insisted on traveling to Jerusalem first. Paul's refusal to listen to the Spirit amounted to internal resistance to gospel expansion. The narrative setting of Paul's arrival in Jerusalem is full of binding, rioting, beating, and general chaos as a result of his resistance. At this point, Luke chose to include a second Damascus narrative through the character Paul.

In the narrative that encompasses the second Damascus account, Paul is depicted as overcome and helpless. Paul was overcome by the crowd, the soldiers, and the chiliarch. He was helpless to defend himself or even speak without permission. Even his efforts to defend himself had little effect, with the crowd calling for his death and the chiliarch's swift transfer of Paul to the Roman barracks.

In the embedded speech, Paul's attempt to defend himself before the crowd, he told of his Damascus experience in an effort to transfer the responsibility for his actions and teachings to God. The content of Paul's speech looks remarkably similar to the narrative of Acts 9:1-26a. However, Luke manipulated the themes. The speech begins just like the narrative of Acts 9:1-26a, with Saul acting in an intentionally forceful manner to persecute the disciples of the Lord. As in 9:1-26a, Saul was overcome through an encounter with Jesus and restored through the healing ministry of Ananias. In 9:1-26a, the overcoming and physical restoration of Saul was followed by Luke's restoration of Paul to the status of an empowered, intentionally forceful actor; however, in 21:33—22:24a, Luke did not complete the transformation of this former persecutor as he had in 9:1-26a. He interrupted Paul's speech at the moment of Saul's refusal to follow God's direction for the location of bearing witness. The effect of the interruption was to portray Saul the witness as not fully transformed and resisting the place of witness. In the speech, Saul was not empowered as an intentionally forceful actor who bore witness. Thus, the portrait of Saul matches that of Paul. Currently, Paul also was resisting his place of witness and found himself overcome and helpless. He was not an empowered and intentionally forceful actor who bore witness.

Luke left Paul in chains, arguing his case before the Sanhedrin and then Roman governors. Stevens notes that in the midst of this extended trial narrative Paul experienced a vision of the Lord (23:11). He argues that this vision set Paul back on track. That is, Paul would have begun to accept his appointed location of witness. Thus, the narrative ethos of Paul should begin to change. In the last trial narrative (25:23—26:32), one finds the third and final Damascus narrative. Luke constructed this narrative as a speech encompassed by a trial narrative. In the trial account, Luke portrayed Paul as overpowered, though headed for Rome. He was innocent but would remain in chains. Ironically, Paul was overpowered and would remain in chains because of his own actions. In the middle of this narrative of Paul's overpowering, Luke included the third Damascus narrative in the form of a defense speech. The main content of the story remains the same as that of 9:1-26a; however, Luke once again manipulated the themes through a suppression of details and emphasis on the obedience of Saul to his divine commission. Saul formerly was a persecutor and was overcome. Through an encounter with Jesus, Saul received a new commission to bear witness. Saul faithfully fulfilled this commission. Saul bore witness as God had directed. In the speech, Luke emphasized the final element of transformed resistance—Saul's empowered and intentionally forceful witness—and downplayed the first two elements of transformation. Luke suppressed Saul's resistance and subsequent overcoming. Further, Luke utilized Festus to interrupt Paul's speech, leaving the portrait of Saul fulfilling his appointed role as witness. Interestingly, the portrait of Saul within the speech does not match that of Paul within the encompassing narrative. The Saul of the speech is an empowered witness. The Paul of the narrative is an overcome and helpless prisoner. Nevertheless, Paul had experienced a "vision of grace" and was headed to Rome. The "vision of grace" worked to transform the Saul of the Damascus narrative but not the Paul of the encompassing trial narrative. Paul is a character in tension with the projected narrative trajectory of once again becoming an empowered and intentionally forceful witness.

Luke used the repetition of the Damascus narrative as a literary device identifying Pauline disobedience and resistance and the transformation of these characteristics. With the first Damascus narrative, Luke provided the reader with a paradigmatic image of resistance transformed. This transformation included three movements or themes:

(1) empowered and intentionally forceful resistance to the expansion of the gospel;
(2) subsequent overcoming and vacating of power of the resistant one by God; and
(3) empowerment and restoration of intentional action to the former resistant one as a witness for God.

Luke used the Damascus narratives and these themes to bracket the *Paulusbild*, fashioning the trial narrative into an extended period of transformation of Pauline resistance. Beginning in 19:21, Paul resisted the leading of the Holy Spirit and his appointed location of witness. He was an intentionally forceful actor resisting God. God bound this intentionally forceful actor in chains. In this opening scene of the *Paulusbild* Luke included the second Damascus narrative (21:33—22:24a). The themes emphasized in the narrative were those of Saul intentionally resisting gospel expansion and God's subsequent overcoming of Saul. Saul was physically restored through Ananias but not fully transformed. He is not yet an empowered and intentionally forceful witness. At the end of the *Paulusbild*, as Paul is headed to Rome, Luke included the final

Damascus narrative (25:23—26:32). Paul was headed to Rome, but not in the freedom intended by God. He remained in chains because of his own actions. Thus, his character was one of tension. The Damascus narrative that Luke included demonstrates Saul's intentionally forceful resistance to the gospel. However, the vacating of power and overcoming of Saul is suppressed, and the theme of the transformation of resistance to empowered witness is emphasized. Nonetheless, the character of Saul in the speech does not match the character of Paul in the narrative. Tension remains, but the projected direction of transformation is evident. Paul is headed to Rome. The "vision of grace" has effected a transformation in Saul but not yet in Paul. If the trajectory of transformation continues, then Paul should once again be an intentionally forceful, empowered witness for the gospel when he arrives in Rome. Therefore, the Lukan literary use of the triple Damascus narrative might be portrayed as follows the Figure 4 below.

Lukan Literary Use of the Damascus Narratives

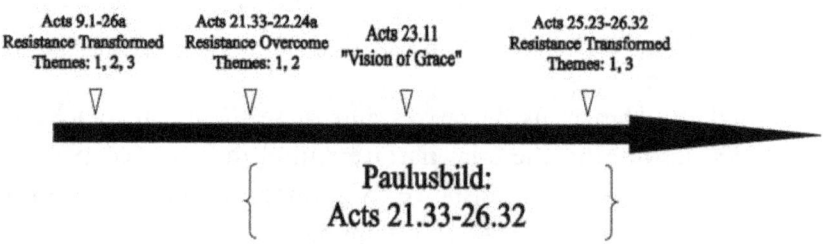

Fig. 4. Lukan Literary Use of the Damascus Narrative

Several implications for further areas of study arise out of the preceding investigation. First, the trajectories of the themes identified in the above study need to be traced through the Gospel of Luke and to the end of the Book of Acts. Did Luke incorporate the theme of the advancing gospel in his Gospel? What role might this theme have in light of Jesus' statements at the inception of his ministry (Luke 4:16-30)? Do the themes of *God Resisted* and *God Active* play a central role in the Gospel of Luke? Do these themes continue to the end of Acts? Further, what is the end result of the proposed projected transformation of Paul's resistance? Is Paul's resistance ever fully transformed? Does he once again act intentionally with force as a witness? Finally, does one find similar instances of resistance transformed in Luke-Acts? If so, does the paradigm found in Acts 9:1-26a function for these characters?

A second area of research exists in the comparison of the above results to those of historical-critical research. This is a literary study of the Damascus accounts in Acts. Therefore, the text of Acts alone was considered. At some point, Acts must be compared to the letters of Paul. Does Luke's portrait of the last Jerusalem visit by Paul match what Paul wrote about the visit? If not, what are the differences and why do they exist? What would be the historical, literary, and theological implications if one encounters two different characterizations of the same event?

Third, a great number of interpretive possibilities await the interpreter who will consider Luke-Acts as a single storyline. Luke should be viewed as an author in his own right with his own theological emphases and agendas. New avenues of interpretation might be discovered if one would consider the Gospel of Luke apart from the other Gospels and as one with Acts. Involved in this research would be an investigation into the genre of Luke-Acts. Further work needs to be done developing the concept of Luke-Acts as a "theography," as the comparison of the Gospel and Acts to the extant Greco-Roman genres yields little fruit. Also, a thorough study of Lukan repetition must be undertaken. In Acts, Luke used repetition for more than just emphasis. With the Damascus narrative, Luke employed repetition to mark character transformation for the reader. Is this the case in the Peter and Cornelius episode as well? Did Luke utilize repetition in his Gospel, and if so, in what manner?

A final area of future research lies in the application of the methodology proposed here. Biblical scholarship would be served well if interpreters would conduct an in-depth analysis of Greco-Roman education. Through this investigation new tools for literary analysis could be discovered in an attempt to work backwards through the process of constructing literary works similar to those of the New Testament. Further, the proposed methodology should be applied to other New Testament genres in test cases. Does this methodology adequately serve the interpreter who is studying the Pauline Epistles, the Gospels, the General Epistles, and the Apocalypse? Can this methodology give new direction to rhetorical criticism? One should note that the principles of future analysis based upon Theon's *Progymnasmata* would differ depending upon the type of text one encountered. The above principles, including the use of tables, should work for narratives, but one should return to Theon's principles when interpreting *synkrisis, chreia, ekphrasis,* or some other elementary exercise. This study has been conducted in the fond hope that the use of rhetoric as an interpretive tool holds much promise for the interpreter who can correctly marshal the methodology.

Appendix
Rhetorical Criticism: A New Direction

Survey of Rhetoric and Biblical Interpretation

Rhetorical Approaches: Early Christianity through Early Twentieth Century

The marshaling of rhetorical canons for the purpose of biblical interpretation is anything but a new phenomenon. Ancient Christian interpreters, trained in the classical rhetorical tradition, did not set their rhetorical training aside when they expounded biblical texts. One of the earliest examples is that of Caius Marius Victorinus Rhetor. Victorinus made use of his rhetorical training to write a series of biblical commentaries on the Pauline Epistles a decade after his conversion in AD 355.[1] In

---

[1] Victorinus may have been one of the first to apply standard rules of rhetoric for the purpose of interpreting biblical texts. For a good introduction to the work of Victorinus as well as a discussion of his conclusions as applicable to Galatians, see Stephen A. Cooper, "*Narratio* and *Exhortatio* in Galatians According to Marius Victorinus Rhetor," *ZNW* 91 (2000) 107–35.

addition, Augustine, also classically trained as a rhetorician, sought to apply his knowledge of the art of rhetoric to Scripture. In his work *On Christian Doctrine*, he urged expositors to use rhetoric in the presentation of the biblical texts.[2] Further, he observed the presence of rhetorical figures in Paul and of tropes in Scripture in general.[3] While no formal method guiding the application of rhetorical canons to Scripture existed, early interpretersschooled within the classical tradition naturally turned to rhetoric as a means of interpreting biblical texts.

This practice did not end with the early Christian interpreters but continued through the Middle Ages and into the early twentieth century. The most notable Middle Age scholar to use rhetoric in biblical interpretation was Philip Melanchthon. He chose to use his own textbooks of rhetoric, based upon classical canons, to interpret Scripture.[4] The rhetorical approach to scriptural interpretation continued in the nineteenth century, perhaps reaching the climax of this endeavor in that period when Christian Wilke considered tropes and figures of speech in the New Testament, while C. F. Georg Heinrici noted Paul's relationship to rhetorical theory in his commentary on 2 Corinthians.[5]

The employment of rhetorical canons for biblical interpretation ceased for a period with an article by Thomas Duncan published in the early twentieth century.[6] Duncan argued that Paul was *rhetorical*, recording the presence of stylistic figures and figures of thought within the Pauline Epistles. His purpose was not to employ rhetorical principles strictly for interpreting Scripture but to find and identify rhetorical forms in Paul. Therefore, his approach had more in common with form criticism than earlier rhetorical approaches and modern literary methods.

---

[2]Augustine, *On Christian Doctrine* 4.4.6.

[3]Ibid., 4.7.11 and 4.7.20–21.

[4]Carl Classen has thoroughly documented the rhetorical approach of Philip Melanchthon to biblical interpretation. See Carl Joachim Classen, *Rhetorical Criticism of the New Testament*, WUNT 128 (Tübingen: Mohr/Siebeck, 2000).

[5]Christian Gottlob Wilke, *Die Neutestamentliche Rhetorik: ein Seitenstück zur Grammatik des neutestamentlichen Sprachidiams* (Dresden: Arnoldische Buchhandlung, 1843); and C. F. Georg Heinrici, *Das zweite Sendschreiben des Apostel Paulus an die Korinthier* (Berlin: Besserche, 1887).

[6]Thomas Shearer Duncan, "The Style and Language of Saint Paul in His First Letter to the Corinthians," *BibSac* 83 (1926) 129–43.

Appendix

The cessation of utilizing rhetorical approaches for biblical interpretation occurred in the early twentieth century for a number of reasons beyond the purview of this survey. One must note that the rise of form and redaction criticisms, coupled with the decline of the instruction of classical rhetoric in European and American higher institutions, contributed greatly to the arrest of this approach. For some forty years after Duncan's article, rhetoric, as a means of interpreting Scripture, lay dormant. However, this means of interpretation gained new life and a fresh voice through a series of events that coalesced in the final years of the 1960s.

Rebirth of the Rhetorical Approach

Early Soundings

The final years of the 1960s provided the fertile soil for the birth of modern literary methods, including rhetorical criticism. Prior to this period, historical, form, and redactional approaches reigned supreme among those critically interpreting biblical texts. Yet some scholars began to grow dissatisfied with these traditional approaches and looked to new horizons of biblical interpretation. One of these new horizons was not actually new but a rediscovery of the ancient strategy of the rhetorical approach to scriptural interpretation.

In an article published in the *Australian Biblical Review*, Edwin A. Judge issued the call for the analysis of the rhetoric of the New Testament. He stated, "If New Testament scholars regard as essential the definitive handbooks of lexicography (e.g. Bauer/Arndt/Gingrich) and of grammar (e.g. Blass/Debrunner), they must equally demand a complete analysis of New Testament rhetoric."[7] Judge had in mind more of a literary study of the stylistics of the New Testament than a formal application of rhetorical principles. Yet Judge viewed his call as going beyond the simple identification of stylistic forms as in of the practice of form criticism.

---

[7] Edwin A. Judge, "Paul's Boasting in Relation to Contemporary Professional Practice," *ABR* 16 (October 1968) 45.

Several months later, James Muilenburg gave the 1969 presidential address at the national meeting of the Society of Biblical Literature. In his address, Muilenburg urged scholars to view biblical texts in their persuasive contexts and labeled the endeavor "rhetorical criticism."[8] Muilenburg was speaking within the parameters of form criticism, and many Old Testament scholars heeded his call for a revision of this method. However, New Testament scholars interpreted Muilenburg's address as a call to return to the classical rhetorical handbooks as instruments for interpreting biblical texts. For the first time in over forty years, the use of rhetoric to interpret biblical texts was again a viable alternative.

Two years later, Amos Wilder gave further stimulus to New Testament scholars for the use of rhetorical approaches. He implored interpreters to go beyond the form critical approach, adopting a more literary method that emphasized the significance of rhetorical patterns present in the biblical text. Wilder wrote: "All such findings of technical form-criticism we shall keep in mind. But we would like to go behind this kind of observation to the question of language itself. How does the whole phenomenon of language, speech, communication, rhetoric present itself in the rise of Christianity? What modes of discourse are specially congenial to the Gospel? What is the special role of oral as against written discourse? What is the theological significance of particular rhetorical patterns used or neglected by the Early Church?"[9] Wilder's counsel was similar to that of Muilenburg. The present application of the form critical approach was not satisfactory. Both Wilder and Muilenburg looked expectantly to the literary analysis—rhetorical in a broad sense—of biblical texts.

The dissatisfaction with traditional critical approaches that led to the calls of these three scholars might not have been enough to entice scholars to begin utilizing rhetorical principles to interpret Scripture. However, the translation and publication of Chaim Perelman and L. Olbrechts-Tyteca's *The New Rhetoric* insured the rebirth of this approach.[10] *The New*

---

[8]James Muilenburg, "Form Criticism and Beyond," *JBL* 88 (1969) 1–18.
[9]Amos N. Wilder, *Early Christian Rhetoric: The Language of the Gospel* (Cambridge: Harvard University Press, 1971), 3.
[10]Chaim Perelman and L. Olbrechts-Tyteca, *The New Rhetoric: A Treatise on Argumentation*, trans. John Wilkinson and Purcell Weaver (Notre Dame: University of Notre Dame Press, 1971).

Appendix

Rhetoric was a philosophical approach to rhetoric in the tradition of Aristotle. Through Neo-Aristotelean lenses, Perelman and Olbrechts-Tyteca viewed all rhetoric as argumentation, an interaction between speaker and audience aimed at gaining the adherence of all addressees, whether orally or through literary means.[11]

While maintaining the broad categories of Aristotle, Perelman and Olbrechts-Tyteca's work varied greatly from the principles set forth in *On Rhetoric*. This new work reintroduced philosophical rhetoric in modern terms and thus established a style and understanding of rhetoric clearly distinguishable from classical rhetoric. The publication of this book with the focus of persuasion as the ultimate end of all rhetoric matched neatly, both in time and intent, with the emphases of Muilenburg in his presidential address. The result was that New Testament scholars sought to tap rhetorical canons, both ancient and modern, as means of interpreting Scripture.

New Beginnings, Bold Strides, and Methodological Chaos

Scholars were somewhat slow to follow the new direction illuminated by Muilenburg and others, due in part to the uncertainty of how to proceed methodologically. How different was this new rhetorical criticism from form criticism? How far beyond form criticism was one to proceed and in what manner? David Greenwood expressed this level of uncertainty unknowingly in his article published in the *Journal of Biblical Literature*.[12] Greenwood attempted to chart a methodological course for the new application of rhetorical criticism, but his attempt differed little from the traditional form critical approach. The field of New Testament interpretation would have to wait several years for guidance in the proposed use of rhetorical criticism.

The methodological guidance needed was provided by Hans Dieter Betz in his article "The Literary Composition and Function of Paul's Letter to the Galatians."[13] Betz had interpreted the call to practice rhetorical

---

[11]Ibid., 6–19.
[12]David Greenwood, "Rhetorical Criticism and Formgeschichte: Some Methodological Considerations," *JBL* 89 (1970) 418–26.
[13]Hans Dieter Betz, "The Literary Composition and Function of Paul's Letter to the Galatians," *NTS* 21 (1975) 353–79.

criticism as a call to apply the canons of classical rhetoric to biblical texts. He chose the letter of Galatians as his first subject. Betz analyzed the letter according to the guidelines of both Greco-Roman rhetoric and ancient epistolography. He claimed that such an approach had never been attempted before, except, perhaps by Joseph Barber Lightfoot.[14] In this article, Betz posited that the letter to the Galatians was an example of an "apologetic letter." He contended that the epistolary framework separated easily from the body of the letter, which then divided into the component parts of a typical Greco-Roman speech.[15]

With his article, Betz provided some methodological direction to other scholars who wished to apply rhetorical criticism to texts. He demonstrated that insight could be gained through the application of the canons of Greco-Roman rhetoric to biblical texts. What Betz did not supply was his explicit method for employing these canons. Neither did he define which aspects of classical rhetoric were acceptable for applying to the New Testament, nor did he adequately explain the interconnectedness of Greco-Roman rhetoric and ancient epistolary theory.

Betz's approach could be termed a classical approach to rhetorical criticism. That is, Betz sought to interpret the biblical text through the application of rhetorical principles drawn from the same historical period of the production of these texts. His purpose was to read the biblical text as an ancient reader would. Several scholars followed Betz, utilizing this classical approach, yet each demonstrated the same methodological shortcomings of Betz. Each applied canons of ancient rhetoric to Scripture without defining for their audience how they implemented these canons.[16] The result was that rhetorical criticism existed only in the practice of each individual interpreter. Each defined rhetorical criticism and the application of such in an idiosyncratic manner as the interpreter approached the biblical text. Nonetheless, none permitted their readers insight into their procedures. Further, none of those who employed rhetorical criticism provided their implicit and individual definition for this method. Thus,

---

[14]Ibid., 353.
[15]Ibid., 354–55.
[16]See F. Forrester Church, "Rhetorical Structure and Design in Paul's Letter to Philemon," *HTR* 71 (1978) 17–33; Charles J. Robbins, "Rhetorical Structure of Philippians 2:6-11," *CBQ* 42 (1980) 73–82; Long, "Trial of Paul"; and Betz, *Galatians*.

Appendix

the application of rhetorical criticism, within this classical camp, differed widely from scholar to scholar; the state of the field of rhetorical criticism lay in methodological chaos.

Some interpreters, dissatisfied with this classical approach to rhetorical criticism, argued that the ancient canons of rhetoric were not adequate interpretive tools for the modern reader. Therefore, these interpreters turned to modern rhetorical theory as a means of illuminating biblical texts.[17] However, these interpreters fell into the same methodological pitfall as those employing the classical approach. Not one interpreter provided an adequate program outlining the application of rhetorical criticism, nor did any interpreter define rhetorical criticism. Therefore, in the early 1980s, rhetorical criticism, as a method, was somewhat nebulous. The need existed for an adequate definition and formal method for practicing rhetorical criticism.

Methodological Consistency, Diverging Agendas, Criticism, and a Return to Methodological Chaos

Kennedy and the classical approach

George Kennedy provided the first programmatic outline for, and definition of, rhetorical criticism, thus supplying clarity where ambiguity had reigned. Kennedy, a classicist by training, encountered a series of students wishing to learn classical rhetoric for the purpose of interpreting biblical texts. Kennedy was surprised with the lack of consistency and total absence of formal method in the field. Therefore, Kennedy sought to provide methodological cohesion with his work *New Testament Interpretation through Rhetorical Criticism*.[18]

Scholars quickly noticed the importance of Kennedy's work for rhetorical criticism. Wilhelm Wuellner stated, "With Kennedy's proposal

---

[17]See Raymond A. Humphries, "Paul's Rhetoric of Argumentation in I Corinthians 1–4" (Ph.D. diss., Graduate Theological Union, 1979); and Martin Kessler, "A Methodological Setting for Rhetorical Criticism," in *Art and Meaning: Rhetoric in Biblical Literature*, ed. David J. A. Clines, David M. Gunn, and Alan J. Hauser, JSOTSS 19 (Sheffield: JSOT Press, 1982), 1–19.

[18]Kennedy, *New Testament Interpretation*, 3–38.

for NT interpretation through rhetorical criticism, publications with rhetoric in their titles will likely reach tidal-wave proportions."[19] The attractiveness of Kennedy's method to scholars was the simplicity of his model.

Kennedy defined rhetoric as "that quality of discourse by which a speaker or writer seeks to accomplish his purposes."[20] He noted that by definition, rhetoric involves the spoken word. While the Bible was a collection of written texts, these texts could be interpreted as oral speeches because the Bible was truly oral in nature.[21] His argument hinged upon the grounds of the oral nature of all reading in the first century.[22] Thus, he concluded the Bible should have oral qualities, designed as such by New Testament authors for oral reading. Kennedy went so far as to state, "In practicing rhetorical criticism we need to keep in mind that intent and that original impact, and thus to read the Bible as speech."[23]

Kennedy posited that the canons of Greco-Roman rhetoric were an adequate source for interpreting New Testament documents even if the authors of the New Testament had not received official training in classical rhetoric. His argument was two-fold. First, Kennedy asserted that all rhetoric was universal in matters of invention. Rhetoric differed from culture to culture only in matters of style and arrangement.[24] Thus, interpreters should gain insight from using guidelines for invention from Greco-Roman rhetoric in interpreting New Testament texts, even if the authors of said texts had no knowledge of these matters. Second, Kennedy contended that even if New Testament authors had received no formal training in matters of Greco-Roman rhetoric, the pervasive influence of rhetoric in the first century would have been impossible to avoid. The average citizen, including the authors of the New Testament, would have picked up rhetorical principles simply by going about their everyday lives. Kennedy wrote:

---

[19] Wilhelm Wuellner, "Where Is Rhetorical Criticism Taking Us?" *Catholic Biblical Quarterly* 49 (1987) 453.
[20] Kennedy, *New Testament Interpretation*, 3.
[21] Ibid., 5.
[22] Ancient readers read texts out loud, sounding out words, rather than silently like the modern reader.
[23] Ibid., 6.
[24] Ibid., 8.

Appendix

> Even if he [Paul] had not studied in a Greek school, there were many handbooks of rhetoric in common circulation which he could have seen. He and the evangelists as well would, indeed, have been hard put to escape an awareness of rhetoric as practiced in the culture around them, for the rhetorical theory of the schools found its immediate application in almost every form of oral and written communication: in official documents and public letters, in private correspondence, in the law courts and assemblies, in speeches at festivals and commemorations, and in literary composition in both prose and verse.[25]

Kennedy proposed that Paul and the other New Testament authors could have learned rhetoric in an osmosis-like process, absorbing rhetorical theory from the culture around them.

After justifying the application of Greco-Roman rhetoric as an interpretive tool, Kennedy laid out several procedural steps for engaging in the practice of rhetorical criticism. Kennedy did not clearly define these steps, leading to some disagreement as to how many separate steps he intended. The most common interpretation of Kennedy identifies five separate steps. First, one was to determine the rhetorical unit. The guidelines for such a unit were that a unit had to have a beginning, middle, and end. In addition, this unit should be a minimum of five or six verses. Kennedy urged the interpreter to realize that small rhetorical units converged to make up larger rhetorical units.[26]

After defining the unit to be studied, the interpreter was to define the rhetorical situation of the unit. For this step Kennedy relied upon the definition of rhetorical situation provided by Lloyd F. Bitzer.[27] In Kennedy's interpretation of Bitzer, a rhetorical situation centered upon the exigence of a situation, that is, the complex of events, persons, and other items that coalesced to form the need for the current rhetorical unit.[28]

Identifying the rhetorical situation, the interpreter was then to discover the rhetorical problem. In order to identify the rhetorical problem, one was to consider *stasis* theory and the three species of rhetoric. The complex

---

[25]Ibid., 10.
[26]Ibid., 33–34.
[27]Lloyd F. Bitzer, "The Rhetorical Situation," *Philosophy and Rhetoric* 1 (1968) 1–14.
[28]Kennedy, *New Testament Interpretation*, 34–36.

stasis theory of Greco-Roman rhetoric would provide the overarching rhetorical approach drawn from a singular or complex problem that necessitated the unit. Further, the species or genre of the speech unit would indicate the desired outcome of the speech unit as well as the setting for the unit.[29]

After defining the rhetorical problem, the interpreter was then to proceed by considering the arrangement of the speech unit. This process included undertaking a line-by-line analysis of the text, identifying devices of style as well as the persuasive flow of the text.[30]

The final step was to review the success of the arrangement in light of the rhetorical situation and problem. Basically, the interpreter was to ask whether the unit was successful in accomplishing the intended purpose. Did the speech successfully persuade, praise, blame, or convict?[31] Following this methodological delineation, Kennedy then gave examples of how his method could be used on selected New Testament texts.[32]

Kennedy's method falls within the classical approach to rhetorical criticism, and is similar to that of Betz. With his method, Kennedy sought to interpret the New Testament in light of rhetorical principles drawn from the same historical period. The difference between Kennedy's classical approach and that of Betz and other early interpreters was that now, for the first time, interpreters could replicate and test rhetorical analyses of New Testament texts.

Classical approach after Kennedy

The impact of Kennedy's proposals upon the field of rhetorical criticism is hard to overstate. Biblical scholars seized upon his method and, as Wuellner had predicted, the number of articles, dissertations, and monographs employing Kennedy's proposals quickly swelled. In recent days, in light of criticism of Kennedy's method, the number of scholars

---

[29]Ibid., 36–37.
[30]Ibid., 37.
[31]Ibid., 38.
[32]Ibid., 39–156.

Appendix

employing this method has drastically dropped. Nevertheless, publications continue to surface following Kennedy's methodology.[33]

Kennedy's proposals have by no means united all attempts to employ rhetorical criticism as an interpretive method in the classical vein. Following the precedent of Betz, a number of scholars have continued to apply the canons of classical rhetoric as interpretive tools following their own, often unstated, method of application; this approach thus returned the field of rhetorical criticism to a state of methodological chaos.[34] The number of

---

[33]The following is a broad—but by no means complete—sampling of published works that employ the methodology proposed by George Kennedy. See Duane Frederick Watson, *Invention, Arrangement, and Style: Rhetorical Criticism of Jude and 2 Peter*, SBLDS 104 (Atlanta: Scholars, 1988); Rollin Grams, "The Temple Conflict Scene: A Rhetorical Analysis of Matthew 21–23," in *Persuasive Artistry: Studies in New Testament Rhetoric in Honor of George A. Kennedy*, JSNTSS 50, ed. Duane F. Watson, (Sheffield: Sheffield Academic, 1991), 41–65; Marty L. Reid, "A Rhetorical Analysis of Romans 1:1–5:21 with Attention Given to the Rhetorical Function of 5:1-21," *Perspectives in Religious Studies* 19 (1992) 255–72; Watson, "Paul's Speech," 184–208; Joseph A. Morris, "Irony and Ethics in the Lukan Narrative World: A Narrative Rhetorical Reading of Luke 4:14-30" (PhD diss., Graduate Theological Union, 1992); Jongseon Kwon, "A Rhetorical Analysis of the Johannine Farewell Discourse" (PhD diss., Southern Baptist Theological Seminary, 1993); J. Ian H. McDonald, "Rhetorical Issue and Rhetorical Strategy in Luke 10:25-37," in *Rhetoric and the New Testament: Essays from the 1992 Heidelberg Conference*, ed. Stanley E. Porter and Thomas H. Olbricht, JSNTSS 90 (Sheffield: Sheffield Academic Press, 1993), 59–73; Duane Frederick Watson, "James 2 in Light of Greco-Roman Schemes of Argumentation," *NTS* 39 (1993) 94–121; Tim Lantzy, "The Case for Christianity: A Rhetorical Study of Luke 15:1–17:10" (Ph.D. diss., Southwestern Baptist Theological Seminary, 1995); Marty L. Reid, "Paul's Rhetoric of Mutuality: A Rhetorical Reading of Romans," in SBLSP, ed. Eugene H. Loverling, Jr. (Atlanta: Scholars, 1995), 117–39; William S. Griffin, "Seeing and Perceiving: The Narrative Rhetoric of a Theme in Mark 15:20b-41" (PhD diss., Graduate Theological Union, 1996); Johann D. Kim, *God, Israel, and the Gentiles: Rhetoric and Situation in Romans 9–11*, SBLDS 176 (Atlanta: Society of Biblical Literature, 2000); and Maryono, "Biblical History."

[34]James D. Hester, "The Rhetorical Structure of Galatians 1:11–2:14," *JBL* 103 (1984) 223–33; Robert G. Hall, "The Rhetorical Outline for Galatians: A Reconsideration," *JBL* 106 (1987) 277–87; Frank Witt Hughes, *Early Christian Rhetoric and 2 Thessalonians*, JSNTSS, 30 (Sheffield: Sheffield Academic, 1989); Thomas H. Olbricht, "An Aristotelian Rhetorical Analysis of 1 Thessalonians," in *Greeks, Romans, and Christians: Essays in Honor of Abraham J. Malherbe*, ed. David L. Balch, Everett Ferguson, and Wayne A. Meeks (Minneapolis: Fortress, 1990), 216–36; Jan Smit, "The Genre of 1 Corinthians 13 in the Light of Classical Rhetoric," *NovT* 33 (1991) 193–216; Duane Litfin, *St.*

applications of this approach as well as those following Kennedy swelled in the 1980s and 1990s but declined in recent days to the point of a near cessation of the classical approach. The abatement of the classical approach is due to the perceived failure of this approach by contemporary scholars.

Criticism of the classical approach

The work of Kennedy provided new life to the rhetorical approach to scriptural interpretation, but recent criticisms have all but destroyed this strategy. Such a result, due to the failure of rhetorical critics to answer the criticisms leveled against them, is tragic, since of all the various rhetorical approaches to interpretation the classical approach holds the most promise for understanding biblical texts within their literary-historical context.[35] The first charge one must raise against the classical approach, specifically against Kennedy's method, is that of the ambiguity of the method. Dean Anderson critiqued Kennedy's approach: "Such a method seems virtually self-explanatory, but one thing is startlingly lacking. There appears to be no distinction made between the study of the rhetoric or argumentation of a unit in general, and the relationship or contribution of *ancient* rhetoric to the unit."[36] Anderson's critique is on target. Kennedy at no point, perhaps purposefully, instructed his readers as to how ancient rhetoric informed and influenced the construction of the New Testament texts by their authors.

That Kennedy assumed such an influence is clear in his statements regarding reading the Bible as speech and the pervasive influence of Greco-Roman rhetoric in first-century society. Yet, to what extent were the authors

---

Paul's Theology of Proclamation: 1 Corinthians 1–4 and Greco-Roman Rhetoric (Cambridge: Cambridge University Press, 1994); Lorin L. Cranford, "A Rhetorical Reading of Galatians," *SWJT* 37 (Fall 1994): 4–10; and Craig R. Koester, *Hebrews: A New Translation with Introduction and Commentary*, AB 36 (New York: Doubleday, 2001).

[35]Classical rhetorical criticism is not the only method that one may employ to interpret Scripture. Nevertheless, this form of rhetorical criticism alone provides a series of literary principles consistent with the historical context of the New Testament authors. Thus, the classical rhetorical approach allows one to use principles that might have been known—if any were known—by the New Testament authors.

[36]R. Dean Anderson, Jr., *Ancient Rhetorical Theory and Paul: Revised Edition*, Contributions to Biblical Exegesis and Theology 18 (Leuven: Peters, 1998), 28.

Appendix

affected by this influence? Should one limit the influence to matters of style, or should one extend the influence to the use of *stasis*, genre, and formal rhetorical divisions? The decision is left up to the interpreter, thus resulting in diverse levels of application of rhetorical principles. Those exegetes who assume a high level of influence strictly and formally apply all rhetorical guidelines.[37] Those interpreters who assume less influence apply rhetorical principles less stringently.[38]

Kennedy's ambiguity is perhaps due to his understanding of the universality of rhetoric. Kennedy had to remain purposefully ambiguous if he truly believed that rhetoric was universal in all matters of invention. If he explicitly stated the dependence of New Testament authors upon Greco-Roman rhetoric, he might have been viewed as excluding the interpretation of biblical texts with other rhetorical systems, a real possibility in light of Kennedy's statements. Such ambiguity, though, results in methodological chaos, the very state of affairs Kennedy tried to avoid. With no formal guidelines, each interpreter is left to judge for himself or herself how to use the rhetorical handbooks, the sources for Greco-Roman rhetorical theory, in the interpretive process.

A second criticism of Kennedy's method is his dependence upon modern rhetorical theory in the delineation of his steps and the false dichotomy such a dependence creates in light of Greco-Roman rhetoric. Kennedy's second step, as outlined above, was to define the rhetorical situation.[39] For this step, Kennedy relied upon Lloyd F. Bitzer's definition of the rhetorical situation. However, Bitzer's understanding of the rhetorical situation, specifically exigence, was based upon modern rhetorical theory, not ancient.[40]

Bitzer had described the rhetorical situation as follows:

---

[37]See as examples Watson, *Invention, Arrangement, and Style*; Hall, "Rhetorical Outline"; and Cranford, "A Rhetorical Reading."
[38]Litfin, *St. Paul's Theology of Proclamation*.
[39]Kennedy, *New Testament Interpretation*, 34–6.
[40]See a similar observation by Insawn Saw, *Paul's Rhetoric in 1 Corinthians 15: An Analysis Utilizing the Theories of Classical Rhetoric* (Lewiston, Me.: Mellen Biblical, 1995), 76.

> Hence, to say that rhetoric is situation means: (1) rhetorical discourse comes into existence as a response to a situation, in the same sense that an answer comes into existence in response to a question, or a solution in response to a problem; (2) a speech is given *rhetorical* significance by the situation, just as a unit of discourse is given significance *as* answer or *as* solution by the question or problem; (3) a rhetorical situation must exist as a necessary condition of rhetorical discourse, just as a question must exist as a necessary condition of an answer.[41]

Ancient rhetorical theorists had no conception of Bitzer's exigence or rhetorical situation. The closest the ancient theorists came to Bitzer's rhetorical situation was in their explanation of *stasis* theory and genres of rhetoric. Quintilian recorded that the term *stasis* "seems to be derived from the fact that it is on it that the first collision between the parties to the dispute takes place, or that it forms the *basis* or *standing* of the whole case."[42] Further, he stated, "But in my opinion the origin of the *basis* varies and depends on the circumstances of the individual case."[43] As for the genre or species of rhetoric, Pseudo-Cicero noted, "There are three kinds of causes which the speaker must treat: Epideictic, Deliberative, and Judicial. The epideictic kind is devoted to the praise or censure of some particular person. The deliberative consists in the discussion of policy and embraces persuasion and dissuasion. The judicial is based on legal controversy, and comprises criminal prosecution or civil suit, and defence."[44]

Much of what Bitzer defined as the rhetorical situation is found in the ancient understanding of *stasis* and species or genres of rhetoric. Nevertheless, Kennedy separated the defining of the rhetorical situation from the defining of the rhetorical problem: *stasis* and species.[45] This separation creates a false dichotomy in the understanding of ancient rhetoric. Instead of this separation, if one wishes to achieve historical consistency with Kennedy's approach, he or she must excise Kennedy's

---

[41] Bitzer, "Rhetorical Situation," 5–6.
[42] Quint. *Inst.* 3.6.4.
[43] Ibid., 3.6.15.
[44] [Cic.] *Rhet. Her.* 1.2.2.
[45] Kennedy, *New Testament Interpretation*, 34–36.

Appendix

second step altogether, allowing the investigation of *stasis* and rhetorical species to inform the rhetorical situation.

One must level a third charge against Kennedy's philosophical assumption of the universality of rhetoric that underlies his method. Kennedy held that rhetoric was a universal phenomenon, especially in matters of invention. He observed, "Although the word 'rhetoric' is a Greek coinage, most ancient cultures had some concept of persuasion and artistic speech or writing and of the differing abilities of speakers."[46] Kennedy elsewhere remarked, "Rhetoric is a historical phenomenon and differs somewhat from culture to culture, more in matters of arrangement and style than in basic devices of invention."[47] Though Kennedy acknowledged that some differences existed from culture to culture, and from one period to another, all rhetoric contained a common uniting thread found in the matters of invention. That is, people conceive or arrive at rhetorical arguments and proofs in a similar manner.

The logical outcome of this view of rhetoric led to a blending of rhetorical theories and canons by interpreters. If rhetoric is truly universal in matters of invention, then any handbook, theory, or concept of rhetorical invention may be brought to bear in the task of rhetorical criticism. Thus, one should not be surprised at the number of interpreters claiming to follow Kennedy who also incorporate the canons of modern rhetoric in their interpretation.[48] In blending rhetorical canons within an interpretive scheme, one places modern conceptions of speech theory, which differ greatly from those of ancient theorists, side by side with ancient conceptions. Such a process fails to maintain a consistent classical/historical approach to the biblical text.

Kennedy's understanding of the universality of rhetoric also led to the incorporation of ancient rhetorical streams that had little or no influence upon Hellenistic Greco-Roman rhetoric, the historical scheme of rhetoric surrounding the writing of the New Testament. The most consistent evidence of this incorporation is the use of Aristotle's *On Rhetoric,* a work

---

[46]George A. Kennedy, "Historical Survey of Rhetoric," in *Handbook of Classical Rhetoric in the Hellenistic Period: 330 B.C.–A.D. 400,* ed. Stanley E. Porter (Leiden: Brill, 1997), 6.

[47]Kennedy, *New Testament Interpretation,* 8.

[48]Lantzy, "Case for Christianity," 64–9; Griffin, "Seeing and Perceiving"; Morris, "Irony and Ethics"; and Maryono, "Biblical History," 87–99.

upon which Kennedy himself relied. However, in light of the statements of ancient and modern historians, Aristotle's *On Rhetoric* had little if any influence upon the canons of Hellenistic rhetoric. Plutarch wrote, "The older Peripatetics were evidently of themselves accomplished and learned men, but they seem to have had neither a large nor exact acquaintance with the writings of Aristotle and Theophrastus, because the estate of Neleus of Scepsis, to whom Theophrastus bequeathed his books, came into the hands of careless and illiterate people."[49]

The lack of awareness of Aristotle by Hellenistic rhetoricians has not escaped the notice of Kennedy, who expressed, "Even if the *Rhetoric* was available to scholars between 300 and 100 BC, new developments in rhetorical theory had rendered it obsolete as a school text. Hermagoras of Temnos, in the middle of the second century, had worked out stasis theory, a systematic way to determine the central question at issue in a speech."[50] Kennedy also argued that, while Aristotle's work is important for the modern reader to understand ancient rhetoric, Aristotle's theories had little influence on the classical rhetorical tradition.[51] In spite of the acknowledgment of the lack of influence upon and knowledge of Aristotle by Hellenistic rhetoricians, Kennedy consistently utilized principles of Aristotle's *On Rhetoric* in his interpretive scheme.[52]

Kennedy is not alone in his use of Aristotle. Most classically oriented rhetorical critics utilize Aristotle extensively in their interpretive procedures. Thomas Olbricht went so far as to equate Hellenistic rhetoric with Aristotle's *On Rhetoric*.[53] The use of Aristotle as an interpretive tool for rhetorical criticism under the assumption that the precepts contained

---

[49]Plutarch *The Life of Sulla*, trans. Bernadotte Perrin, vol. 4, LCL (Cambridge: Harvard University Press, 1916. Reprint, Cambridge: Harvard University Press, 1950), 26.1–2. See also Strab. 13.1.54. Quintilian demonstrated only a tacit awareness of Aristotle in his *Institutes*. Cicero displayed a lack of understanding and awareness of Aristotle in his early works and only in later works demonstrated limited knowledge. Yet, even then his rhetorical theory varies at points from that of Aristotle, specifically in the explication of *stasis* theory.

[50]George A. Kennedy, "The Composition and Influence of Aristotle's *Rhetoric*," in *Essays on Aristotle's Rhetoric*, ed. Amélie Oksenberg Rorty (Berkely: University of California Press, 1996), 422.

[51]Kennedy, "Historical Survey," 22.

[52]Kennedy, *New Testament Interpretation*, 12–33.

[53]Olbricht, "Aristotelian Rhetorical Analysis," 221.

Appendix

therein are indicative and in step with those of Hellenistic rhetoric displays a lamentable lack of classical training among biblical scholars. Scholars have continued to employ the precepts found in *On Rhetoric,* claiming historical continuity with biblical texts in spite of ancient historical evidence, shallow knowledge of Aristotle and his theories in Hellenistic rhetorical handbooks, and strong caveats from Anderson.[54] If scholars wish to interpret biblical texts within a rhetorical framework contemporary to the production of the New Testament documents, then they must follow Anderson's critiques and limit themselves to the works of Pseudo-Cicero, Quintilian, Theon, and the early work of Cicero.[55]

Following the trend begun by Betz, most scholars have applied rhetorical criticism to the letters of Paul, finding them more conducive to rhetorical analysis than biblical narratives. The basic approach, imitating Betz, has been to separate the epistolary opening and closing of these letters from the body of the letter.[56] Once the interpreter has identified the epistolary prescript and postscript, he or she then divides the body of the letter along the standard divisions of rhetorical arrangement.[57] The basis of this approach is rooted in an assumption that the biblical texts may be equated with speech and in an assumption of rhetorical knowledge by Paul.[58] The reasoning is that Paul's letters are really speeches sandwiched within an epistolary framework. The

---

[54] Anderson, *Ancient Rhetorical Theory*, 35, 42, 46–47, and 66. Anderson has provided the best survey of rhetorical handbooks to date. He weighed each, concluding which handbooks represented the Hellenistic rhetorical tradition. See Maryono, "Biblical History," as example of a failure to heed the warnings of Anderson.

[55] Anderson, *Ancient Rhetorical Theory*, 96.

[56] See Betz, "Literary Composition," 353.

[57] See Watson, *Invention, Arrangement, and Style*; Reid, "Rhetorical Analysis"; and Koester, *Hebrews*, as examples.

[58] The concept of the biblical text, especially the letters of Paul, as speech begins with the watershed article of Robert W. Funk, "The Apostolic *Parousia:* Form and Significance," in *Christian History and Interpretation: Studies Presented to John Knox*, ed. W. R. Farmer (Cambridge: Cambridge University Press, 1967), 249–68. Funk argued that the letter and emissary are the medium of apostolic authority, a surrogate for the presence of the apostle Paul himself. Thus, in the reading of the letter one should hear Paul himself speaking. Rhetorical critics grasped this concept coupled with the oral nature of first-century reading and identified all biblical texts as speech. For Pauline knowledge of rhetorical theory see Kennedy, *New Testament Interpretation*, 10. Kennedy assumed that even if Paul was not properly schooled in rhetoric, he would have gained rhetorical knowledge through an osmosis-like process or through the study of rhetorical handbooks.

result of such assumptions is the subsuming of epistolary categories by rhetorical divisions. To these assumptions and their outcome, epistolary theorists and scholars have cried foul.

As early as the late nineteenth century, scholars noted the lack of formal rhetorical knowledge displayed by Paul. Eduard Norden wrote:

> Paulus ist ein Schrifsteller, den wenigstens ich nur sehr schwer verstehe; das erklärt sich mir aus zwei Gründen: einmal ist seine Art zu argumentieren fremdartig, und zweitens ist auch sein Stil, als Ganzes betrachtet, unhellenisch. Mir bestätigt sich diese Erklärung durch die Tatsache, daß wenigstens ich den sog. Hebräerbrief, an dem man schon in alter Zeit eine ganz andere, unter hellenischem Einfluß stehende Stilistik bemerkte, von Anfang bis Ende ohne jede Schwierigkeit durchlese, ebenso den sog.[59]

Norden's statement of the unhellenistic writing style of Paul has been ignored by rhetorical critics, who argue instead that Paul could have gained rhetorical knowledge by observing rhetoric practiced in his time.[60] Scholars who make this argument not only ignore Norden's conclusion concerning Paul but also display a lack of understanding of ancient rhetoric. Hellenistic rhetoric was so complex, due to *stasis* theory and the importance of stylistics, that no person could gain enough rhetorical insight through casual observation to argue effectively as an orator. Quintilian himself noted the stark contrast in style alone of the trained and untrained speaker.[61] If Paul

---

[59]Eduard Norden, *Die Antike Kunstprosa: Vom VI. Jahrhundert V. Chr. Bis in die Zeit der Renaissance*, vol. 2, 3d ed. (Leipzig: Teubner, 1915; reprint, 1995), 499 (page citations are to the reprint edition). " Paul is an author, that I understand only with difficulty; this is clear to me for two reasons: first, his type is strangely argued, and his style is secondly as, considered as a whole, is unhellenistic. This explanation confirms itself for me through this fact, that at least I am convinced. Hebrews, already for a long time quite different, stands noticed under the Hellenic influence of stylistics, from beginning until end reads through without any difficulty, in the same way as these."

[60]For the most recent argument along these lines see Charles A. Wanamaker, "Epistolary vs. Rhetorical Analysis: Is a Synthesis Possible?" in *The Thessalonians Debate: Methodological Discord or Methodological Synthesis?* ed. Karl P. Donfried and Johannes Beutler (Grand Rapids: Eerdmans, 2000), 283.

[61]Quint. *Inst.* 2.12.1–12.

Appendix

demonstrated no formal rhetorical training in his style, then one would not expect, nor should they expect to find, evidence of Pauline knowledge of *stasis*, species, or formal proofs in his letters. This evidence should move interpreters towards caution in labeling portions of the Pauline Epistles along formal divisions of Hellenistic oratory.[62]

Furthermore, the subsuming of epistolary categories to rhetorical categories fails to recognize the literary nature and epistolary genre of Paul's letters with the formal divisions of this genre. Scholars have discovered that the typical Greco-Roman letter, including those of Paul, followed a set format, including the opening, body, and closing.[63] The Greco-Roman letter was a means for maintaining conversation in a literary format, a format that had little to do with Greco-Roman rhetoric.[64] Stanley Porter sounded one of the strongest warnings about the overlap of rhetorical and epistolary theory when he asserted, "It is possible—though difficult to defend—that some rhetorical practices of the orators may have influenced ancient letter writers. That formal rhetorical categories were systematically applied to analysis of Epistles, and that there was a precedent for this in the literary analyses of the ancient world, are open to serious question."[65] In the Hellenistic world, epistolary and rhetorical theory had little if any formal overlap and contact. Therefore, one commits a severe injustice when approaching the Pauline Epistles as rhetoric, as oral speech, and not as epistles, written communication.

---

[62]Scholars continue to argue for a Pauline knowledge of formal rhetoric. See especially, Kim, *God, Israel, and the Gentiles*. Often the reasoning of these interpreters is circular. Paul would have known rhetoric because of the pervasive influence of rhetoric in the Greco-Roman world. Since rhetoric was part of everyday life, rhetorical features are present in Paul's Epistles. Because rhetorical features are present in Paul's Epistles, rhetoric was a pervasive influence in the Greco-Roman world that influenced Paul.

[63]John L. White, "The Greek Documentary Letter Tradition Third Century B.C.E. to Third Century C.E.," *Semeia* 22 (1982) 91.

[64]Abraham J. Malherbe, *Ancient Epistolary Theorists*, ed. Bernard Brandon Scott, SBLSBS, 19 (Atlanta: Scholars, 1988), 3.

[65]Stanley E. Porter, "The Theoretical Justification for Application of Rhetorical Categories to Pauline Epistolary Literature," in *Rhetoric and the New Testament: Essays from the 1992 Heidelberg Conference*, ed. Stanley E. Porter and Thomas H. Olbricht, JSNTSS 90 (Sheffield: Sheffield Academic, 1993), 115.

Some rhetorical critics have heeded the warnings of White, Malherbe, and Porter. They have withdrawn from formally applying strict rhetorical divisions to the Pauline Epistles all the while attempting to salvage the application of rhetorical criticism to the New Testament Epistles. However, their attempts are simply a passive nod to the cautions. Jeffrey Reed maintained that the parts of an Epistle could work functionally like the formal parts of oratory while not formally identified as such.[66] The argument is an acknowledgment that the Pauline Epistles do not demonstrate a formal rhetorical arrangement. Still, the consequence of functionally equating epistolary and rhetorical categories is to subsume the epistolary categories for rhetorical divisions in practice, if not in name.

In light of the strong criticisms leveled against the present use of rhetorical criticism in the interpretation of the Epistles, one might be tempted to discard this method. Total rejection, however, may be going too far. Instead, one should approach the analysis of the letters in the one area of crossover between epistolary and rhetorical theory, namely, the area of style. "If one wants to consider the epistles as the ancients would have, so far as their explicit relation to rhetoric was concerned, one must analyse style."[67] Style (elocution), for the ancient orator, was the greater part of rhetoric, a point to be discussed in detail below.

A final critique of the classical approach to rhetorical criticism is the inadequacy of this approach in handling New Testament narratives such as the Gospels and Acts. One may not strictly apply the principles of Greco-Roman rhetoric, especially matters of division, to broad sections of biblical narrative without violating the nature of the biblical text.[68]

---

[66]Jeffrey T. Reed, "Using Ancient Rhetorical Categories to Interpret Paul's Letters: A Question of Genre," in *Rhetoric and the New Testament: Essays from the 1992 Heidelberg Conference*, ed. Stanley E. Porter and Thomas H. Olbricht, JSNTSS 90 (Sheffield: Sheffield Academic, 1993), 292–324; and *idem*, "The Epistle," in *Handbook of Classical Rhetoric in the Hellenistic Period: 330 B.C.–A.D. 400*, ed. Stanley E. Porter (Leiden: Brill, 1997), 174–78. See also Samuel Byrskog, "Epistolography, Rhetoric and Letter Prescript: Romans 1.1-7 as a Test Case," *JSNT* 65 (1997) 26–46; and Frank Witt Hughes, "The Rhetoric of Letters," in *The Thessalonians Debate: Methodological Discord or Methodological Synthesis?* ed. Karl P. Donfried and Johannes Beutler (Grand Rapids: Eerdmans, 2000), 194–240.
[67]Porter, "Theoretical Justification," 116.
[68]See Grams, "Temple Conflict Scene." Grams provided a heavy-handed application of Greco-Roman rhetoric in matters of division to Matthew 21–23. The result was that

Appendix

Further, as noted by David Young, Kennedy's method is insufficient to examine the blend of primary and secondary rhetoric, that is, narration and direct speech, found in the New Testament narratives.[69] Finally, as recognized by Frank Hughes and William Kurz, the New Testament narratives rhetorically are not openly persuasive like a forensic speech or even a letter but are subtle in their approach and persuasive strategies.[70] Biblical narratives differ in approach and agenda from classical rhetoric, rendering such an approach inappropriate.

Given the above critiques leveled against the classical approach to rhetorical criticism, one can understand why the number of interpreters employing the method is dwindling. In fact, faced with the continued lack of methodological cohesion, one is tempted to discard this approach altogether. Nonetheless, caution must be shown. Much good remains in the classical approach. As stated above, the classical rhetorical approach holds the best means of understanding the biblical texts rhetorically in their historical context. Of all the rhetorical approaches, the classical approach uses oral and literary principles that were accessible to the New Testament authors. The classical approach may be salvaged, including some aspects of Kennedy's method, if the above-mentioned critiques are answered.[71]

---

formal rhetorical categories were forced upon the text, even though this pericope does not include even one continuous speech by Jesus.

[69] David M. Young, "Whoever Has Ears to Hear: The Discourses of Jesus in Mark as Primary Rhetoric of the Greco-Roman Period" (PhD diss., Graduate School of Vanderbilt University, 1994), 80.

[70] Frank Witt Hughes, "The Parable of the Rich Man and Lazarus (Luke 16:19-31) and Graeco-Roman Rhetoric," in *Rhetoric and the New Testament: Essays from the 1992 Heidelberg Conference*, ed., Stanley E. Porter and Thomas H. Olbricht, JSNTSS 90 (Sheffield: Sheffield Academic, 1993), 29–41; and William S. Kurz, "Narrative Models for Imitation in Luke-Acts," in *Greeks, Romans, and Christians: Essays in Honor of Abraham J. Malherbe,* ed. David L. Balch, Everett Ferguson, and Wayne A. Meeks (Minneapolis: Fortress, 1990), 171–89.

[71] In the conclusion of this chapter, a new direction will be proposed for the classical approach to rhetorical criticism, utilizing key components of Kennedy's method.

The new rhetoric and the modern rhetorical approach

From the beginning of the rebirth of rhetorical criticism, the application of modern canons of rhetoric has been a consistently utilized approach. Wilhelm Wuellner has been the greatest proponent of this approach, arguing that the divisions and practices of ancient rhetorical theorists do not fit modern understandings.[72] Much like the classical approach, the modern approach suffers from a lack of methodological cohesion. The one common thread unifying all modern practitioners is the understanding of all rhetoric as persuasion. This concept is due to the influence of Perelman and Olbrechts-Tyteca and their *New Rhetoric*.

At least four main approaches exist within the modern rhetorical camp. The first is that of understanding rhetoric in broad terms and analyzing texts according to exigence, persuasion, and topics.[73] A second approach is the combination of modern canons of rhetoric with contemporary models of speech and discourse theory, creating axes of "power" by which to analyze the biblical texts.[74] A third modern rhetorical approach is the combination of modern canons of rhetoric with modern concepts of fiction and literature.[75] The final modern rhetorical approach is solely to employ modern canons of rhetoric.[76]

---

[72] Wilhelm Wuellner, "Biblical Exegesis in the Light of the History and Historicity of Rhetoric and the Nature of Rhetoric of Religion," in *Rhetoric and the New Testament: Essays from the 1992 Heidelberg Conference*, ed. Stanley E. Porter and Thomas H. Olbricht, JSNTSS 90 (Sheffield: Sheffield Academic, 1993), 503.

[73] See Neil Elliott, *The Rhetoric of Romans: Argumentative Constraint and Strategy and Paul's Dialogue with Judaism*, JSNTSS 45 (Sheffield: Sheffield Academic, 1990).

[74] See Elisabeth Schüssler Fiorenza, *Rhetoric and Ethic: The Politics of Biblical Studies* (Minneapolis: Fortress, 1999).

[75] Morris, "Irony and Ethics"; Young, "Whoever Has Ears."

[76] James J. Murphy, "Early Christianity as a 'Persuasive Campaign': Evidence from the Acts of the Apostles and the Letters of Paul," in *Rhetoric and the New Testament: Essays from the 1992 Heidelberg Conference*, ed. Stanley E. Porter and Thomas H. Olbricht, JSNTSS 90 (Sheffield: Sheffield Academic, 1993), 90–99; Dennis L. Stamps, "Rethinking the Rhetorical Situation: The Entertextualization of the Situation in the New Testament Epistles," in *Rhetoric and the New Testament: Essays from the 1992 Heidelberg Conference*, ed. Stanley E. Porter and Thomas H. Olbricht, JSNTSS 90 (Sheffield: Sheffield Academic, 1993), 192–210; and Wilhelm Wuellner, "The Rhetorical Genre of Jesus' Sermon in Luke 12.1–13.9," in *Persuasive Artistry: Studies in New Testament Rhetoric in Honor of*

Appendix

Criticism of the modern rhetorical approach

With rhetorical criticism, one may choose to interpret the biblical text employing whichever rhetorical canon he or she wishes, so long as the interpreter does not ask of the text more than can be expected historically and socially. Such questioning is often the downfall of the modern approach. The major catalyst for the modern approach is the assumption that the ancient rhetorical categories are not sufficient for understanding the biblical text. In other words, modern society has developed a style of writing, speaking, and communicating that outstrips that of the ancient theorists. Therefore, a new system, one that fits the modern concepts of speech communication, must be employed. As long as the interpreter approaches the text acknowledging that the modern system of speech communication he or she is applying to the text includes concepts, tropes, figures, and forms that the ancient author did not nor could not have known, then the application of the modern approach is sound. However, more often than not, the modern critic approaches the text placing constraints upon the ancient authors, reading them and asking questions of them as if they were twenty-first century authors.[77]

Furthermore, modern rhetorical critics are not above placing formal divisional constraints upon biblical texts, especially the Epistles, divisional constraints that subsume obvious literary forms.[78] In addition, just like rhetoricians who follow classical models, modern critics blend ancient and modern rhetorical canons, often equating them.[79] In critiquing the modern rhetorical approach, one should consider the arguments marshaled above against similar methodological tendencies of the classical rhetorical approach.

The application of the modern approach does show promise. This approach aids one in interpreting and presenting biblical texts in terms that fit the modern setting. In addition, much potential exists in the combination of speech theory with rules for fiction. Such an approach

---

George A. Kennedy, ed. Duane F. Watson, JSNTSS 50 (Sheffield: Sheffield Academic, 1991), 93–118.
[77]See Wuellner, "Biblical Exegesis"; and especially Fiorenza, *Rhetoric and Ethic*, 123–28.
[78]Humphries, "Paul's Rhetoric," 118–28.
[79]See Young, "Whoever has Ears"; and Griffin, "Seeing and Perceiving."

can aid the interpreter in illuminating biblical narratives. Nevertheless, the interpreter who wishes to understand the biblical text according to the rhetorical principles known by a first-century reader or to comprehend the avenues of invention that the biblical author would have traversed conceptually may not wish to employ the modern approach.

Socio-rhetorical criticism

A third approach has appeared recently upon the horizon of rhetorical criticism, that of socio-rhetorical criticism. This method is an interpretive methodology that Vernon Robbins has developed over the past two decades. Robbins, in his effort to find a forum for his methodology, has attempted to equate socio-rhetorical criticism with rhetorical criticism.[80] The result is that now, in both regional and national meetings of the Society of Biblical Literature, one is as likely to hear a socio-rhetorical presentation in a seminar on rhetorical approaches as a traditional classical or modern interpretation. However, socio-rhetorical criticism should not be identified with rhetorical criticism. Interpreters who employ this method deserve their own forum, as do interpreters employing traditional rhetorical criticism.

Robbins's first major attempt at what was to become socio-rhetorical criticism was his work *Jesus the Teacher*.[81] At this point, Robbins's thoughts and the application of his method were in embryonic stage, resembling only faintly the formal explanation of his theory in later years.[82] In later works, Robbins has come to view socio-rhetorical criticism as an opportunity and "challenge to integrate major strategies of the new movements and methods through a rhetorical approach that focuses on literary, social, cultural and ideological issues in the texts."[83] Specifically, this challenge is to integrate as many critical approaches as possible to view a text from several different textual "arenas."

---

[80]Vernon K. Robbins, "Rhetorical Argument about Lamps and Light in Early Christian Gospels," in *Context: Essays in Honour of Peder Johan Borgan*, ed. P. W. Böckman and R. E. Kristiansen, Relieff 24 (Tapir: Tapir Publishers, 1987), 177–95.

[81]Vernon K. Robbins, *Jesus the Teacher: A Socio-Rhetorical Interpretation of Mark* (Philadelphia: Fortress, 1984).

[82]See Robbins, *Exploring the Texture of Texts*, 1–4; idem, *Tapestry of Early Christian Discourse*, 1–41.

[83]Robbins, *Tapestry of Early Christian Discourse*, 1.

Appendix

The goal of socio-rhetorical criticism, according to Robbins, is to interpret a text along four textual arenas or angles: (1) Inner texture; (2) Intertexture; (3) Social and Cultural Texture; and (4) Ideological Texture.[84] The need to analyze a text along these various angles arises because of Robbins's view of the biblical text as a network or matrix of meanings. Traditional critical approaches applied individually are inadequate because "these networks extend far beyond the boundaries we construct to analyze and interpret phenomena; they interconnect phenomena inside and outside of texts in ways quite difficult for us even to imagine. Therefore, no interpreter should allow one arena of texture to be an environment for creating boundaries that separate this arena permanently from other arenas of texture."[85] In order to avoid interpreting a text in any one exclusive manner, Robbins posited that one must use as many critical disciplines as possible on their own terms and allow these critical disciplines to interact and inform each other.[86] Thus, a socio-rhetorical critic will combine "literary criticism, social-scientific criticism, postmodern criticism, and theological criticism together into an integrated approach to interpretation."[87]

At the surface level, one immediately recognizes discontinuity between the traditional rhetorical approach and that of Robbins. He has attempted to bring as many critical disciplines to bear upon a single text as possible, while rhetorical criticism seeks only to apply rhetorical canons, modern or ancient. Rhetorical criticism is interested in communicating with other disciplines only after interpretive results are generated, while the whole concept of socio-rhetorical criticism is to generate results through communication with other disciplines. Finally, rhetorical criticism has roots in historical and literary approaches to Scripture, while the socio-rhetorical approach is an attempt by Robbins to push biblical interpretation beyond these domains into a postmodern agenda.[88] Socio-rhetorical criticism, as explained by Robbins and applied by interpreters, is a separate

---

[84]Ibid., 27–43. Robbins lists a fifth arena, Sacred Texture, in Robbins, *Exploring the Texture of Texts*, 3.
[85]Robbins, *Tapestry of Early Christian Discourse*, 20.
[86]Ibid., 41.
[87]Robbins, *Exploring the Texture of Texts*, 2.
[88]Vernon K. Robbins, "The Present and Future of Rhetorical Analysis," in *The Rhetorical Analysis of Scripture: Essays from the 1995 London Conference*, ed. Stanley E. Porter and Thomas H. Olbricht, JSNTSS 146 (Sheffield: Sheffield Academic, 1997), 25–30.

and unique methodology that must be set aside as such. To interpret socio-rhetorical criticism as rhetorical criticism as recent scholars have done is to invite the subsuming of the traditional rhetorical approach by the socio-rhetorical approach.

Critiquing the socio-rhetorical method is beyond the scope of the current discussion, in light of the differences between the traditional rhetorical approach to interpretation and the socio-rhetorical approach. However, a few brief cautions are offered to the socio-rhetorical critic. Those engaging in socio-rhetorical interpretation must be wary of certain pitfalls inherent in the method. The socio-rhetorical critic must avoid the postmodern tendencies of socio-rhetorical criticism to destroy boundaries between critical methodologies, thus corrupting interpretive analysis. The socio-rhetorical critic also must avoid the postmodern tendency latent in this method toward reader-oriented interpretations, which destroy the social and literary dimensions and intentions of this method. Finally, the socio-rhetorical critic must avoid becoming overextended in his or her application of multiple methodologies to a single text. One cannot specialize in all areas and all methodologies, though one may have a general understanding of many methodologies. When one tries to marshal many critical methods in a simultaneous manner, the result is often a shallow interpretive reading of the text due to the general knowledge of many methodologies rather than in-depth knowledge of one or two.

Need for a new direction

At present, a new direction is needed for the traditional rhetorical approach to biblical interpretation. A new methodological strategy that illuminates the biblical texts in their historical context is possible if one begins with an adequate understanding of Hellenistic rhetoric and its influence upon biblical texts. In this task, one must provide methodological consistency as well as an appreciation for the various genres present within the New Testament. Such is the purpose of the rest of this discussion.

Appendix

Literary-Rhetorical Criticism: A New Direction

For the most part, rhetorical critics begin their application of rhetorical criticism to biblical texts with an evaluation and explanation of ancient rhetorical theory. This evaluation contains explanations of terms such as *enthymeme, inventio, elocutio, narratio, dispositio, ethos, pathos, logos,* and other related words.[89] The beginning of the practice of rhetorical criticism at this point reveals an unstated assumption on the part of interpreters. The underlying assumption is that Hellenistic rhetorical theory, specifically that found in the school handbooks, had a direct impact upon the construction of the New Testament texts. This assumption further implies that the authors of the New Testament were educated along classical lines and modes of thought, including advanced rhetorical training. Such an assumption has little in common with historical reality. Instead of beginning with a discussion of rhetoric, rhetorical critics should begin with a survey of Hellenistic education in an effort to perceive the level of education of the New Testament authors. With an historical understanding of the educational level of the New Testament authors one is on firmer ground in applying a limited number of rhetorical canons, those to which the authors—in light of their educational experience—would have had some exposure.[90]

---

[89] See Kennedy, *New Testament Interpretation,* 7–33; Church, "Rhetorical Structure," 17–20; Steve Walton, "Rhetorical Criticism: An Introduction," *Themelios* 21 (January 1996) 4–6; and Kwon, "Rhetorical Analysis of Johannine Farewell Discourse," 31–76.

[90] The following is a brief survey of Hellenistic educational practices. This survey is not intended to be all-inclusive, for the Hellenistic practices and levels of education varied widely from one region to the next. Instead, the following is an attempt to highlight the major components of Hellenistic rhetoric in order to delimit the application of Hellenistic rhetorical canons. If one desires a more in-depth survey of Hellenistic education, one should consider the following: Quint. *Inst.*1–2; Henri Irenée Marrou, *A History of Education in Antiquity,* trans. George Lamb (London: Sheed and Ward, 1956); John T. Townsend, "Ancient Education in the Time of the Early Roman Empire," in *The Catacombs and the Colosseum: The Roman Empire as the Setting of Primitive Christianity,* ed. Stephen Benko and John J. O'Rourke (Valley Forge: Judson, 1971), 139–63; Teresa Morgan, *Literate Education in the Hellenistic and Roman Worlds* (Cambridge: Cambridge University Press, 1998); Raffaella Cribiore, *Gymnastics of the Mind: Greek Education in Hellenistic and Roman Egypt* (Princeton: Princeton University Press, 2001); and Donald Lemen Clark, *Rhetoric in Greco-Roman Education* (Morningside Heights, N.Y.: Columbia University Press, 1957).

Hellenistic Education: The Ἐγκύκλιος Παιδεία

No central body governed educational practices during the Hellenistic era. No one person set out to define what did and did not constitute a proper Hellenistic education. The closest extant attempt at such a formal definition of education is found in the first two books of Quntilian's *Institutes*. Therefore, in order to formulate a view of Hellenistic education one must sift through the records provided by archaeology and the papyri, coupling them with the offhand remarks of ancient authors.

According to Quintilian, the Hellenistic educational system fell into three somewhat overlapping parts.[91] The first level of education began when a child was young, perhaps four or five, but as late as seven, and involved the instruction by a pedagogue or grammatist.[92] The duty of the pedagogue was to instruct the child in the alphabet and basic literary phrases. This instructor, usually a family slave, taught a child to read and write and gave limited ethical instruction through the teaching of simple aphorisms.[93] The pedagogue taught these rudiments of literacy through the use of alphabets, syllabaries, and word lists.[94]

As soon as a child could read and write, he was sent to the teacher of literature or *grammaticus*.[95] The *grammaticus* completed the greater part of the educational cycle, which for most students was the limit of educational exposure. Raffaella Cribiore has contended that most people did not advance far enough in the educational cycle even to study under this teacher.[96] Quintilian divided the professional tasks of the *grammaticus* or grammarian into two parts: the art of speaking correctly, and the interpretation of literature.[97] The art of speaking correctly was in reality training in the formal principles of grammar. The interpretation of literature was the training of

---

[91]Quint. *Inst.* 1–2.
[92]Ibid., 1.1.8; and Marrou, *History of Education*, 160.
[93]Quint. *Inst.* 1.1.12–36.
[94]Teresa Morgan, "Dionysius Thrax and the Educational Uses of Grammar," in *Dionysius Thrax and the Technē Grammatikē*, The Henry Sweet Society Studies in the History of Linguistics, ed. John Flood, Werner Hüllen, Vivien Law, Michael K. C. MacMahon, and Robert Robins, vol. 1 (Münster: Nodus, 1995), 77.
[95]Quint. *Inst.* 1.4.1.
[96]Cribiore, *Gymnastics of the Mind*, 187.
[97]Quint. *Inst.* 1.4.2.

Appendix

children to read and interpret the poets and historians and included some exposure to composition and rhetorical theories through the *progymnasmata*. As is readily apparent, the subject matter taught by the grammarian was far-reaching and widely divergent. Therefore, the *grammaticus* was often a highly educated person, having a knowledge of literature, orthography, music, astronomy, and other sciences.[98]

For the teaching of the formal rules of grammar, a Hellenistic grammarian might have followed a similar educational format as that found in the grammar of Dionysios Thrax, a systematic textbook used in the Hellenistic schools.[99] Dionysios Thrax wrote, "Grammar is an experimental knowledge of the usages of language as generally current among poets and prose writers."[100] He went on to divide the teaching of grammar into six parts, each building upon the previous, leading up to the practice of ancient literary criticism. Within Dionysios's grammar, one finds instructions not only of the elements of grammar but of reading tone, rhapsody, and stops. The ultimate purpose of the grammar was not to teach grammar for grammar's sake but to teach grammar so the student might read with understanding. Thus, the teaching of grammar served the purpose of enabling the student to interpret, critique, and compose literature. The ability to read and understand literature was of the utmost importance, since literature would be a prime source for rhetorical theory, moral examples, and literary models to be imitated.[101]

In addition to teaching grammar, which was designed for future literary applications, the grammarian taught his students how to interpret literature. Part of this training included the reading and recitation of poetry, history, and speeches. However, a great part of this training was accomplished through the use of the *progymnasmata* or elementary exercises. The *progymnasmata* were a graded series of exercises that were "supposed to teach a student how to write on set themes: they were meant to warm up his muscles, stretch his power of discourse, and build his vigor."[102] The *progymnasmata* probably represented the final stages of

---

[98]Ibid., 1.4-9.
[99]Dionysios Thrax, "The Grammar of Dionysios Thrax," trans. Thomas Davidson, *Journal of Speculative Philosophy* 8 (1874) 326–39.
[100]Ibid., 366.
[101]Morgan, "Dionysius Thrax," 84.
[102]Cribiore, *Gymnastics of the Mind*, 223.

literary training, designed to move the student from the tutelage of the grammarian to that of the rhetorician. The student began by learning how to paraphrase a story, a more literary-oriented exercise, and then gradually moved to more complex, rhetorically oriented exercises such as *ekphrasis* and *prosopopoeia*.

The one extant example of *progymnasmata* from the first century AD is that of Theon, probably of Alexandria, Egypt. James Butts placed the writing of this graded set of exercises sometime shortly before the writing of Quintilian's *Institutes*.[103] According to Theon, his *progymnasmata* were of the utmost benefit for those who took up the art of rhetoric.[104] However, he also stated that the "practice in the exercises is absolutely necessary, not only for those who intend to be orators, but also if someone wants to be a poet or prose-writer, or if he wants to acquire facility with some other form of writing. For these exercises are, so to speak, the foundation stones for every form of writing."[105] In Hellenistic education, the grammarian—not the rhetorician—with his use of the *progymnasmata* prepared students to engage in literary activities.

In Quintilian's time, and in the years before him, rhetoric had become so complex and cumbersome that grammarians began to teach the most elementary aspects of rhetoric, including primitive attempts at declamation.[106] Quintilian lamented this handing over of the rhetorical art to the grammarian. Instead, he directed that advanced students study under both a rhetorician and a grammarian at the same time, with each school day divided between the two instructors.[107] The outcome—though certainly varying from one location to the next—was a limited exposure to rhetoric by those trained by a grammarian.

The final step in the educational process was that of studying under a rhetorician. Few of those who studied under a grammarian ever went as far as studying with a rhetorician. Those who did, did so with the objective of serving in the law courts or deliberative bodies.[108] Only those who had

---

[103]James R. Butts, "The Progymnasmata of Theon: A New Text with Translation and Commentary" (PhD diss., Claremont Graduate School, 1986), 3–6.
[104]Theon 1.25–26.
[105]Ibid., 2.139–43.
[106]Quint. *Inst.* 2.1.1–3; see also Marrou, *History of Education*, 160.
[107]Quint. *Inst.* 2.1.12–13.
[108]Tacitus claimed that rhetoric was used primarily within the law courts. See Tac. *Dial.* 5. He also claimed that, in his time, oratory and law had been equated and that the

trained under a rhetorician—watching, listening, declaiming, imitating, and again watching—were themselves prepared for this role.[109] The literary exercises, no matter how rhetorical in nature, did not provide enough training to equip a person "to conduct lawsuits, debate laws in the senate or give displays of epideictic oratory in public places."[110] Instead, those who had completed the written exercises, such as the *progymnasmata*, were fit only to serve as "bureaucratic middlemen in a variety of posts, to read and analyse complicated texts, to articulate and pass on information in a clear and concise form."[111] At issue was the difficulty of rhetorical theory, which could be grasped only through much instruction and practice as well as natural ability.[112]

Rhetorical training had little impact upon those wishing to engage in literary endeavors, nor was rhetorical training required for such a task. In addition, few ever learned the complicated and complex art of rhetoric. Those who did learn the rhetorical art did so for the purpose of serving as lawyers and statesmen. On the other hand, a far greater number of students studied under the grammarian, learning the basic principles of literary analysis and composition through the use of the *progymnasmata*. If the authors of the New Testament received any education in the classical vein, they were more likely to have progressed through the level of the grammarian rather than the rhetorician. The literary nature, agenda, and genres of the New Testament do suggest some exposure to advanced literary training. Further, due to the complex nature and limited forum for rhetoric in the first century, New Testament authors were unlikely to have known how to construct judicial, deliberative, and epideictic speeches as taught by a rhetorician. Rhetorical theory was too complex, required too much skill and practice, and was too limited in display to be picked up through osmosis or casual contact. In addition, the New Testament authors engaged in a literary, not oral, agenda by recording history and writing letters. Since the New Testament consists of these literary documents and not

---

rhetorical schools taught only deliberative and judicial rhetoric. See Tac. *Dial.* 8, 33, and 35. He went so far as to claim that if there were no crime, then there would be no need for orators. See Tac. *Dial.* 41.

[109]Quint. *Inst.* 2.5.14–16.
[110]Morgan, *Literate Education*, 225.
[111]Ibid.
[112]Tac. *Dial.* 33.

formal judicial speeches, deliberative addresses, or epideictic orations, one must question the influence and use of the rhetorical arts in the interpretation of literary texts such as the New Testament. One should look to the *progymnasmata* for guidelines in regards to acceptable form, style, and compositional method in interpretation of the New Testament.

The Progymnasmata and Rhetorical Method

Scholars have been so tempted by the straightforward and logical outlines of the rhetorical handbooks that they have overlooked both the literary nature of the New Testament and the *progymnasmata*, those exercises that trained students to engage in literary activities. Kennedy did observe that if "students subsequently undertook serious literary work, they tended to utilize progymnasmatic forms in the development of their thought. Because these forms are common types, found in many cultures, something analogous to them can often be found in the Bible, though they are rarely developed there in accord with the specific suggestions of the Greek and Roman schools."[113] Having acknowledged the possible presence of forms similar to those found in the *progymnasmata*, Kennedy then fully ignored such as an interpretive tool. He commented on most New Testament genres, with the exception of Hebrews, a prime candidate for analysis along the lines of the elementary exercise of *synkrisis* or comparison.

A few scholars have sought to draw connections between the elementary exercises and New Testament texts, but by no means has this task been exhausted. Vernon Robbins and Burton Mack first promoted the usefulness of the *chreia*, an elementary exercise, in the interpretation of the gospel narratives.[114] A *chreia* "is a concise statement of action which

---

[113]Kennedy, *New Testament Interpretation*, 22.
[114]Vernon K. Robbins, "The Chreia," in *Greco-Roman Literature and the New Testament: Selected Forms and Genres*, ed. David E. Aune, SBLSBS 21 (Atlanta: Scholars, 1988), 1–23; Burton L. Mack, "Elaboration of the Chreia in the Hellenistic School," in *Patterns of Persuasion in the Gospels*, ed. Burton L. Mack and Vernon K. Robbins (Sonoma: Polebridge, 1989), 31–67; *idem*, "The Anointing of Jesus: Elaboration within a Chreia," in *Patterns of Persuasion in the Gospels*, ed. Burton L. Mack and Vernon K. Robbins (Sonoma: Polebridge, 1989), 85–106; and Vernon K. Robbins, "Pronouncement Stories and Jesus' Blessing of the Children: A Rhetorical Approach," *Semeia* 29 (1983) 42–74.

is attributed with aptness to some specified character or to something analogous to a character."[115] This form fits neatly with and explains many of the nuances of the pronouncement stories of the gospels, stories which record actions and happenings, culminating with a pronouncement or saying of Jesus.

The use of the *progymnasmata* in the construction of classical literature is readily apparent. Plutarch structured his *Lives* to follow the elementary exercise of *synkrisis*. Ovid's *Heroides* and *Metamorphoses* include myth, *prosopopoeia*, narrative, *synkrisis*, and *ekphrasis*. Elements of the *chreia* appear in Diogenes Laertius's *Lives of the Eminent Philosophers* and in *Bioi* or *Lives* written during the period.[116] Dionysius of Halicarnassus incorporated fables into his *Antiquitates romanae* as did Livy in his *Ab Urbe condita*.[117] Much like Plutarch's use of *synkrisis*, Philostratus's use of *ekphrasis* serves as the key trope in his *Imagines*. For each of these authors, the *progymnasmatic* exercises provided not rules for composition but patterns of available discourse to draw upon and manipulate for their own authorial purposes.

One should not be surprised to discover that New Testament authors also made ready use of these exercises, not in a prescriptive or formulaic manner, but as a source of possible patterns of discourse to be manipulated in keeping with their authorial purposes at hand. Nevertheless, few have investigated the issue at any depth beyond the *chreia*. This lack of investigation exists in spite of the statement of Butts over a decade ago that "there is evidence that the Gospel writers were familiar not only with the *chreia* form, but also knew several of the compositional techniques commonly taught by the rhetoricians as part of their set of 'elementary exercises.'"[118] Only Timothy Seid has branched out, in a formal manner, beyond the *chreia* and beyond the Gospels, to apply the *progymnasmata* as an interpretive tool.[119]

---

[115]Theon 3.2.2–3.
[116]Dion. Laert. *Lives* 2.82 and 4.22.
[117]Dion. Hal. *Ant. rom.* 8.6.1–3 and Livy 2.32.
[118]James R. Butts, "The Chreia in the Synoptic Gospels," *BTB* 16 (1986) 137.
[119]Timothy Wayne Seid, "The Rhetorical Form of the Melchizedek/Christ Comparison in Hebrews 7," (PhD diss., Brown University, 1996). In a private conversation, in November 2000 at the national meeting of the Society of Biblical Literature, Seid contended that the *progymnasmata* were the most overlooked interpretive tool in New Testament exegesis.

Due to the influence of the *progymnasmata* upon the structure and compositional techniques of Hellenistic literature and the demonstration of such effects in the Gospels and Hebrews, any classical rhetorical method should explore the *progymnasmata* as a primary source for interpretive strategies. Except in cases in which the nature of the biblical text is unquestionably oral, such as the forensic speeches of Tertullus and Paul in Acts, the interpreter should forego rhetorical divisions and arrangement techniques and limit discussion to the arrangement and divisions set forth in the *progymnasmata*. This caution includes a foregoing of locating biblical texts within the rhetorical species of forensic, deliberative, and epideictic for the literary genres of myth, narrative, chreia, comparison, description, speech-in-character, and the like.

Style, Style, and More Style

At this point, one might wonder what of the Hellenistic rhetorical handbooks is left to consider in the construction of a rhetorical methodology. The answer is style. Style or *elocutio* was the one area of overlap between literary and oratorical endeavors. Style was present in the literary works of the poets, prose writers, and historians, as well as the great orators of the law courts. In the first century AD, style was the most important aspect of oral and literary occupations. Therefore, any classically oriented rhetorical analysis should center upon style.

This concept startles many rhetorical critics. Jongseon Kwon contended that "when rhetorical criticism becomes confined to 'style' or 'artistry,' it is indistinguishable from literary criticism."[120] This conclusion is due more to a modern conception of stylistics as flowery speech or ornamentation than to a first-century understanding. When one considers and emphasizes style, the emphasis is on what was most important to the first-century audience. One should recognize that in ancient thought style was more than a means of adornment; rather, style was a means to communicate substance.[121]

---

[120] Kwon, "Rhetorical Analysis of the Johannine Farewell Discourse," 24.
[121] Porter, "Theoretical Justification," 116.

Appendix

The importance of style is seen explicitly in the Hellenistic definition of rhetoric. Cicero stated, the "function of eloquence seems to be to speak in a manner suited to persuade an audience, the end is to persuade by speech."[122] If one considered only this definition, then rhetoric would appear to be concerned with persuasion. However, Quintilian stated that "the definition which suits its real character is that which makes rhetoric the science of speaking well."[123] For Quintilian, speaking well involved the character of the orator as well as proper conception, arrangement, and style. Speech or oratory was meant to persuade but in the first century did so primarily through style. Dionysius of Halicarnassus, who composed an entire work that dealt solely with style, wrote that style was more important in communication than theory and the correct arrangement of a speech.[124] Quintilian lamented the overly zealous fascination of his contemporaries with style. "And if we have to spend all our life in the laborious effort to discover words which will at once be brilliant, appropriate and lucid, and to arrange them with exact precision, we lose all the fruit of our studies. And yet we see the majority of modern speakers wasting their time over the discovery of single words and over the elaborate weighing and measurement of such words when once discovered."[125] A few lines later he wrote, "And yet there are some who are never weary of morbid self-criticism, who throw themselves into an agony of mind almost over separate syllables, and even when they have discovered the best words for their purpose look for some word that is older, less familiar, and less obvious, since they cannot bring themselves to realise that when a speech is praised for its words, it implies that its sense is inadequate."[126] Rhetoricians in the first century were enamored with style.

The importance of style is observed in the statements of Quintilian: "On the other hand, by the employment of skillful ornament the orator commends himself at the same time, and whereas his other accomplishments appeal to the considered judgment of the learned, this gift appeals to the enthusiastic approval of the world at large, and the

---

[122]Cic. *Inv.* 1.5.6.
[123]Quint. *Inst.* 2.15.34.
[124]Dion. Hal. *Comp.* 4.
[125]Quint. *Inst.* 8.Pr.26–27.
[126]Ibid., 8.Pr.31–32.

speaker who possesses it fights not merely with effective, but with flashing weapons."[127] To the contribution of style to persuasion, he recorded, "But rhetorical ornament contributes not a little to the furtherance of our case as well. For when our audience find it a pleasure to listen, their attention and their readiness to believe what they hear are both alike increased, while they are generally filled with delight, and sometimes even transported by admiration."[128]

In spite of modern trepidations, style was an important, if not the most important, component of oral and literary works. Style was the means, in spite of the laments of Quintilian, by which the orator persuaded the audience and the author moved the reader. Audiences longed for good style and could easily recognize poor style.[129] Any rhetorical method that seeks to interpret the biblical texts in light of their historical setting must include an emphasis on style and the first-century use of such style in the task of persuasive communication.

Literary-Rhetorical Criticism

In light of the above surveys of the application of rhetorical criticism, Hellenistic education, the *progymnasmata*, and style, one may now consider some formal methodological statements. The purpose of rhetorical criticism, applied classically, is to read and interpret the biblical text by comprehending the meaning and message intended by the author, appreciating fully the genre of the text, and following Hellenistic literary and rhetorical principles and rules designed for the construction of such texts. Therefore, classical rhetorical criticism is to interpret biblical texts in light of the rhetorical and literary milieu in which they were written.

The first step of any classical rhetorical approach should be the defining of the rhetorical unit. The unit should have a clearly defined beginning, middle, and end. Helpful in defining this unit is the use of *inclusio*, hook words, change in theme, change in topic, change in narrative setting, or other literary, grammatical, or syntactical markers consistent with the practices of the author.

---

[127]Ibid., 8.3.2.
[128]Ibid., 8.3.5.
[129]Ibid., 2.12.1–12 and 4.2.122.

Appendix

One should observe any structural, syntactical, or rhetorical markers that might function in the determination of overall structure of the unit. If no such markers are available, the interpreter should seek to divide the work into thought or argumentative blocks. These blocks can be detected by shifts in themes, subjects, and genre, as these are all ways of denoting change. Before moving to the next step, the interpreter should seek to understand the placement of this unit within the overall movement of the text and whether the present unit consists of even smaller rhetorical units. Somewhat helpful in the determination of these individual units is the determination of the genre of the larger text. Certain genres, such as the epistle, have their own strictly defined units.

The second step of the rhetorical method is to identify the rhetorical situation of the text. One should abstain from identifying the rhetorical situation as Kennedy does, using modern rhetorical theory.[130] If the unit in question is clearly constructed along the lines of a Greco-Roman speech, such as those included in Acts, then one may use *stasis* theory and the species of rhetoric to identify the rhetorical issue at hand as well as the intent of the character making the speech. However, direct speeches are the exception, not the rule, for the New Testament. The New Testament consists of various literary genres such as epistle, narrative, and paraenesis. Therefore, the interpreter should first determine with which genre one is working. Second, one should turn to the guidelines provided by the *progymnasmata*. One should identify as clearly as possible which elementary exercises were employed—if any—in the unit by the author. The interpreter then should follow the persuasive logic of the larger text as a whole to determine how the present literary form was used by the author. In the larger picture, what role does the present literary form serve? What narrative themes necessitate the present literary form? How is argumentative thought flow served by the present form?

The final step is to analyze the style and arrangement of the unit. In this task, the interpreter should turn to the *progymnasmata* for guidelines in the construction of the elementary exercises. These guidelines will provide interpretive handles for distinguishing the literary arrangement of the text. One may draw from the rhetorical guidelines of arrangement

---

[130]Kennedy, *New Testament Interpretation*, 34–36.

only if the unit under consideration is plainly a direct speech, intentionally fashioned by the author along the lines of Greco-Roman rhetoric.

In the analysis of style, one should turn to the devices of style set forth in the Hellenistic rhetorical handbooks of Quintilian, Cicero, Pseudo-Cicero, and if desired, Dionysius, in order to identify the presence of stylistic devices within the text. The interpreter should not be satisfied with the simple identification of a stylistic device, but one must seek to understand how this device functions as a means of persuasion or how such a device contributes to the logical flow of the text. How was the author's turn of a phrase or of repetition used to further the present authorial intent, identified in the previous step? Because of the dependence upon the elementary exercises and the emphasis of the literary nature of the New Testament, this method should be called *Literary-Rhetorical Criticism*.

Bibliography

Primary Literature

Aland, Kurt et al., editors. *The Greek New Testament,* 4th rev. ed. New York: United Bible Societies, 1993.

Aristotle. *On Rhetoric.* Translated by George A. Kennedy. New York: Oxford University Press, 1991.

Augustine. *On Christian Doctrine.* Translated by D. W. Robertson. Indianapolis: Bobbs-Merrill, 1958.

Cicero. *De Inventione.* Translated by H. M. Hubbell. LCL 386. Cambridge: Harvard University Press, 1949. Reprinted, 1993.

———. *Brutus.* Translated by G. L. Hendrickson. LCL 342. Cambridge: Harvard University Press, 1939. Reprinted, 1997.

[Cicero]. *Rhetorica Ad Herennium.* Translated by Harry Caplan. LCL 403. Cambridge: Harvard University Press, 1954. Reprinted, 1989.

Demetrius. *On Style.* Translated by Doreen C. Innes. LCL 199. Cambridge: Harvard University Press, 1995. Reprinted, 1999.

Dionysius of Halicarnassus. *On Literary Composition.* Translated by Stephen Usher. LCL 466. Cambridge: Harvard University Press, 1985.

Plutarch. *The Life of Sulla.* Translated by Bernadotte Perrin. LCL 4. Cambridge: Harvard University Press, 1916. Reprinted, 1950.

Quintilian. *Institutio Oratoria.* 4 vols. Translated by H. E. Butler. LCL 124, 125, 126, 127. Cambridge: Harvard University Press, 1920–21.

Strabo. *The Geography of Strabo.* Translated by Horace Leonard Jones. LCL 6. Cambridge: Harvard University Press, 1929. Reprinted, 1950.

Tacitus. *Dialogus*. Translated by M. Hutton and W. Peterson. Edited by R. M. Ogilivie et al. LCL 34. Cambridge: Harvard University Press, 1914. Reprinted, 1970.
Theon. Θέωνος Σοφιστοῦ Προγυμνάσματα. Translated by James R. Butts. In "The Progymnasmata of Theon: A New Text with Translation and Commentary." PhD diss., Claremont Graduate School, 1986.

Secondary Literature

Alexander, Loveday C. A. "Acts and Ancient Intellectual Biography." In *The Book of Acts in Its Ancient Literary Setting*, edited by Bruce W. Winter and Andrew D. Clarke, 31–63. The Book of Acts in Its First Century Setting 1. Grand Rapids: Eerdmans, 1993.

———. "Fact, Fiction and the Genre of Acts." *NTS* 44 (1998) 380–99.

———. "Formal Elements and Genre: Which Greco-Roman Prologues Most Closely Parallel the Lukan Prologues?" In *Jesus and the Heritage of Israel: Luke's Narrative Claim upon Israel's Legacy*, edited by David P. Moessner and David L. Tiede, 9–26. Luke the Interpreter of Israel 1. Harrisburg, Pa.: Trinity, 1999.

Alexander, Thomas Craig. "Paul's Final Exhortation to the Elders from Ephesus: The Rhetoric of Acts 20:17-38." PhD diss., Emory University, 1990.

Anderson, R. Dean, Jr. *Ancient Rhetorical Theory and Paul*. Rev. ed. Contributions to Biblical Exegesis and Theology 18. Leuven: Peters, 1999.

Atra, Brian Joseph. "An Examination of the Speeches of Peter in Acts: Implications for the Authorship and Thought of First Peter." PhD diss., Mid-America Baptist Theological Seminary, 1998.

Aune, David E. *The New Testament in Its Literary Environment*. LEC. Philadelphia: Westminster, 1987.

Balch, David L. "Comments on the Genre and a Political Theme of Luke-Acts: A Preliminary Comparison of Two Hellenistic Historians." In *SBLSP* 28, 343–61. Atlanta: Scholars, 1989.

———. "The Genre of Luke-Acts: Individual Biography, Adventure Novel, or Political History?" *SWJT* 33 (Fall 1990) 5–19.

Barr, David L., and Judith L. Wentling. "The Conventions of Classical Biography and the Genre of Luke-Acts: A Preliminary Study." In *Luke Acts: New Perspectives from the Society of Biblical Literature Seminar*, edited by Charles H. Talbert, 63–88. New York: Crossroad, 1984.

Barrett, C. K. *A Critical and Exegetical Commentary on the Acts of the Apostles*. 2 vols. ICC. Edinburgh: T. & T. Clark, 1994–98.

Bauernfeind, Otto. *Kommentar und Studien zur Apostelgeschichte*. WUNT 22. Tübingen: Mohr/Siebeck, 1980.

Beck, Norman A. "The Lukan Writer's Stories about the Call of Paul." In *SBLSP* 22, 213–18. Chico: Scholars, 1983.

Bibliography

Betz, Hans Dieter. "The Literary Composition and Function of Paul's Letter to the Galatians." *NTS* 21 (1975) 353–9.

———. *Galatians: A Commentary on Paul's Letter to the Churches in Galatia*. Hermeneia. Philadelphia: Fortress, 1979.

Bitzer, Lloyd F. "The Rhetorical Situation." *Philosophy and Rhetoric* 1 (1968) 1–14.

Black, C. Clifton. "The Rhetorical Form of the Hellenistic Jewish and Early Christian Sermon: A Response to Lawrence Wills." *HTR* 81 (1988) 1–18.

———. "Keeping up with Recent Studies: XVI. Rhetorical Criticism and Biblical Interpretation." *ExpT* 100 (April 1989) 252–58.

———. "Rhetorical Questions: The New Testament, Classical Rhetoric, and Current Interpretation." *Dialog* 29 (Winter 1990) 62–70.

———. "Rhetorical Criticism." In *Hearing the New Testament: Strategies for Interpretation*, edited by Joel B. Green, 256–77. Grand Rapids: Eerdmans, 1995.

Black, Robert Allen. "The Conversion Stories in the Acts of the Apostles: A Study of Their Forms and Functions." PhD diss., Emory University, 1985.

Bond, Jeffrey Miller. "Cicero's Critique of Plato: The Quarrel Between Rhetoric and Philosophy Volume One." PhD diss., University of Chicago, 1992.

Bonz, Marianne Palmer. *The Past as Legacy: Luke-Acts and Ancient Epic*. Minneapolis: Fortress, 2000.

Botha, Pieter J. J. "The Verbal Art of the Pauline Letters: Rhetoric, Performance and Presence." In *Rhetoric and the New Testament: Essays from the 1992 Heidelberg Conference*, edited by Stanley E. Porter and Thomas H. Olbricht, 408–28. JSNTSS 90. Sheffield: Sheffield Academic, 1993.

Brawley, Robert L. *Luke-Acts and the Jews: Conflict, Apology, and Conciliation*. SBLMS 33. Atlanta: Scholars, 1987.

———. "Paul in Acts: Aspects of Structure and Characterization." In *SBLSP* 27, 90–105. Atlanta: Scholars, 1988.

Brown, Schuyler. "The Role of the Prologues in Determining the Purpose of Luke-Acts." In *Perspectives on Luke-Acts*, edited by Charles H. Talbert, 99–111. Perspectives in Religious Studies 5. Edinburgh: T. & T. Clark, 1978.

Bruce, F. F. *The Book of the Acts*. Rev. ed. NICNT. Grand Rapids: Eerdmans, 1988.

Bechtler, Steven Richard. "The Meaning of Paul's Call and Commissioning in Luke's Story: An Exegetical Study of Acts 9, 22, and 26." *Studia Biblica et Theologica* 15 (1987) 53–77.

Budesheim, Thomas L. "Paul's *Abschiedsrede* in the Acts of the Apostles." *HTR* 69 (1976) 9–30.

Burfeind, Carsten. "Paulus *Muß* nach Rom: Zur Politischen Dimension der Apostelgeschichte." *NTS* 46 (2000) 75–91.

Burridge, Richard A. "Biography." In *Handbook of Classical Rhetoric in the Hellenistic Period: 330 B.C.–A.D. 400*, edited by Stanley E. Porter, 371–91. Leiden: Brill, 1997.

———. "The Gospels and Acts." In *Handbook of Classical Rhetoric in the Hellenistic Period: 330 B.C.–A.D. 400*, edited by Stanley E. Porter, 507–32. Leiden: Brill, 1997.

Butts, James R. "The Chreia in the Synoptic Gospels." *BTB* 16 (1986) 132–38.

———. "The Progymnasmata of Theon: A New Text with Translation and Commentary." PhD diss., Claremont Graduate School, 1986.

Byrskog, Samuel. "Epistolography, Rhetoric and Letter Prescript: Romans 1.1-7 as a Test Case." *JSNT* 65 (1997) 26–46.

Cadbury, Henry J. "Four Features of Lucan Style." In *Studies in Luke-Acts: Essays Presented in Honor of Paul Schubert*, edited by Leander E. Keck and J. Louis Martyn, 87–102. Nashville: Abingdon, 1966.

———. *The Making of Luke-Acts.* New York: Macmillan, 1927; reprinted, London: SPCK, 1968.

Callan, Terrance. "The Preface of Luke-Acts and Historiography." *NTS* 31 (1985) 576–81.

Campbell, Douglas A. "A Rhetorical Suggestion Concerning Romans 2." In *SBLSP*, 140–67. Atlanta: Scholars, 1995.

Cancik, Hubert. "The History of Culture, Religion, and Institutions in Ancient Historiography: Philological Observations Concerning Luke's History." *JBL* 116 (1997) 673–95.

Carroll, John T. "Literary and Social Dimensions of Luke's Apology for Paul." In *SBLSP* 27, 106–18. Atlanta: Scholars, 1988.

Church, F. Forrester. "Rhetorical Structure and Design in Paul's Letter to Philemon." *HTR* 71 (1978) 17–33.

Clark, Donald Lemen. *Rhetoric in Greco-Roman Education.* Morningside Heights, N.Y.: Columbia University Press, 1957.

Classen, Carl Joachim. *Rhetorical Criticism of the New Testament.* WUNT 128. Tübingen: Mohr/Siebeck, 2000.

Collins, Raymond F. "Paul's Damascus Experience: Reflections on the Lukan Account." *Louvain Studies* 11 (1986) 99–118.

Conzelmann, Hans. *Acts of the Apostles: A Commentary on the Acts of the Apostles.* Translated by James Limburg et al. Hermeneia. Philadelphia: Fortress, 1987.

Cooper, Stephen, A. "*Narratio* and *Exhortatio* in Galatians according to Marius Victorinus Rhetor." *ZNW* 91 (2000) 107–35.

Cosgrove, Charles H. "The Devine *dei* in Luke-Acts: Investigations into the Lukan Understanding of God's Providence." *NovT* 26 (1984) 168–90.

Cranford, Lorin L. "A Rhetorical Reading of Galatians." *SWJT* 37 (Fall 1994) 4–10.

Cribiore, Raffaella. *Gymnastics of the Mind: Greek Education in Hellenistic and Roman Egypt.* Princeton: Princeton University Press, 2001.

Crouch, Frank. "The Persuasive Moment: Rhetorical Resolutions in Paul's Defense Before Agrippa." In *SBLSP* 35, 333–42. Atlanta: Scholars, 1996.

Cunningham, Scott. *"Through Many Tribulations": The Theology of Persecution in Luke-Acts.* JSNTSS 142. Sheffield: Sheffield Academic, 1997.

Czachesz, Istv·n. "Socio-Rhetorical Exegesis of Acts 9:1-30." *Communio Viatorum* 37 (1995) 5–32.

Dawsey, James M. "Characteristics of Folk-Epic in Acts." In *SBLSP* 28, 317–25. Atlanta: Scholars, 1989.

de Romilly, Jacqueline. *Magic and Rhetoric in Ancient Greece*. Cambridge: Harvard University Press, 1975.

Dibelius, Martin. *Studies in the Acts of the Apostles*. Translated by Mary Ling. Edited by Heinrich Greeven. London: SCM, 1956. Revised as: *The Book of Acts*. Edited by K. C. Hanson. Fortress Classics in Biblical Studies. Minneapolis: Fortress Press, 2005.

Dobschütz, Ernst von. "Die Berichte über die Bekehrung des Paulus." *ZNW* 29 (1930) 144–47.

Downing, F. Gerald. "Contemporary Analogies to the Gospels and Acts: 'Genres' or 'Motifs'?" In *Synoptic Studies: The Ampleforth Conferences of 1982 and 1983*, edited by C. M. Tuckett, 51–65. JSNTSS 7. Sheffield: JSOT Press, 1984.

Duncan, Thomas Shearer. "The Style and Language of Saint Paul in His First Letter to the Corinthians." *BibSac* 83 (1926) 129–43.

Dunn, James D. G. *The Acts of the Apostles*. NarrComm. Valley Forge, Pa.: Trinity, 1996.

Dupont, Jacques. "La structure oratoire du discours d'Étienne." *Bib* 66 (1985) 153–67.

Durbin, Daniel Timothy. "Clouds of Witnesses: A Rhetorical Analysis of Narrated Witness in the Gospels." PhD diss., University of Southern California, 1996.

Easton, Burton Scott. *The Purpose of Acts*. London: SPCK, 1936.

Elliott, Neil. *The Rhetoric of Romans: Argumentative Constraint and Strategy and Paul's Dialogue with Judaism*. JSNTSS 45. Sheffield: Sheffield Academic, 1990.

Fiorenza, Elisabeth Schüssler. *Rhetoric and Ethic: The Politics of Biblical Studies*. Minneapolis: Fortress, 1999.

Fitzmyer, Joseph A. *The Acts of the Apostles: A New Translation with Introduction and Commentary*. AB 31. New York: Doubleday, 1998.

Foakes-Jackson, F. J., and Kirsopp Lake. "The Internal Evidence of Acts." In *The Beginnings of Christianity: Part 1, The Acts of the Apostles,* vol. 2: *Prolegomena II, and Criticism*, edited by F. J. Foakes-Jackson and Kirsopp Lake, 121–206. London: Macmillan, 1922.

Foster, Barry M. "The Contribution of the Conclusion of Acts to the Understanding of Lucan Theology and the Determination of Lucan Purpose." PhD diss., Trinity International University, 1997.

Fowl, Stephen E. "Who's Characterizing Whom and the Difference This Makes: Locating and Centering Paul." In *SBLSP* 32, 537–53. Atlanta: Scholars, 1993.

Funk, Robert W. "The Apostolic *Parousia:* Form and Significance." In *Christian History and Interpretation: Studies Presented to John Knox*, edited by W. R. Farmer, 249–68. Cambridge: Cambridge University Press, 1967.

Gaventa, Beverly Roberts. "The Overthrown Enemy: Luke's Portrait of Paul." In *SBLSP* 24, 439–49. Atlanta: Scholars, 1985.

———. *From Darkness to Light: Aspects of Conversion in the New Testament*. Overtures to Biblical Theology. Philadelphia: Fortress, 1986.

Gempf, Conrad. "Public Speaking and Published Accounts." In *The Book of Acts in Its Ancient Literary Setting*, edited by Bruce W. Winter and Andrew D. Clarke, 259–303. The Book of Acts in Its First Century Setting 1. Grand Rapids: Eerdmans, 1993.

Gill, David. "The Structure of Acts 9." *Bib* 55 (1974) 546–48.
Grams, Rollin. "The Temple Conflict Scene: A Rhetorical Analysis of Matthew 21–23." In *Persuasive Artistry: Studies in New Testament Rhetoric in Honor of George A. Kennedy*, edited by Duane F. Watson, 41–65. JSNTSS 50. Sheffield: Sheffield Academic, 1991.
Greenwood, David. "Rhetorical Criticism and Formgeschichte: Some Methodological Considerations." *JBL* 89 (1970) 418–26.
Griffin, William S. "Seeing and Perceiving: The Narrative Rhetoric of a Theme in Mark 15:20b-41." PhD diss., Graduate Theological Union, 1996.
Haenchen, Ernst. *The Acts of the Apostles: A Commentary*. Translated by Bernard Noble et al. Philadelphia: Westminster, 1971.
Hall, Robert G. "The Rhetorical Outline for Galatians: A Reconsideration." *JBL* 106 (1987) 277–87.
———. "Ancient Historical Method and the Training of an Orator." In *The Rhetorical Analysis of Scripture: Essays from the 1995 London Conference*, edited by Stanley E. Porter and Thomas H. Olbricht, 103–18. JSNTSS 146. Sheffield: Sheffield Academic, 1997.
Hamm, Dennis. "Paul's Blindness and Its Healing: Clues to Symbolic Intent (Acts 9, 22 and 26)." *Bib* 71 (1990) 63–72.
Hansen, G. Walter. "The Preaching and Defence of Paul." In *Witness to the Gospel: The Theology of Acts*, edited by I. Howard Marshall and David Peterson, 295–324. Grand Rapids: Eerdmans, 1998.
Harrisville, Roy A. "Acts 22:6-21." *Int* 42 (1988) 181–85.
Hedrick, Charles W. "Paul's Conversion/Call: A Comparative Analysis of the Three Reports in Acts." *JBL* 100 (1981) 415–32.
Heil, Christoph. "Arius Didymus and Luke-Acts." *NovT* 42 (2000) 358–93.
Heinrici, C. F. Georg. *Das zweite Sendschreiben des Apostel Paulus an die Korinthier*. Berlin: Bessersche, 1887.
Hengel, Martin. *Acts and the History of Earliest Christianity*. Translated by John Bowden. Philadelphia: Fortress, 1979. Reprint, Eugene, Ore.: Wipf and Stock, 2003.
Hester, James D. "The Rhetorical Structure of Galatians 1:11—2:14." *JBL* 103 (1984) 223–33.
Hickling, Colin J. A. "The Portrait of Paul in Acts 26." In *Les Actes des ApÙstres*, edited by J. Duculot, 499–503. BETL 48. Leuven: Leuven University Press, 1979.
Hilgert, Earle. "Speeches in Acts and Hellenistic Canons of Historiography and Rhetoric." In *Good News in History: Essays in Honor of Bo Reicke*, edited by Ed. L. Miller, 83–109. Atlanta: Scholars, 1993.
Hirsch, Emanuel. "Die drei Berichte der Apostelgeschichte über die Bekehrung des Paulus." *ZNW* 28 (1929) 305–12.
Hock, Ronald F. "The Greek Novel." In *Greco-Roman Literature and the New Testament: Selected Forms and Genres*, edited by David E. Aune, 127–46. SBLSBS 21. Atlanta: Scholars, 1988.

Bibliography

———. "The Rhetoric of Romance." In *Handbook of Classical Rhetoric in the Hellenistic Period: 330 B.C.–A.D. 400,* edited by Stanley E. Porter, 445–65. Leiden: Brill, 1997.

Hubbard, Benjamin J. "The Role of Commissioning Accounts in Acts." In *Perspectives on Luke-Acts,* edited by Charles H. Talbert, 187–98. Perspectives in Religious Studies 5. Edinburgh: T. & T. Clark, 1978.

Huffman, Douglas Scott. "The Theology of the Acts of the Apostles: Lukan Compositional Markedness as a Guide to Interpreting Acts." PhD diss., Trinity Evangelical Divinity School, 1994.

Hughes, Frank Witt. *Early Christian Rhetoric and 2 Thessalonians.* JSNTSS 30. Sheffield: Sheffield Academic, 1989.

———. "The Parable of the Rich Man and Lazarus (Luke 16.19-31) and Graeco-Roman Rhetoric." In *Rhetoric and the New Testament: Essays from the 1992 Heidelberg Conference,* edited by Stanley E. Porter and Thomas H. Olbricht, 29–41. JSNTSS 90. Sheffield: Sheffield Academic, 1993.

———. "The Rhetoric of Letters." In *The Thessalonians Debate: Methodological Discord or Methodological Synthesis?* edited by Karl P. Donfried and Johannes Beutler, 194–240. Grand Rapids: Eerdmans, 2000.

Humphries, Raymond A. "Paul's Rhetoric of Argumentation in 1 Corinthians 1–4." PhD diss., Graduate Theological Union, 1979.

Jervell, Jacob. *Luke and the People of God: A New Look at Luke-Acts.* Minneapolis: Augsburg, 1972.

———. *The Theology of the Acts of the Apostles.* New Testament Theology. Cambridge: Cambridge University Press, 1996.

Jervell, Jacob. *Die Apostelgeschichte.* KEKNT 17. Göttingen: Vandenhoeck & Ruprecht, 1998.

Johnson, Luke Timothy. *The Acts of the Apostles.* Sacra Pagina 5. Collegeville, Minn.: Liturgical, 1992.

Judge, E. A. "Paul's Boasting in Relation to Contemporary Professional Practice." *ABR* 16 (October 1968) 37–50.

Jüngst, Johannes. *Die Quellen der Apostelgeschichte.* Gotha: Perthes, 1895.

Kelley, Shawn. "And Your Young Will See Visions: A Functionalist Literary Reading of the Visions to Saul and Peter in Acts." PhD diss., Vanderbilt University, 1991.

Kennedy, George A. *New Testament Interpretation through Rhetorical Criticism.* Chapel Hill: University of North Carolina Press, 1984.

———. *A New History of Classical Rhetoric.* Princeton: Princeton University Press, 1994.

———. "The Composition and Influence of Aristotle's *Rhetoric.*" In *Essays on Aristotle's Rhetoric,* edited by Amélie Oksenberg Rorty, 416–24. Philosophical Traditions 6. Berkeley: University of California Press, 1996.

———. "Historical Survey of Rhetoric." In *Handbook of Classical Rhetoric in the Hellenistic Period: 330 B.C.–A.D. 400,* edited by Stanley E. Porter, 3–41. Leiden: Brill, 1997.

———. *Classical Rhetoric and Its Christian and Secular Tradition from Ancient to Modern Times,* 2d ed. Chapel Hill: University of North Carolina Press, 1999.

Kessler, Martin. "An Introduction to Rhetorical Criticism of the Bible: Prolegomena." *Semitics* 7 (1980) 1–27.

———. "A Methodological Setting for Rhetorical Criticism." In *Art and Meaning: Rhetoric in Biblical Literature*, edited by David J. A. Clines et al., 1–19. JSOTSS 19. Sheffield: JSOT Press, 1982.

Kilgallen, John J. "Paul before Agrippa (Acts 26.2-23) Some Considerations." *Bib* 69 (1988) 170–95.

Kim, Johann D. *God, Israel, and the Gentiles: Rhetoric and Situation in Romans 9–11.* SBLDS 176. Atlanta: Society of Biblical Literature, 2000.

Koester, Craig R. *Hebrews: A New Translation with Introduction and Commentary.* AB 36. New York: Doubleday, 2001.

Kremer, Jacob. "Die Dreifache Wiedergabe des Damaskuserlebnisses Pauli in der Apostelgeschichte: Eine Hilfe für das Rechte Verständnis der Lukanischen Osterevangelien." In *The Unity of Luke-Acts*, edited by J. Verheyden, 329–55. BETL 142 Leuven: Leuven University Press, 1999.

Kurz, William S. "Hellenistic Rhetoric in the Christological Proof of Luke-Acts." *CBQ* 42 (1980) 171–95.

———. "Luke-Acts and Historiography in the Greek Bible." In *SBLSP* 19, 283–300. Atlanta: Scholars, 1980.

———. "Narrative Models for Imitation in Luke-Acts." In *Greeks, Romans, and Christians: Essays in Honor of Abraham J. Malherbe*, edited by David L. Balch, et al., 171–89. Minneapolis: Fortress, 1990.

———. *Reading Luke-Acts: Dynamics of Biblical Narrative.* Louisville: Westminster John Knox, 1993.

Kwon, Jongseon. "A Rhetorical Analysis of the Johannine Farewell Discourse." PhD diss., Southern Baptist Theological Seminary, 1993.

Lake, Kirsopp. "The Conversion of Paul and the Events Immediately Following It." In *The Beginnings of Christianity: Part I, The Acts of the Apostles*, vol. 5: *Additional Notes to the Commentary*, edited by F. J. Foakes-Jackson and Kirsopp Lake, 188–95. London: Macmillan, 1933.

———, and Henry J. Cadbury. *The Beginnings of Christianity: Part I, The Acts of the Apostles*, vol. 4: *English Translation and Commentary.* London: Macmillan, 1933.

Lambrecht, Jan. "Rhetorical Criticism and the New Testament." *Bijdragen tijdschrift voor filosofie en theologie* 50 (1989) 239–53.

Lantzy, Tim, "The Case for Christianity: A Rhetorical Study of Luke 15:1—17:10." PhD diss., Southwestern Baptist Theological Seminary, 1995.

Law, Vivien. "The *Techne* and the Grammar in the Roman World." In *Dionysius Thrax and the Technē Grammatikē*, edited by John Flood et al., vol. 1, 111–19. The Henry Sweet Society Studies in the History of Linguistics. Münster: Nodus, 1995.

Leeman, A. D. *Orationis Ratio: The Stylistic Theories and Practice of the Roman Orators Historians and Philosophers.* Vol. 1. Amsterdam: Hakkert, 1963.

Litfin, Duane. *St. Paul's Theology of Proclamation: 1 Corinthians 1–4 and Greco-Roman Rhetoric.* SNTSMS 79. Cambridge: Cambridge University Press, 1994.

Bibliography

Lohfink, Gerhard. *The Conversion of St. Paul: Narrative and History in Acts*. Translated by Bruce J. Malina. Herald Scriptural Library. Chicago: Franciscan Herald, 1976.

Lohse, Eduard. "Lukas als Theologe der Heilsgeschichte." *EvTh* 14 (1954) 256–75.

Long, William R. "The Trial of Paul in the Book of Acts: Historical, Literary, and Theological Considerations." PhD diss., Brown University, 1982.

———. "The *Paulusbild* in the Trial of Paul in Acts." In *SBLSP* 22, 87–105. Chico, Calif.: Scholars, 1983.

Löning, Karl. *Die Saulustradition in der Apostelgeschichte*. Neutestamentliche Abhandlungen 9. Münster: Aschendorff, 1973.

Lösch, Stephen. "Die Dankesrede des Tertullus, Apg 24.1-4." *ThQ* 112 (1931) 295–319.

Lundgren, Sten. "Ananias and the Calling of Paul in Acts." *StTh* 25 (1971) 117–22.

Mack, Burton L. "The Anointing of Jesus: Elaboration within a Chreia." In *Patterns of Persuasion in the Gospels*, edited by Burton L. Mack and Vernon K. Robbins, 85–106. Foundations and Facets: Literary Facets. Sonoma: Polebridge, 1989.

———. "Elaboration of the Chreia in the Hellenistic School." In *Patterns of Persuasion in the Gospels*, edited by Burton L. Mack and Vernon K. Robbins, 31–67. Foundations and Facets: Literary Facets. Sonoma: Polebridge, 1989.

Mack, Burton L. *Rhetoric and the New Testament*. GBS. Minneapolis: Fortress, 1990.

Maddox, Robert. *The Purpose of Luke-Acts*. FRLANT 126. Göttingen: Vandenhoeck & Ruprecht, 1982.

Malherbe, Abraham J. "'Not in a Corner': Early Christian Apologetic in Acts 26:26." *SecCent* 5 (1985–86) 193–210.

———. *Ancient Epistolary Theorists*. SBLSBS 19. Atlanta: Scholars, 1988.

Marguerat, Daniel. "Saul's Conversion (Acts 9, 22, 26) and the Multiplication of Narrative in Acts." In *Luke's Literary Achievement: Collected Essays*, edited by C. M. Tuckett, 127–55. JSNTSS 116. Sheffield: Sheffield Academic, 1995.

Marrou, Henri Irenée. *A History of Education in Antiquity*. Translated by George Lamb. London: Sheed and Ward, 1956.

Maryono, Petrus. "Luke's Use of Biblical History and Promise in Acts 13.16-41." PhD diss., Dallas Theological Seminary, 2001.

Mather, P. Boyd. "Paul in Acts as 'Servant' and 'Witness.'" *BR* 30 (1985) 23–43.

McCormick, Larry David. "Paul's Addresses to Jewish Audiences in the Acts of the Apostles: Luke's Model Witness and His Calling to Testify to 'The Hope of Israel.'" PhD diss., Fordham University, 1996.

McDonald, J. Ian H. "Rhetorical Issue and Rhetorical Strategy in Luke 10.25-37." In *Rhetoric and the New Testament: Essays from the 1992 Heidelberg Conference*, edited by Stanley E. Porter and Thomas H. Olbricht, 59–73. JSNTSS 90. Sheffield: Sheffield Academic, 1993.

Mealand, David L. "Hellenistic Historians and the Style of Acts." *ZNW* 82 (1991) 42–66.

———. "Style, Genre, and Authorship in Acts, the Septuagint, and Hellenistic Historians." *Literary and Linguistic Computing* 14 (1999) 479–506.

Meierding, Paul, "Jews and Gentiles: A Narrative and Rhetorical Analysis of the Implied Audience in Acts (Luke-Acts)." PhD diss., Luther Northwestern Theological Seminary, 1992.

Meyer, Donald Galen. "The Use of Rhetorical Technique by Luke in the Book of Acts." 2 vols. PhD diss., University of Minnesota, 1987.

Moessner, David P. "'The Christ Must Suffer': New Light on the Jesus-Peter, Stephen, Paul Parallels in Luke-Acts." *NovT* 28 (1986) 220–56.

Morgan, Teresa. "Dionysius Thrax and the Educational Uses of Grammar." In *Dionysius Thrax and the Technē Grammatikē*, edited by John Flood et al., vol. 1, 73–94. The Henry Sweet Society Studies in the History of Linguistics. Münster: Nodus, 1995.

———. *Literate Education in the Hellenistic and Roman Worlds*. Cambridge Classical Studies. Cambridge: Cambridge University Press, 1998.

Morris, Joseph A. "Irony and Ethics in the Lukan Narrative World: A Narrative Rhetorical Reading of Luke 4:14-30." PhD diss., Graduate Theological Union, 1992.

Muilenburg, James, "Form Criticism and Beyond." *JBL* 88 (1969) 1–18.

Munck, Johannes. *The Acts of the Apostles: Introduction, Translation, and Notes*. AB 31. Garden City, N.Y.: Doubleday, 1967.

Murphy, James J. "Early Christianity as a 'Persuasive Campaign': Evidence from the Acts of the Apostles and the Letters of Paul." In *Rhetoric and the New Testament: Essays from the 1992 Heidelberg Conference*, edited by Stanley E. Porter and Thomas H. Olbricht, 90–99. JSNTSS 90. Sheffield: Sheffield Academic, 1993.

Neyrey, Jerome H. "The Forensic Defense Speech and Paul's Trial Speeches in Acts 22–26: Form and Function." In *Luke-Acts: New Perspectives from the Society of Biblical Literature Seminar*, edited by Charles H. Talbert, 210–24. New York: Crossroad, 1984.

Nielsen, Anders E. *Until It Is Fulfilled Lukan Eschatology according to Luke 22 and Acts 20*. WUNT 2/126. Tübingen: Mohr/Siebeck, 2000.

Norden, Eduard. *Die Antike Kunstprosa: Vom VI. Jahrhundert V. Chr. Bis in die Zeit der Renaissance*. 2 vols. 3d ed. Leipzig: Teubner, 1915; reprinted, 1995.

Olbricht, Thomas H. "An Aristotelian Rhetorical Analysis of 1 Thessalonians." In *Greeks, Romans, and Christians: Essays in Honor of Abraham J. Malherbe*, edited by David L. Balch et al., 216–36. Minneapolis: Fortress, 1990.

O'Toole, Robert F. *The Christological Climax of Paul's Defense*. Analecta biblica 78. Rome: Biblical Institute Press, 1978.

Palmer, Darryl W. "Acts and the Ancient Historical Monograph." In *The Book of Acts in Its Ancient Literary Setting*, edited by Bruce W. Winter and Andrew D. Clarke, 1–29. The Book of Acts in Its First Century Setting 1. Grand Rapids: Eerdmans, 1993.

Parsons, Mikeal C., and Richard I. Pervo. *Rethinking the Unity of Luke and Acts*. Minneapolis: Fortress, 1993.

Penner, Todd C. "Narrative as Persuasion: Epideictic Rhetoric and Scribal Amplification in the Stephen Episode in Acts." In *SBLSP* 35, 352–67. Atlanta: Scholars, 1996.

Bibliography

Perelman, Chaim, and L. Olbrechts-Tyteca. *The New Rhetoric: A Treatise on Argumentation.* Translated by John Wilkinson and Purcell Weaver. Notre Dame: University of Notre Dame Press, 1971.
Pervo, Richard I. "Must Luke and Acts Belong to the Same Genre?" In *SBLSP* 28, 309–16. Atlanta: Scholars, 1989.
———. *Luke's Story of Paul.* Minneapolis: Fortress, 1990.
———. "Israel's Heritage and Claims upon the Genre(s) of Luke and Acts: The Problems of a History." In *Jesus and the Heritage of Israel*, edited by David P. Moessner and David L. Tiede, 127–43. Luke the Interpreter of Israel 1. Harrisburg, Pa.: Trinity, 1999.
Pesch, Rudolf. *Die Apostelgeschichte.* Vol. 1, *Teilband (Apg 1–12).* EKKNT. Zürich: Benziger, 1986.
———. *Die Apostelgeschichte.* Vol. 2, *Teilband (Apg 13–28).* EKKNT. Zürich: Benziger, 1986.
Plümacher, Eckhard. "Eine Thukydidesreminiszenz in der Apostelgeschichte (Act 20,33-35–Thuk. II 97,3f.)." *ZNW* 83 (1992) 270–75.
———. "*Terateia*: Fiktion und Wunder in der hellenistisch-römischen Geschichtsschreibung und in der Apostelgeschichte." *ZNW* 89 (1998) 66–90.
———. "Cicero und Lukas: Bemerkungen zu Stil un Zweck der historischen Monographie." In *The Unity of Luke-Acts*, edited by J. Verheyden, 759–75. BETL 142. Leuven: Leuven University Press, 1999.
Polhill, John B. *Acts.* New American Commentary 26. Nashville: Broadman, 1992.
Porter, Stanley E. "Thucydides 1.22.1 and Speeches in Acts: Is There a Thucydidean View?" *NovT* 32 (1990) 121–42.
———. "The Theoretical Justification for Application of Rhetorical Categories to Pauline Epistolary Literature." In *Rhetoric and the New Testament: Essays from the 1992 Heidelberg Conference*, edited by Stanley E. Porter and Thomas H. Olbricht, 100–22. JSNTSS 90. Sheffield: Sheffield Academic, 1993.
———. *The Paul of Acts: Essays in Literary Criticism, Rhetoric, and Theology.* WUNT 115. Tübingen: Mohr/Siebeck, 1999.
Rackham, Richard Belward. *The Acts of the Apostles.* Westminster Commentaries. London: Methuen, 1901; reprinted, Grand Rapids: Baker, 1964.
Reasoner, Mark. "The Theme of Acts: Institutional History or Divine Necessity in History?" *JBL* 118 (1999) 635–59.
Rebenich, Stefan. "Historical Prose." In *Handbook of Classical Rhetoric in the Hellenistic Period: 330 B.C.–A.D. 400*, edited by Stanley E. Porter, 265–337. Leiden: Brill, 1997.
Reed, Jeffrey T. "Using Ancient Rhetorical Categories to Interpret Paul's Letters: A Question of Genre." In *Rhetoric and the New Testament: Essays from the 1992 Heidelberg Conference*, edited by Stanley E. Porter and Thomas H. Olbricht, 292–324. JSNTSS 90. Sheffield: Sheffield Academic, 1993.
———. "The Epistle." In *Handbook of Classical Rhetoric in the Hellenistic Period: 330 B.C.–A.D. 400*, edited by Stanley E. Porter, 171–93. Leiden: Brill, 1997.

Reid, Marty L. "A Rhetorical Analysis of Romans 1:1—5:21 with Attention Given to the Rhetorical Function of 5:1-21." *Perspectives in Religious Studies* 19 (1992) 255-72.

———. "Paul's Rhetoric of Mutuality: A Rhetorical Reading of Romans." In *SBLSP* 34, 117-39. Atlanta: Scholars, 1995.

Reinhardt, Tobias. "Rhetoric in the Fourth Academy." *Classical Quarterly* 50 (2000) 531-47.

Reymond, Sophie. "Paul sur le chemin de Damas (*Ac 9,22 et 26*)." *Nouvelle revue Théologique* 118 (1996) 520-38.

Robbins, Charles J. "Rhetorical Structure of Philippians 2:6-11." *CBQ* 42 (1980) 73-82.

Robbins, Vernon K. "Pronouncement Stories and Jesus' Blessing of the Children: A Rhetorical Approach." *Semeia* 29 (1983) 42-74.

———. *Jesus the Teacher: A Socio-Rhetorical Interpretation of Mark*. Philadelphia: Fortress, 1984.

———. "Rhetorical Argument about Lamps and Light in Early Christian Gospels." In *Context: Essays in Honour of Peder Johan Borgen*, edited by P. W. Böckman and R. E. Kristiansen, 177-95. Relieff 24. Trondheim: Tapir, 1987.

———. "The Chreia." In *Greco-Roman Literature and the New Testament: Selected Forms and Genres*, edited by David E. Aune, 1-23. SBLSBS 21. Atlanta: Scholars, 1988.

———. "Rhetorical Composition and the Beelzebul Controversy." In *Patterns of Persuasion in the Gospels*, edited by Burton L. Mack and Vernon K. Robbins, 85-106. Foundations and Facets: Literary Facets. Sonoma: Polebridge, 1989.

———. "Writing as a Rhetorical Act in Plutarch and the Gospels." In *Persuasive Artistry: Studies in New Testament Rhetoric in Honor of George A. Kennedy*, edited by Duane F. Watson,142-68. JSNTSS 50. Sheffield: Sheffield Academic, 1991.

———. *Exploring the Texture of Texts: A Guide to Socio-Rhetorical Interpretation*. Valley Forge, Pa.: Trinity, 1996.

———. "Narrative in Ancient Rhetoric and Rhetoric in Ancient Narrative." In *SBLSP* 35, 368-84. Atlanta: Scholars, 1996.

———. *The Tapestry of Early Christian Discourse: Rhetoric, Society and Ideology*. London: Routledge, 1996.

———. "The Present and Future of Rhetorical Analysis." In *The Rhetorical Analysis of Scripture: Essays from the 1995 London Conference*, edited by Stanley E. Porter and Thomas H. Olbricht, 24-52. JSNTSS 146. Sheffield: Sheffield Academic, 1997.

———. "The Claims of the Prologues and Greco-Roman Rhetoric: The Prefaces to Luke and Acts in Light of Greco-Roman Rhetorical Strategies." In *Jesus and the Heritage of Israel*, edited by David P. Moessner and David L. Tiede, 63-83. Luke the Interpreter of Israel 1. Harrisburg, Pa.: Trinity, 1999.

Rordorf, Willy. "Paul's Conversion in the Canonical Acts and in the Acts of Paul." *Semeia* 80 (1997) 137-44.

Bibliography

Rosenblatt, Marie-Eloise. "Recurrent Narration as a Lukan Literary Convention in Acts: Paul's Jerusalem Speech in Acts 22:1-21." In *New Views on Luke and Acts*, edited by Earl Richard, 94–105. Collegeville, Minn.: Liturgical, 1990.

———. *Paul the Accused: His Portrait in the Acts of the Apostles.* Collegeville, Minn.: Liturgical, 1995.

Rosner, Brian S. "Acts and Biblical History." In *The Book of Acts in Its Ancient Literary Setting*, edited by Bruce W. Winter and Andrew D. Clarke, 65–82. The Book of Acts in Its First Century Setting 1. Grand Rapids: Eerdmans, 1993.

———. "The Progress of the Word." In *Witness to the Gospel: The Theology of Acts*, edited by I. Howard Marshall and David Peterson, 215–33. Grand Rapids: Eerdmans, 1998.

Rowe, Galen O. "Style." In *Handbook of Classical Rhetoric in the Hellenistic Period: 330 B.C.–A.D. 400*, edited by Stanley E. Porter, 121–57. Leiden: Brill, 1997.

Sandnes, Karl Olav. "Paul and Socrates: The Aim of Paul's Areopagus Speech." *JSNT* 50 (1993) 13–26.

Satterthwaite, Philip E. "Acts Against the Background of Classical Rhetoric." In *The Book of Acts in Its Ancient Literary Setting*, edited by Bruce W. Winter and Andrew D. Clarke, 337–79. The Book of Acts in Its First Century Setting 1. Grand Rapids: Eerdmans, 1993.

Saw, Insawn. *Paul's Rhetoric in 1 Corinthians 15: An Analysis Utilizing the Theories of Classical Rhetoric.* Lewiston, Me.: Mellen Biblical, 1995.

Schiappa, Edward. *The Beginnings of Rhetorical Theory in Classical Greece.* New Haven: Yale University Press, 1999.

Schillebeeckx, Edward. *Jesus: An Experiment in Christology.* Translated by Hubert Hoskins. New York: Crossroad, 1979.

Schmidt, Daryl D. "The Historiography of Acts: Deuteronomistic or Hellenistic?" In *SBLSP* 24, 417–27. Atlanta: Scholars, 1985.

———. "Rhetorical Influences and Genre: Luke's Preface and the Rhetoric of Hellenistic Historiography." In *Jesus and the Heritage of Israel*, edited by David P. Moessner and David L. Tiede, 27–60. Luke the Interpreter of Israel 1. Harrisburg, Pa.: Trinity, 1999.

Schmidt, Karl Ludwig. *The Place of the Gospels in the General History of Literature.* Translated by Byron R. McCane. Columbia: University of South Carolina Press, 2002.

Schubert, Paul. "The Final Cycle of Speeches in the Book of Acts." *JBL* 87 (1968) 1–16.

Segal, Alan F. *Paul the Convert: The Apostolate and Apostasy of Saul the Pharisee.* New Haven: Yale University Press, 1990.

Seid, Timothy Wayne. "The Rhetorical Form of the Melchizedek/Christ Comparison in Hebrews 7." PhD diss., Brown University, 1996.

Smit, Jan. "The Genre of 1 Corinthians 13 in the Light of Classical Rhetoric." *NovT* 33 (1991) 193–216.

Soards, Marion L. "The Speeches in Acts in Relation to Other Pertinent Ancient Literature." *ETL* 70 (1994) 65–90.

———. *The Speeches in Acts: Their Content, Context, and Concerns*. Louisville: Westminster John Knox, 1994.
Songer, Harold S. "Acts 20–28: From Ephesus to Rome." *RevExp* 87 (1990) 451–63.
Spencer, Floyd Albert. "The Influence of Isocrates in Antiquity." PhD diss., University of Chicago, 1923.
Spitta, Friedrich. *Die Apostelgeschichte: Ihre Quellen und deren Geschichtlicher Wert*. Halle: Waisenhaus, 1891.
Stagg, Frank. *The Book of Acts: The Early Struggle for an Unhindered Gospel*. Nashville: Broadman, 1955.
Stamps, Dennis L. "Rethinking the Rhetorical Situation: The Intertextualization of the Situation in the New Testament Epistles." In *Rhetoric and the New Testament: Essays from the 1992 Heidelberg Conference*, edited by Stanley E. Porter and Thomas H. Olbricht, 192–210. JSNTSS 90. Sheffield: Sheffield Academic, 1993.
———. "Rhetorical and Narratological Criticism." In *Handbook to Exegesis of the New Testament*, edited by Stanley E. Porter, 219–39. NTTS 25. Leiden: Brill, 1997.
Stanley, David M. "Paul's Conversion in Acts: Why the Three Accounts?" *CBQ* 15 (1953) 315–38.
Steck, Odil Hannes. "Formgeschichtliche Bemerkungen zur Darstellung des Damaskusgeschehens in der Apostelgeschichte." *ZNW* 67 (1976) 20–28.
Sterling, Gregory E. "Luke-Acts and Apologetic Historiography." In *SBLSP* 28, 326–42. Atlanta: Scholars, 1989.
———. *Historiography and Self-Definition: Josephos, Luke-Acts and Apologetic Historiography*. NovTSup 64. Leiden: Brill, 1992.
Stevens, Gerald L. "Luke's Perspective on Paul's Jerusalem Visit in Acts 19–23." AAR/SBL Southwest Regional Meeting, Dallas, 1999. Photocopied.
Stowers, Stanley K. *Letter Writing in Greco-Roman Antiquity*. LEC 5. Philadelphia: Westminster, 1986.
Swiggers, Pierre. "Poetics and Grammar: From *Technique* to 'Tekne'." In *Greek Literary Theory after Aristotle: A Collection of Papers in Honour of D. M. Schenkeveld*, edited by J. G. J. Abbenes et al., 17–41 Amsterdam: VU University Press, 1995.
Tajra, Harry W. *The Trial of St. Paul*. WUNT 35. Tübingen: Mohr/Siebeck, 1989.
Talbert, Charles H. *Literary Patterns, Theological Themes and The Genre of Luke-Acts*. SBLMS 20. Missoula, Mont.: Scholars, 1974.
———. *Reading Acts: A Literary and Theological Commentary on the Acts of the Apostles*. New York: Crossroad, 1997.
Tannehill, Robert C. *The Narrative Unity of Luke-Acts: A Literary Interpretation*. Vol. 2: *The Acts of the Apostles*. Minneapolis: Fortress Press, 1994.
Thrax, Dionysios. "The Grammar of Dionysios Thrax." Translated by Thomas Davidson. *Journal of Speculative Philosophy* 8 (1874) 326–39.
Townsend, John T. "Ancient Education in the Time of the Early Roman Empire." In *The Catacombs and the Colosseum: The Roman Empire as the Setting of Primitive*

Christianity, edited by Stephen Benko and John J. O'Rourke, 139–63. Valley Forge: Judson, 1971.

Trocmé, Étienne. *Le "Livre des Actes" et L'Histoire*. EHPR 45. Paris: Presses Universitaires de France, 1957.

———. "The Beginnings of Christian Historiography and the History of Early Christianity." *ABR* 31 (October 1983) 1–13.

Veltman, Fred. "The Defense Speeches of Paul in Acts." In *Perspectives on Luke-Acts*, edited by Charles H. Talbert, 243–56. Perspectives in Religious Studies 5. Edinburgh: T. & T. Clark, 1978.

Walker, Jeffrey. *Rhetoric and Poetics in Antiquity*. Oxford: Oxford University Press, 2000.

Walton, Steve. "Rhetorical Criticism: An Introduction." *Themelios* 21 (January 1996) 49.

Wanamaker, Charles A. "Epistolary vs. Rhetorical Analysis: Is a Synthesis Possible?" In *The Thessalonians Debate: Methodological Discord or Methodological Synthesis?* edited by Karl P. Donfried and Johannes Beutler, 255–86. Grand Rapids: Eerdmans, 2000.

Wansbrough, Dom Henry. "The Book of the Acts and History." *Downside Review* 39 (April 1995) 96–103.

Watson, Duane Frederick. *Invention, Arrangement, and Style: Rhetorical Criticism of Jude and 2 Peter*. SBLDS 104. Atlanta: Scholars, 1988.

———. "Paul's Speech to the Ephesian Elders (Acts 20.17-38) Epideictic Rhetoric of Farewell." In *Persuasive Artistry: Studies in New Testament Rhetoric in Honor of George A. Kennedy*, edited by Duane F. Watson, 184–208. JSNTSS 50. Sheffield: Sheffield Academic, 1991.

———. "James 2 in Light of Greco-Roman Schemes of Argumentation." *NTS* 39 (1993) 94–121.

———. "Amplification Techniques in 1 John: The Interaction of Rhetorical Style and Invention." *JSNT* 51 (1993) 99–123.

Webber, Randall C. "'Why Were the Heathen So Arrogant?' The Socio-Rhetorical Strategy of Acts 3–4." *BTB* 22 (1992) 19–25.

Wellhausen, Julius. *Kritische Analyse der Apostelgeschichte*. AKGWG 15/2. Berlin: Weidmann, 1914.

Wendt, Hans Hinrich. *Die Apostelgeschichte*. KEKNT 5. Göttingen: Vandenhoeck & Ruprecht, 1899.

White, John L. "The Ancient Epistolography Group in Retrospect." *Semeia* 22 (1982) 1–14.

———. "The Greek Documentary Letter Tradition Third Century B.C.E. to Third Century C.E." *Semeia* 22 (1982) 89–106.

Wilder, Amos N. *Early Christian Rhetoric: The Language of the Gospel*. Cambridge: Harvard University Press, 1971.

Wilke, Christian Gottlob. *Die neutestamentliche Rhetorik: ein Seitenstück zur Grammatik des neutestamentlichen Sprachidiams*. Dresden: Arnold, 1843.

Wills, Lawrence. "The Form of the Sermon in Hellenistic Judaism and Early Christianity." *HTR* 77 (1984) 277–99.

Wilson, J. Daniel. "Jesus' Rhetoric of Authority in the Temple Conflict Narrative: A Rhetorical Analysis of Matthew 21–23." PhD diss., Mid-America Baptist Theological Seminary, 1993.

Winter, Bruce W. "Official Proceedings and the Forensic Speeches in Acts 24–26." In *The Book of Acts in Its Ancient Literary Setting*, edited by Bruce W. Winter and Andrew D. Clarke, 305–36. The Book of Acts in Its First Century Setting 1. Grand Rapids: Eerdmans, 1993.

Witherington, Ben III. "Finding Its Niche: The Historical and Rhetorical Species of Acts." In *SBLSP* 35, 67–97. Atlanta: Scholars, 1996.

———. *The Acts of the Apostles: A Socio-Rhetorical Commentary*. Grand Rapids: Eerdmans, 1998.

Witherup, Ronald D. "Functional Redundancy in the Acts of the Apostles: A Case Study." *JSNT* 48 (1992) 67–86.

———. "Cornelius Over and Over and Over Again: 'Functional Redundancy' in the Acts of the Apostles." *JSNT* 49 (1993) 45–66.

Wouters, Alfons. "The Grammatical Papyri and the *Technē Grammatikē* of Dionysius Thrax." In *Dionysius Thrax and the Technē Grammatikē*, edited by John Flood et al., vol. 1, 73–94. The Henry Sweet Society Studies in the History of Linguistics. Münster: Nodus, 1995.

Wuellner, Wilhelm. "Where Is Rhetorical Criticism Taking Us?" *CBQ* 49 (1987) 448–63.

———. "The Rhetorical Genre of Jesus' Sermon in Luke 12.1—13.9." In *Persuasive Artistry: Studies in New Testament Rhetoric in Honor of George A. Kennedy*, edited by Duane F. Watson, 93–118. JSNTSS 50. Sheffield: Sheffield Academic, 1991.

———. "Biblical Exegesis in the Light of the History and Historicity of Rhetoric and the Nature of the Rhetoric of Religion." In *Rhetoric and the New Testament: Essays from the 1992 Heidelberg Conference*, edited by Stanley E. Porter and Thomas H. Olbricht, 492–513. JSNTSS 90. Sheffield: Sheffield Academic, 1993.

Yamada, Kota. "A Rhetorical History: The Literary Genre of the Acts of the Apostles." In *Rhetoric, Scripture and Theology: Essays from the 1994 Pretoria Conference*, edited by Stanley E. Porter, 230–50. JSNTSS 131. Sheffield: Sheffield Academic, 1996.

Young, David M. "Whoever Has Ears to Hear: The Discourses of Jesus in Mark as Primary Rhetoric of the Greco-Roman Period." PhD diss., Vanderbilt University, 1994.

Zweck, Dean. "The *Exordium* of the Areopagus Speech, Acts 17.22, 23." *NTS* 35 (1989) 94–103.

www.ingramcontent.com/pod-product-compliance
Lightning Source LLC
Chambersburg PA
CBHW020850160426
43192CB00007B/860